KINGSHIP OF GOD

*the text of this book is printed
on 100% recycled paper*

MARTIN BUBER

KINGSHIP
OF GOD

Third, newly enlarged Edition
Translated by
RICHARD SCHEIMANN

HARPER TORCHBOOKS

Harper & Row, Publishers

New York, Evanston, San Francisco, London

To the friends who have helped me to read the scriptures, Florens Christian
Rang 1864–1924 and Franz Rosenzweig 1885–1929.

KINGSHIP OF GOD is a translation from the German KONIGTUM GOTTES, the
third German edition, Heidelberg, Lambert Schneider, 1956. A hardcover
edition of this book is published by Harper & Row, Publishers, Inc.

First HARPER TORCHBOOK edition published 1973.

STANDARD BOOK NUMBER: 06–131717–9

TRANSLATOR'S FOREWORD

If I were asked why I undertook the arduous task of translating *Königtum Gottes* I would reply: 'Because I once met Martin Buber.' When I was a graduate student in History of Religions at the University of Chicago my teacher and friend, Prof. Joachim Wach, had as his guests for an evening Martin Buber and a small circle of students. Our distinguished visitor did not give us a prepared speech, but instead responded to our interests and questions. I do not remember anything that was said on that occasion. I remember only that Dr. Buber spoke slowly and softly, gazing intently into the eyes of each one who addressed him. I would not have said (as some have) that he looked like an Old Testament prophet, but he certainly looked like a German university professor of a certain vintage, with his black suit of very heavy wool cloth and his massive gold watch chain draped across the front of his vest. At any rate I came away that evening convinced that I had met a genuine charismatic.

When, years later, Harper and Row asked me to consider translating this book, I was given the opportunity to become more closely acquainted with Martin Buber in one of his many roles, namely, as interpreter of sacred scripture. Although I am unable to assess his achievement in terms of the history of Old Testament studies, it seems to me that Dr. Buber moves with confidence through a maze of historical and textual hypotheses and arguments which bear upon our knowledge of Israel's history. What emerges is a portrayal of the people's experience of the divine kingship, a portrayal made more than plausible by reason of its concreteness and internal consistency. Dr. Buber conveys to the reader a sense of the core of Israel's experience, an experience of being addressed by God, of being drawn into dialogue with God, in and through the community's experience of captivity, wandering, conquest and settlement, and of the bestowing and withdrawing of charismatic leadership. According to Buber it was this experience of dialogue between God and man which welded a loose and shifting confederation of tribes into a people and which kept on constituting Israel as a people through the epoch of its human kingship and through so many centuries of the failure of its political aspirations— experiences which attended upon the birth of Messianic expectation.

It seems to me that in this little book Martin Buber shows himself to be a virtuoso of *Verstehen*. One sees in these pages how the man who can portray so vividly a people's encounter and dialogue with the divine Thou would also understand how to depict the ebb and flow of dialogue between man and man, both when God is manifest and when He is in eclipse.

When I first began the work of translating *Kingship of God* I sought to break up Dr. Buber's long, periodic sentences into smaller units which would somehow approximate a rather straightforward, crisp English. I soon discovered, however, that this could not be done without distorting the author's meaning and, of course, obscuring his style of thought. He himself asked that I translate as literally as possible. This I have done even when it makes the English rather clumsy. Because English is less inflected than German I had in some complex sentences, for the sake of clarity, to repeat antecedents when the pronouns or adjectives meant to refer to them could not do so in English without ambiguity or distortion of meaning. Furthermore, in order to reflect something of the rudimentary character of Israelitish social structure I have in nearly every case translated the German word 'Volk' as 'people' rather than 'nation,' not only because Buber sees Israel's early consciousness of itself as 'pre-political,' but also because I feared that the words 'nation' and 'national' would inevitably suggest features of modern political experience which would be misleading. For similar reasons I have rendered 'königlich' as 'kingly' rather than 'royal.' Names of Biblical persons and places have been given spellings current in English versions of the Bible when it seemed to me that more accurate transliterations from the Hebrew would confuse many readers. With many misgivings I have followed this policy in rendering the Tetragrammaton with the familiar JHWH rather than the more accurate YHVH.

Before his death Dr. Buber read and gave his sanction to my translation of the text, but he did not see the translation of the notes. The responsibility for errors is, of course, mine.

Valparaiso, Indiana
December, 1966

CONTENTS

PREFACE TO THE FIRST EDITION *

I WANTED originally to combine the results of many years of Bible studies in a theological commentary which would have to treat Old Testament problems in the exact order of succession in which the text presents them; since these were entirely, directly or indirectly, problems of faith, it was to be called *The Biblical Faith*. Thus I had arranged it with Franz Rosenzweig when, together, we translated into German the first ten books of the Scriptures. I continued to work on this plan for a year after his death until I realized that my strength was not sufficient for an adequate discussion of all the questions, but that in a discussion of a different kind precisely those questions which to me are the most important would not be done justice. Thus it proved to be my duty to abandon the all too wide-ranging work and to dedicate an independent presentation to those subjects which seemed of special consequence to me and on which I would soonest have something to say which would advance knowledge. Of most importance to me, in me most deeply matured, and therefore to be placed at the beginning was the question of the origin of 'messianism' in Israel. It touched on another, concerning which I had begun, more than twenty years ago, a slowly growing, subsequently postponed, essay-project and which

* This preface was sent out in advance of the book when it still was constituted as the first volume of a work projected to three volumes—under the general title *Das Kommende. Untersuchungen zur Entstehungsgeschichte des messianischen Glaubens* [*The Coming One. Investigations with Reference to the Genetic History of the Messianic Faith*]. The second volume entitled *Der Gesalbte* [*The Anointed*], was half finished in 1938 and had already been set up in type when the Schocken Press, Berlin, which published the work was officially dissolved. For many years external and internal causes hindered continuation of the work; not until recently could it be resumed. Sections from the still uncompleted second volume have been printed in advance in German and Hebrew publications. I plan to publish it as a separate book. I have abandoned the writing of the third volume; nevertheless its fundamental ideas have been set forth in my book *Der Glaube des Propheten* (1950), 180–334 (cf. also my book *Zwei Glaubensweisen*, 1950, pp. 103–16).

now—in a special connection, but supplementing these investigations —begged to be taken up again anew, the christological question. The question itself, namely of the origin of Israelitish messianism, I had for seven years repeatedly attempted to clarify in lectures and addresses, most particularly in a course of lectures at Frankfurt in the winter semester of 1924–25 and, in substantially deeper penetration, in a course for an invited circle held in August 1928 at Ponte Tresa, a course whose notes, recorded by my friend Carl Theil, later facilitated for me the written composition.

As I went about this, there soon emerged the three-fold division of the subject which is expressed in the fact that the first volume which I introduce with these remarks is to be followed by two others. The first volume will verify the religious idea of a folk-kingship of God as an actual-historical one for the early period of Israel. The second will show how the sacral character of the Israelitish king as one 'anointed' of JHWH is related to this. It is left to the third to portray how both conceptions—already in the period of the kings—change from history into eschatology. For the 'eschatological' hope—in Israel, the 'historical people par excellence' (Tillich), but not in Israel alone—is first always historical hope; it becomes eschatologized only through growing historical disillusionment. In this process faith seizes upon the future as the unconditioned turning point of history, then as the unconditioned overcoming of history. From this point of vantage it can be explained that the eschatologization of those actual-historical ideas includes their mythicization. For just as soon as faith seeks to express more than and something other than its actual relationship to the divine, as soon, accordingly, as it seeks to report and describe and not simply to invoke and proclaim, it must mythicize its object. Myth is the spontaneous and legitimate language of expecting, as of remembering, faith. But it is not its substance. In terms of mythical plasticity one can understand the *images* of eschatology, but not its impetus and power. The genuine eschatological life of faith is—in the great labour-pains of historical experiences—born from the genuine historical life of faith; every other attempt at derivation mistakes its character. This insight, too, my book will have to verify, and, primarily in its third volume, defend against the encroachment of a 'mythological' theory which is legitimate within the boundaries drawn for it.

The messianic faith of Israel is, as is to be shown, according to its central content the being-oriented-toward the fulfilment of the relation between God and world in a consummated kingly rule of God. That Israel perceives this believing expectation and its living expression as belonging to, and entrusted most peculiarly to, it among all the nations is based upon the believing memory that it once proclaimed JHWH as its direct and exclusive folk-king. Whether the memory— necessarily mythicizing—of such an occurrence originated from its historical actuality or signifies only a late illusion, a theological art-product, is decisively important for our method of proceeding; for only if the memory is historical can the expectation, even in its oldest utterances, be traced back to it. But the proclamation of an eternal folk-kingship of JHWH and its development are no longer to be surveyed on a merely 'religious' level; they impinge upon the political existence of the nationality. The problem has progressed from a religio-historical into an historical one. One must attempt to establish anew, upon the basis of critical research, the thesis of an early direct-theocratic tendency in Israel, a thesis penalized because of its untenable precritical formulation—a thesis by means of which, allegedly, 'a real insight into the folk history of Israel' becomes 'impossible'.[1] It will have to stand a double test: whether its taking with historical serious-ness the Biblical pre-kingly texts of direct-theocratic tendency—in their being dated contrary to the prevailing opinion and in their inter-pretations which likewise diverge from that opinion in many ways— is philologically justified; and whether this taking-seriously, where (inevitably with the aid of materially supported hypotheses), it pro-gresses to historical reconstruction, attains an historical picture which can be scientifically justified (for an epoch of Israelitish existence which has since Wellhausen become quite empty).

The first volume is devoted to the discussion of this epoch, be-ginning with the Book of Judges and then adducing historical texts of the Pentateuch and of the Book of Joshua as well. The final crisis of this epoch is treated in the second volume in its initial part which is based upon the Books of Samuel; its task is to explain how the con-ception of a human governor of God[2] intersects with and transforms

[1] Caspari, 'Der Herr ist König', *Christentum und Wissenschaft*, IV (1928), 23ff.
[2] Caspari polemicizes NKZ, XLVI (1935) against the 'unclarified' concept, allegedly used by me, of a 'deputy' of God which I never use except in citation (pp. 52 and 56) and not in relation to Israel. The concept of a governor—accord-ing to the nature of the case to be discussed first in the second volume—is cer-

that primitive-theocratic tendency—both common to the ancient
Orient and both nevertheless occurring here in a configuration of a
peculiarly new nature. How the resulting scale of ideas and strivings
enters into the eschatologization is the one theme of the third volume
which involves the first of the eschatological tensions; its other theme
is the relation between the folk-kingship and the world kingship of
JHWH and with it the second of the eschatological tensions; its third
and last theme are the changes in form of the messianic person up until
the Deutero-Isaiah mystery with the consideration of which the book
is to close—to these also corresponds one of the tensions. The fourth
tension, that between the completion of creation and, connected with
its conclusion, the establishment of a new aeon, no longer belongs, as
being of post-exilic origin, in its context.

Within its philological foundation the book, in accordance with
the literary-critical standpoint of its first and second volume, will
naturally be regarded essentially as a contribution to the problem of
the 'Elohist' or 'Elohists'. I can only indicate there how this problem
appears to me.[1] If I also am not able to believe in a separable, coherent
original document to be regarded as 'Elohistic', and if everything
adduced for it only leads me on to greater and smaller pieces and fragments quite different from one another in style, I nevertheless regard
as a secure discovery the discrimination of two great fundamental types
of tradition-compilation coming to expression in the differentiation of
J and E (independently of the question of how far these logograms are
justified: I can accord to them, as is to be substantiated elsewhere, only
a very conditional justification; moreover, the Ephraimite does not
appear to me to stand in opposition to the Judaean in E).[2] These types
which accordingly signify not sources, but trends of literature, originate

tainly not unclear (cf. in Caspari himself, *op. cit.*, 196). A governor rules a pro-
vince of the empire, unconditionally responsible to the ruler for actions delegated
to him, having in relation to subordinates only conditioned authority since they
can appeal to the prince. (Addendum to the second edition.)

[1] Cf. also my essay 'Genesisprobleme', MGWJ, lxxx (1936), 81ff. (Addendum to the second edition.)

[2] Since Volz, in Volz-Rudolph, *Der Elohist als Erzähler* (1933), 8, finds in
this sentence a certain contradiction, I observe for purposes of clarification that I
can concede to the *designations* only a conditional justification because the duality
of the divine names as criterion for the discrimination of source documents seems
inapplicable, and as criterion for the discrimination of traditions and their compilations only in very limited fashion applicable. Cf. on the subject Cassuto, *La
questione della Genesi* (1934), 1–92. (Addendum to the second edition.)

plainly from two socially and spiritually separated circles: J from the circle of courtly, for the most part early courtly, compilers, poets, and chroniclers, cultivated but rejoicing in legend, resolutely attentive to religious tradition, but in the treatment of contemporary or recent history prone to a profane-political tendency; E from the circle of the $n^e b\bar{u}m$, who had some time earlier entered upon their Word-administrating and poetical office, but literarily active for a far longer time, independent of the court, supported by the people, less gifted in narration, but inspired in message, experiencing and portraying history as a theo-political occurrence, contending for the interpenetration of religion and politics against every principle of partition which would place them in opposition to one another. To this 'prophetic' type, whose origin and social position the first two volumes endeavour to illuminate as well as the scanty material permits, the authenticating texts for the thesis represented here are to be assigned. With the assigning to this type, however, no dating has yet been decided, since we are dealing here not with a source, but with a manner of manipulating traditional material, and indeed with a manner which is *already established in the oldest formation of tradition*. The question about dating was therefore to be established by itself with every text. In the process I had to come to terms with the new and the most recent literature more extensively than would have been necessary in other circumstances. Where I could refer to a substantiation, already at hand, of what appeared to me to be the correct view I have done it. Where expressions, from the most recent period, of an opinion disputed by me have found either no discussion or not sufficient discussion I have inquired into these with the thoroughness required in this case (thus, pp. 186ff., into the pronouncements of von Rad on the problem of the ark and especially, p. 210ff., into those of Mowinckel on the dating of the Balaam passages, which appeared to me also to have a certain exemplary significance).

Fundamentally decisive for me was the analysis of the *historical bias* of the texts and textual structures. I can, indeed, not concur in Winckler's assertion[1] that in the orient 'an historical presentation always' pursues 'a definite goal', namely the 'proof of justification for those political claims which are made by the side which provided the occasions for formulating the whole': a prophetic historical impact

---

[1] *Allg. Evang.-luther. Kirchenzeitung*, 1903, 1198, cited on the authority of Budde, *Geschichte der althebräischen Literatur*, p. 63.

ought not to be understood from this point of view at all. To be sure, I think with Naville[1] that it 'is of fundamental importance to take account of the purpose of a writing, of its ground of existence, and accordingly to consider of what sort the people are to whom it is directed and what sort of influence it is supposed to exercize upon them'. This approach, in which I see one of the guiding principles of the 'methodical critique of subject matter and ideas' demanded by Staerk,[2] is applied in the second chapter of the first volume to Judges, in the second volume to Samuel. The natural result is that the concept of the 'redactor' from this point of view undergoes a considerable modification, but also a considerable differentiation.

On p. 85ff. of this volume I refer to the significance of the 'historical bias' method for the problem of the formation of tradition. I shall have to deal more exhaustively with this and other questions of method in the Foreword to the second volume where I also intend to offer a little something on the problem of tradition which will supplement the presentations of volume one.

The present volume starts out from a particular literary-critical question, that of Judges 8:22ff. (first chapter). In order to clarify this question as far as befits the limitations of this volume (the pertinent texts in Samuel cannot be examined until volume two), the genre, structure, and origin of the Book of Judges must be investigated anew (second chapter). The historical-political concreteness of a fundamental idea of the Biblical faith, disclosed in this manner, is now religio-historically elucidated and confirmed by the consideration of related ancient-oriental ideas in general (third chapter) and west-Semitic ones in particular (fourth chapter). It is then, to be sure, ranged alongside of them (fifth chapter), but only in order to be rightly contrasted with them and to cause the divine kingship of Israel to be recognized in its uniqueness (sixth chapter), a uniqueness to which the beginning of the book had expressly referred—a consciously 'theological', but in every point hermeneutically verified recognition. In order that the origin of this uniqueness, which is not to be sought upon a level of the 'development of ideas', but only in the three-dimensionality of a living fact of folk history, be understood and attested, a literary-critical in-

---

[1] *Actes du congrès international d'histoire des religions*, 1925, i, 424; the uncritical individual assertions of Naville's presentation indeed show how much one can err in the application of a correct principle.

[2] ZAW, NF I (1924), 35.

vestigation is again necessary, this time of several Pentateuch passages (seventh chapter). This clears the way for the venture of an historical outline of the pre-state Canaan-period of Israel in its relation to a primitive-theocratic tendency and to its transformations (eighth chapter) up until the crisis of the tendency which is to be treated in the second volume.

For the subject of the fourth chapter, which with an indispensable categorial sharpness (which, however, does not leave the actually given mixtures unconsidered and unexplained) distinguishes the leader-gods of the West Semitic tribes from the fertility demons encountered by them in the lands of settlement, I had, since 1924, been assembling extensive material which I had intended to add as an appendix to the projected book on the Biblical faith, when 1927–29 Wolf Graf Baudissin's great posthumous work *Kyrios* appeared and made this part of my work superfluous in the most gratifying way. I could now be content to refer here frequently to this work, one of those remarkable monuments of German scholarship. I was obliged, however, to turn against it in several points, especially in one of central significance: it is erroneous to see tribal gods in the *b^ealim*; never, so far as we are able to discover, did a Baal become lord of a tribe other than through theocracy. In order to prevent a possible misunderstanding of my intention I add that the discussions, necessary in the context of this volume, of several Semitic and specifically Israelitish conceptions of God are in no way designed to exhibit the basic forms of Semitic or Israelitish conceptions of God and their relation to one another. Nevertheless probably the most difficult problem of all, that of the historical relationship between the divine names JHWH and Elohim, cannot here be drawn into the visual field at all.[1]

Beside the *Kyrios* of Baudissin I make mention thankfully of another work, significant in another way, the *Aufsätze zur Religionssoziologie* by Max Weber, together with that which his book *Wirtschaft und Gesellschaft* offers in the way of supplementary general insights and pertinent matters which were expanded upon in conversation with the extraordinary man. In the last chapter of this volume I have made use of Weber's concepts and ideas for the presentation of a view essentially

[1] Cf. p. 189, note 14. Of that which I have said on this point in 1912 in the lecture, 'Der Mythos der Juden' (now in *Reden über das Judentum*, complete edition, pp. 125–42) not very much more than the *problem* of 'monopluralism' remains for me. (Addendum to the second edition.)

different from his; I profess, however, to have done no injustice to his primary intention. I shall never forget—it was about 1910—after a lecture on Jewish piety which I had delivered before Heidelberg students, Max Weber, requested by the young people to open the discussion, stepped up to me and asked me whether it were agreeable to me if he spoke now; he could, to be sure, offer 'only science about religion and not religion'. Also my book here is not intended to express faith, but a knowledge about it; it asserts admittedly that one can possess a knowledge about faith legitimately only then when the eye remains directed upon the cosmic margin, never given as object, at which faith is given a habitation.

I cannot here name all those who have generously given advice and information to me in the course of the long preparation and to whom I am thankful on this account. Especially valuable to me—in addition to instructive conversations with Prof. Joseph Horovitz who died a year ago—were the suggestions of Prof. Erich Ebeling, Prof. Alfred Jeremias, Prof. Herman Lommel, Prof. Eugen Mittwoch, Prof. J. H. Mordtmann, Prof. Kurt Sethe, and Prof. Willy Staerk who also read a proof. For bibliographical assistance I have to thank Prof. Aron Freimann, for proof-reading and other assistance Dr. Nahum Norbert Glatzer, Dr. Max Grünewald, Dr. Martin Plessner, Dr. Georg Salzberger, Dr. Eduard Strauss, Dr. Ludwig Strauss, and Dr. Carl Theil.

My work was greatly aided by the high and directly manifested conception which the proprietor of the publishing house in which it is published, Mr Salman Schocken, has also concerning this part of his calling.

Heppenheim on the Bergstrasse, in February, 1932.[1]

---

[1] In order to leave this preface unaltered (except for a few linguistic improvements), I have presented in other places everything which has since proven desirable for purposes of clarification. (Addendum to the second edition.)

PREFACE TO THE SECOND EDITION

THE first edition of this volume was already sold out by the beginning of 1934. I was, however, at that time and for a while thereafter, deterred by community obligations connected with the times from work on the continuation of the book, and consequently also on the preparation of the new edition; both became possible for me again in the last year. In the text I had, to be sure, little to alter, although I examined carefully everything in the nature of objection which confronted me in public and in personal communication. But for that very reason I had to respond to every argument of weight: where only details were involved, in the notes, which in addition to that, especially on the bibliographical side, required expansion; where, however, the whole was involved, in a new preface. This applies, as far as I can see, to five public pronouncements.

I. Ludwig Köhler[1] acknowledges that Judges 8:23 is 'a principle', but attaches an emphatic objection against my interpretation: 'God is the ruler. But He is that because He is the Lord and not the other way around. That God is the ruler is in the Old Testament only an inflection of this, admittedly a very meaningful one.' That God is the ruler because He is the Lord and not the other way around, that is also so very much my conviction that I am not at all able to imagine how it could appear 'the other way around'. But the most essential thing, that which I intended and intend to show is this, that in Israel the 'inflection' attained this strength, this definiteness, this degree of reality and effectiveness. All sorts of communities in the world acknowledge a 'lord' without on that account thinking seriously of conceding to him also the actual lordship over the actual community. The taking-seriously, the believing logicality, the prophetic—according to my interpretation even early-prophetic—rejection of a politically indeterminate belief concerning divine lordship, seems to me to be fundamental for Isreal. To be sure, Varuna of the Vedas is also a

[1] *Theologie des Alten Testaments* (1936), pp. 12ff.

'king', and indeed one who protects 'holy law',[1] but to wish to sub-ordinate the political actuality of the world of men to him would be contrary to his image. To be sure, Ahura Mazda also has his 'lordship', which is one day to attain completion in his victory,[2] but this is not the realm in which political decisions are found. More concretely, as I have set forth in the third chapter of this book, Egypt and, still more, Babylon conceived of divine kingship, but here it is well nigh exhausted in the task of protecting human authority. From time to time, as in post-exilic Judaism, a theocratic conception in the narrower sense degenerates into hierocracy. Only in ancient Israel, so far as I see, is there—certainly not as ruling state of mind, but as a clear, manifest tendency of mind advocated with the passion of the spiritual man—this sublime realism which wants *totally* to deal seriously with faith. This is the paradox of Israel which appears in the pre-state period (the subject of this volume) as the conception of a direct theocracy, in the early-state period (the subject of the second volume) as the conception of an admittedly indirect, but still genuine theocracy.

II. Wilhelm Caspari[3] objects, starting from the *melekh*-passages of Deutero-Isaiah, that I ventured 'two interpretations, one super-imposed on the other, of *mlk* and *Jahwe* in order then to explain the complex *mlk-Jahwe* as a formula of identity'. I rather attach great importance to the point that such a formula of identity does not exist. It is presupposed by *Isaiah* 6:5, but as an unexpressed formula, only intended and believed. That one shrinks from pronouncing it can very well be understood; JHWH is indeed a *melekh*, but He transcends the nature of a Semitic *malk*-god so intrinsically that a formula must be avoided which could threaten to want to restrict Him to it. Whatever is to be said therefore is not said in a noun-expression, but either purely in a verb-form as in Exodus 15:18 or in an historical assertion as in Deuteronomy 33:5. Furthermore, according to Caspari, I reduced 'the *mlk* to the pre-historical chieftain in order to regard *this* office of Jahwe as a most ancient religious idea in which Old Testament piety rests from times immemorial'. But I am not concerned primarily at all with the office and title of the Biblical God. That which I regard as a most ancient religious idea, more correctly as the central one among

[1] Cf. especially Rudolf Otto, *Das Gefühl des Überweltlichen* (1932), 167ff., *Reich Gottes und Menschensohn* (1934), 11ff.

[2] Cf. recently especially Lommel, *Die Religion Zarathustras* (1930), 52ff.

[3] *Lieder und Gottessprüche der Rückwanderer* (1934), 1544.

the ancient religious ideas of Israel, is something which emerges from a wealth of early texts (of which I name in the fifth chapter only a selection by way of example); it can be expressed in the words: *JHWH leads us.* The Exodus report remains in the centre of the Israelitish religious world because it presents the historical warrant of this leading in insurpassable concreteness. Not in theological metaphorics, but in all concreteness is JHWH revered and trusted as *the God who leads the community.* In order to express this fact in religiohistorical categories I have referred to the West-Semitic tribal gods, among whom JHWH is not simply to be counted at any stage that can be literarily documented, who, however, form the background— the only religio-historically reconstructable one—from which He emerges and to which he remains related long after Israel became acquainted with the kingly gods of the ancient oriental major powers. Caspari says[1] that the kingly title of JHWH in Deutero-Isaiah corresponds to 'the political world-situation within which the plan of a new basis for community seeks its actualization', and what is more, 'in spite of the impossibility of thinking additionally of a pantheon, as the government of the gods, after the Babylonian model'. But one must see the title together with such passages as Isaiah 40:3, 43:19; 48:21; 49:10; 52:12. It is nevertheless unmistakable that here the traditional idea of the leading God attained a new vitality in the hope for His leading of the returning multitudes. He is proclaimed as *melekh,* and He appears as leader. Is one to assume that the two elements existed independently next to one another? One will not be able to find features of a Babylonian prince of the gods in the countenance of the JHWH of Deutero-Isaiah. The 'political import in the Godkingship' which Caspari concedes does not suffice here; the essential thing is that this divine Lord even now, as formerly, leads His own Himself, directly, as a sheik leads his wandering tribe.

In a thoughtful essay concerning this volume,[2] Caspari disputes, if I understand him rightly, the historical possibility of a pre-state theocracy and apparently also of a primitive-theocratic tendency of mind. He begins with a definition: 'Bluntschli, *Staatsrecht,* volume I, 1, A., recognizes theocracy only in a state which wants to be directly of God. Thus theocracy occurs only in the state, not previous to it or

---

[1] *Op. cit.,* 154.
[2] 'Der Theokrat', NKZ, xlvi (= *Luthertum,* I, 1935), 193–206. I enter into the more important single arguments in the Notes.

without it.' Theocracy is said to belong typologically to an empire; the supra-national state of a master-folk which consumes other peoples and states is said to incline to the idea of a divine state which represents a unified humanity so that the divinity exercizes the government of the world through the master-folk. Next there arises an indirect theocracy: the king as the representative of the god. This can pass over into a direct theocracy: with the divinization of the king. That which comes to expression in the Biblical reports concerning the pre-state period of Israel is said to be something entirely different. The situation of the eighth chapter of Judges is explained by Caspari as follows:

'Through inquiry a loose federation of communities, at high points of their activity or in crises (Judges 1), placed themselves under a divine leadership. This situation is too original to count as theocracy, namely as a subordination under God resulting in *political* forms.'

On the religio-historical problem of *malk*-piety as such he notes by way of summary: 'God as regent was already in the stateless period an expression of united pious subordination; it did not entail a notion of political forms in which He was thought to rule and to pursue political goals.' If a theocracy combines with the *malk*-religions, then it does so only 'by reason of political analogies', that is, probably under the influence of theocratic empires. 'There is no folk-political, but only a state-political meaning of *mlk*; in terms of this meaning the bridge to Sinai is certainly absent.'

The entire discussion of Caspari rests upon a definition: theocracy is something which can only be found in the state; thus it cannot have existed in pre-state Israel.[1] But here something else is involved besides concepts. That, in terms of the subject with which I am dealing, I do not have in mind what one is accustomed to call theocracy, has been given unequivocal expression in this book, in the very first chapter (cf. p. 64ff.). One may name that of which I treat something else—it is, however it is named, an historical actuality. In the last chapter p. 137ff) I have characterized a psychic basis for the parallel of pre- and early-Islamic Bedouinism. This is something quite different from the projection of political forms of rulership upon the religious level: it is

[1] Caspari, to be sure, attributes to me (*op. cit.*, p. 194) the opinion that 'the national-state' was in existence 'for a long time' 'as pre-kingly', but one will seek such an absurdity in vain in this book.

the rejection of political forms of rulership which impair a person's immediate relation to God. His immediate relation to God; not a negative freedom, a disorderly lawlessness, but this firm, bold standing under the one authority. That man here again and again breaks down, that he does not tolerate the air of this freedom, that in acting he mistakes it for the other, the empty, freedom, belongs to human nature and to man-less-ness, but it does not touch upon the reality-character of that psychic basis of primitive theocracy. 'Buber's concession,' says Caspari, 'that under the judges the theocracy was a primitive one, avails for his opponent.' This is no concession, but the very core of my thesis. And it avails for my opponent only because he, in the grip of political theories, does not notice that which theology dare never lose sight of: the religious social fertility of those very preliminary forms of the state and of the fringe-formations around it.

If, according to Caspari, there are in the pre-state history of Israel situations in which a 'loose federation of communities' places itself under a divine leadership so that 'God appears as regent', then this is to me enough of a 'concession'; and when he adds that this state of affairs is 'too original to count as theocracy', I willingly surrender for the splendid adjective 'original' the dubious substantive 'theocracy'. I would rather call what I mean kingship of God; and with 'king' I mean precisely the 'primitive' *melekh* which the elders of Israel mean when they (I Samuel 8:19ff.) demand a king, 'that we also become like all the tribes and our king dispense justice for us (sc. against our enemies) and go on before us and fight our battle', whereupon Samuel (12:12) replies: 'But JHWH, your God, is your King!' For thus had they experienced it: JHWH had dispensed justice for them, He had gone on before them and had fought their battle, the *melekh* of an original early period. Certainly with the consolidation of the state a transformation of meaning also occurs with this concept which brings it nearer to the conceptual world of empires. Now, however, it is still the concept which is close to the wandering pastoral tribes which, on a dangerous search for land, moving against lurking enemies, see the invisible Lord of their covenant striding before them.

III. Walter Baumgartner[1] writes: 'If for Buber Jahwe is a *melekh*-god, that is, a tribal god who guides the history of his folk or tribe (chapter 5), this includes something two-fold in itself: that Israel already in Moses' times existed as a fixed and independent magnitude,

[1] DLZ III/4 (1933), 1348-55.

and that Jahwe already before, from times immemorial, was its God, its 'primeval God' p. 97). Are these presuppositions so assured that they can bear the entire further construction? The much-discussed question when and how the 'folk Israel' originated does not move Buber strongly. That Jahwe was for Israel no new God he maintains on p. 125 where, of the counter arguments, he enters only into the one drawn from the covenant-ceremony of Exodus 24. That which for some time and from the most diverse directions has been adduced in favour of the 'Kenite hypothesis', he has not refuted. Over against the consciousness of many of the prophets that the relationship of Jahwe and Israel originates from the time of Moses his reference to the 'God of the fathers' does not weigh heavily.'

In order that JHWH be a *melekh*-god Israel does not at all have to exist already in Moses' times 'as a fixed and independent magnitude'. Rather one need only assume: first, that an association of blood-related tribes wanders together and regards as the common leader of these wanderings a God who is perhaps named only with a war-cry-like shout 'ya-hu!' perhaps ('Ha, He!') a cry which at once recognizes and proclaims Him;[1] second, that in the process this association of tribes, or at least a major part thereof, comes historically into a common bondage, for such half-nomads the most grievous fate thinkable; third, that the common experience of the liberation and of the exodus, recognized and proclaimed by the helper, who arises in the situation, as the deed of that God, the experience of common deliverance by the God, formerly so indefinite, establishes the bond for an association, as its Lord appears in the name changed into the verbal form, or as having become visible through the name—this also an act of mediation of the helper—'He is here', that is, 'He is with us'; fourth, that through common covenant with this Lord, covenant-order and covenant-mentality, the real becoming of a people takes place. With all this the people is certainly not yet a fixed and independent magnitude; but nevertheless unified enough to be able also, after the occupation, to incorporate related elements, which perhaps did not participate in this historical event, into its life of tradition, its cultic-political assembly and formation, in order to be celebrated in the Song of Deborah as the magnitude 'Israel', whose leader is called JHWH.

But whence this God? Old Testament scholarship dares not close its eyes to the insight which the general history of religion has possessed

[1] Cf. below p. 105, 190ff.

for a long time: that the origin of a specific piety is not to be ascertained, indeed that questions of origin are boundary-questions which the investigator as such must acknowledge if his very investigation is not to become problematic. To answer a question of origin by derivation from another historical sphere, where one does not need to ask the question of origin, means to answer it only in pro forma fashion. For centuries people have wanted to derive the religious achievement which is connected with the name of Moses from Egypt, of whose religion they knew all sorts of things; but the more they discovered about it, the more futile the undertaking proved to be. Since then derivation from the Kenites has taken its place, of whose religion they know nothing at all.[1] Therefore in their argumentation they had practically to confine themselves to the interpretation of Old Testament texts, and a verification can proceed in a purely exegetical fashion.[2] So far as the literature[3] is known to me, essentially five arguments of this sort have been brought forward: (1) that of the prophetic texts mentioned by Baumgartner; (2) that of the name (Exodus 3:13ff. and 6:3); (3) that of the person and significance of Jethro (Exodus 18); (4) that of the concluding of the covenant (Exodus 24); and (5) that of the mountain of God (Exodus 33). They will be discussed in that order.

(1) Of the approximately twenty passages (if one disregards mere references and allusions) in which the exodus is spoken about in prophetic texts, no more is said, with the exception of one single passage, than what is said in the texts of the Pentateuch. 'That the relationship of Jahwe and Israel stems from the time of Moses' is suggested in none of them in any other sense than the one which is the leitmotif of the Pentateuch composition: that JHWH first chooses a people for Himself—in the fathers—in order that it may come to be, then, however, once again, by way of actualization, after it has come to be, and that the anticpating covenant with the fathers, involving the

[1] 'That is an explanation of ignotum ab ignoto', remarks Montgomery on this point, *Arabia and the Bible* (1934), p. 10, n. 19.

[2] Hypotheses like those advocated by Schmökel, 'Jahwe und die Keniter', JBL, lii (1933), 212ff., for example those about a Kenitic origin of the 'order of Levites', presuppose the exegetical provability of the Kenite thesis and can, if this presupposition does not prove true, make no claim to an independent proof. For that reason I dare to forego a discussion of them here.

[3] Since Richard v.d. Alm (= Fr. W. Ghillany), *Theologische Briefe an die Gebildeten der deutschen Nation* (1863), i, 216, 321, and Tiele, *Vergelijkende geschiedenis der Egyptische en Mesopotamische godsdiensten* (1869–72), 588ff.

'seed', can only be completed with a partner when there is an Israel as partner, so that only now really does JHWH take this Israel fo. Himself as people and give Himself to it as God (Exodus 6:7). Even so radical a formulation as that of Hosea's (12:10; 13:4) 'I JHWH am thy God from the land of Egypt' has no other content than this, just as his 'from Egypt I called My son' (11:1) only echoes the adoption-proclamation of Exodus 4:22. The exception to which I have referred is Ezekiel 20:5ff. (cf. 23:19) which, however, occupies a special position only with reference to an idol-worship of Israel in Egypt; besides, it does not go beyond Hosea. In any case the late passage can certainly not be traced back to an independent tradition.

(2) The argument based on Exodus 3 is treated by me in the fifth chapter. It will not do to attribute to the one responsible for a centrally important text, to the author or redactor, the suggestion that it is in the imagination of Moses that the people of Israel addresses to him the question how the God of the fathers is to be called. 'Moses' expectation that his compatriots would inquire after the name of the God who was commissioning him, ... is a contradiction in itself' (Alt[1]). This contradiction is not dissolved, however, by deleting (along with Alt), verse 6. Even if one, as is obviously intended,[2] omits the two following verses and thus omits the 'ammi of verse 7 as well, nevertheless the 'ammi of verse 10 remains unremovable[3]—in the mouth of a 'strange' God impossible in *this* moment—and demands almost a preceding explanation of *who* is thus speaking of Israel; no other than an already originated God can, long before the establishing of the covenant, even before direct contact, say 'my people'. It is not a source-critical analysis of the section, but only an analysis of the meaning of the question itself which can lead further here. With the same *ma* the son in Deuteronomy 6:20 is said to ask—not for the wording, but for the meaning and basis of the laws, as is shown by the answer. Moses has the people ask for the (magically usable) meaning-secret of the name; to this verse 14 gives the answer. And, in the same way, 6:3 is not to be overcome with source-criticism: we do not dis-

---

[1] *Der Gott der Väter* (1929), 12.   [2] *Op. cit.*, 13.

[3] Morgenstern, 'The Elohist Narrative in Ex 3, 1–15' (AJSL, xxxvii, 1920/21), 249, wants, to be sure, to ascribe it to a jahwistic redactor with the substantiation that in verses 11, 13, and 15 no 'ammi occurs—as though it were in place in one of these verses. On the other hand in verse 6 Morgenstern wants to read only *elohe chothn°kha*: the God of thy father-in-law!

cover the Pentateuch redactorship otherwise to be so questionable that we could regard it as possible that it yoked passages like Genesis 12:8 together with this one, if this one declares that the fathers did not know the name JHWH. On the other hand, it is quite probably to be assumed that texts like Genesis 12:8 are to be understood in terms of the original trigramm-tradition. The development in meaning of the name through its expansion to the tetragramm, that is, through the changing of an exclamation into a verb form, is in terms of the situation such a tremendous happening that the following word could very well be connected with it:

'I gave Myself to Abraham, Isaac and Jacob to be seen as El-Shaddai [which, since El-Shaddai certainly cannot yet be understood as a form which God assumes, can only mean: I gave to them to be perceived My Shaddai-property in My Shaddai-name—whatever this property be, the meaning of this name in contradistinction to the meaning of the JHWH-name was not handed down], but according to My name JHWH I did not give Myself to them to be known.' (Cf. below, p. 190, n. 25.)

(3) According to the Kenite hypothesis Jethro (18:10ff.) gives 'expression to his proud joy that *his* God, the God of the Kenites Jahwe, has proved Himself mightier than all the other gods'.[1] But in verse 11 Jethro says: 'Now I have discovered ...' or 'Now I know ...' According to this he would declare that until now he has not known that his, the God of the Kenites, is greater than all! Which devotee of a god speaks thus of him?[2] Furthermore according to this hypothesis Jethro, in 18:12, brings sacrifice to God, he leads the holy communal meal with Aaron and the elders of Israel, the sacrifice 'is performed not by Aaron, nor by Moses, but by the Kenite; thus it is not he who turns to a new god, but it is Israel which does so'.[3] This interpretation is based on a conjecture according to which not *way-yiqqach*, 'which occurs nowhere and yields no reasonable meaning', but *way-yisbach* is to be read 'with certainty',[4] whereas Gressmann[5] regards this as 'most

[1] Budde, *Die altisraelitische Religion* (1912), 12.

[2] The *'atha yadathi* of Judges 17:13, Psalm 20:7, says something quite different: the assistance of God is recognized, not His greatness (which the believer confesses again and again, but never as something recognized 'now for the first time').

[3] *Op. cit.* [4] *Op. cit.*, p. 132.

[5] *Mose und seine Zeit* (1913), 166, note 1.

probably a dogmatic correction of the original *way-yaqrib'*. But a related *laqach* as a term of the ritual of sacrifice occurs, for example, in Leviticus 12:8 and designates the bringing forward of sacrificial animals on the part of the one *for whom* a sacrifice is offered. Jethro donates the animals with which, for his benefit, a sacrifice is offered to JHWH. Functioning as offerer one may think of Moses (cf. Targum Jer.) who, in terms of verse 7, is certainly already on the spot, namely, in the tent of the leader;[1] from the fact that Aaron and the elders (who must come out of the camp) are named as the ones coming to the meal but Moses is not named, one in no case needs to conclude that Moses as semi-official member of the tribe of the Kenites 'had for a long time before participated in the worship of Jahwe' and 'no longer needed acceptance into His community'.[2] And finally it follows, of course, from the report concerning Jethro's tendering of advice, verses 14–26, 'that in the wilderness tribe into which Moses married a political organization existed earlier than with the Israelites',[3] by no means, however, that 'the theocracy, that is, the rule of priests', is 'represented here already in full clarity as the only authorized organization of the people'[4] and 'is to be traced back to foreign influence'.[5] Even the equation, theocracy = rule of priests, rests upon an error which is fatal for the knowledge of biblical reality. The pre-exilic theocratic constitutional tendency is not to be equated at any point, not even at its beginning, with hierocracy.[6] Even if the concept of 'prophetocracy'[7] is not correct because—as I showed in the eighth chapter of this volume—the post-Mosaic pre-state *nebiim* were in general not possessors of power, but were the circle supporting the charismatic possessors of power; if Moses, however, is not simply to be ranked typologically among the prophets, still the designation would be atmospherically far more appropriate to the Moses-story than the hierocratic one. After this, however, in the interpretation of Jethro's tendering of advice its character is mistaken. In the tradition which lies at the base of the report two stages of original compositon are obviously to be dis-

---

[1] Cf. below, p. 133.

[2] Budde, *op. cit.*, p. 12; cf. Gressmann, *op. cit.*, p. 167.

[3] Ed. Meyer, *Die Israeliten und ihre Nachbarstämme* (1906), p. 97, note 3.

[4] *Op. cit.*, p. 98; cf. in addition below, pp. 204ff.

[5] W. Vischer, *Jahwe der Gott Kains* (1929), p. 9.

[6] Cf. pp. 136, 160, and J. Kaufmann, 'Probleme der israelitisch-jüdischen Religionsgeschichte', ZAW, NF vii (1930), 23ff.

[7] *Op. cit.*, p. 27.

tinguished: one of the unlimited power of the charismatic leader and one of its limitation by 'specified division of power'.[1] Here it is not 'the spiritual leadership' which crowds, also in law, 'between the divinity and the people',[2] but contrariwise the sphere of decision of this leadership is diminished (since indeed the *ssarim* have to determine what from time to time belongs before the central authority and what does not), and it is this diminishing which is traced back to Midianite influence: the inclination to freedom of the 'wilderness tribe' asserts itself against every extension of authority. To be sure, there is connected with this in the text a purely arithmetical form of organization, strange to nomads, which obviously belongs first to the period of the kings (cf. I Samuel 8:12) and seeks after a primeval justification; the last six words of the 21st and 25th verses of Exodus 18 appear to be grafted upon the original tradition out of such motives.[3]

(4) The argument of the establishing of the covenant has, as Baumgartner mentions, been treated sufficiently by me in the seventh chapter. A refutation of my exposition has to my knowledge not been attempted.

To conclude a *bᵉrith* does not mean biblically that two who have hitherto not known one another now agree to have dealings with one another. It means that between two, no matter in which relation they have hitherto stood toward one another, now this secure legal relationship of common 'limitation' is founded, or one founded earlier is renewed in a new, changed situation. The tribes of Israel already knew JHWH just as wandering tribes know their leader-god; now, however, in the grip of the historical hour and of its interpreter, the solemn union occurs, by virtue of which a covenant of the tribes and the union's covenant with the *melekh*, order and constitution, folk-spirit and community-spirit, become one.

5. Against my observations in the fifth chapter on JHWH's alleged original 'attachment to the mountain of God' Baumgartner objects that my interpretation of the primeval 'accompanying' God will not do justice to the fearful uncertainty over who will lead the

[1] Max Weber, *Wirtschaft und Gesellschaft* (1922), 165.

[2] Ed. Meyer, *op. cit.*, p. 98.

[3] Cf. in addition Phythian-Adams, *The Call of Israel* (1934), p. 72ff., which certainly represents, in this point as well as also with reference to the historical content of the Jethro-tradition, a wide-ranging critique; his final conclusion, however, is also my own: 'there is no particle of evidence to be found here for assuming that Moses derived his religion from a priest of Midian'.

people farther through the wilderness (Exodus 33:1–6, 12–23; cf. Gressmann, *Mose*, 218ff.), and to the wandering of Elijah to Horeb. Exodus 33:3 is already by itself, still more, however, in connection with verses 14–17 (the untenableness of the Gressmann analysis has indeed been amply appreciated by Old Testament scholarship; on the literary unity of the entire pericope, cf. my introductory analysis: Buber and Rosenzweig, *Die Schrift und ihre Verdeutschung*, 1936, pp. 262ff.), an indication against the idea of a God attaching to the mountain, which, however, is by no means thereby attested as the original Israelitish idea (see below, p. 34ff.). That Israel 'after long discussion' had to be content 'that the angel of Jahwe moves with them while Jahwe remains in His home-land'[1] can be read only from texts jumbled without sufficient warrant. And Elijah wanders, 1 Kings 19:8ff., to Horeb, into 'the [known] cave', in order to die at the holy place (that which he says before this, verse 4, is no mere figure of speech!) not in order 'to make complaint' to JHWH 'about all of his hardship and trouble' (Eissfeldt in Kautsch-Bertholet): that he had already done in verse 4, a day's journey from Beersheba; the rest results only because JHWH speaks to him.[2]

To the direct arguments for the Kenite-hypothesis another indirect one may be joined, which is supported by the beginning passage of the prayer, Deuteronomy 26:5ff., which is translated 'An Aramaean ready to perish was my father' and to which is remarked[3]:

'The prevailing opinion that the ancestor of Deuteronomy 26 is the Jacob of Genesis is untenable. An Israelite would hardly have called one blessed by the fathers (Genesis 27:29) an *'obed 'arami*. The song is not acquainted with the sojourn of the patriarchs in the promised land; it is therefore—at least with the tradition deposited in it—older than the Genesis-tradition.'

But when we compare Genesis 20:13a with our passage it dawns on us that *obed* is to be understood here just as it is in Jeremiah 50:6; Ezekiel 34:4, 16; Psalm 119:176: gone astray, like a sheep from the herd.[4] Precisely this Abraham expresses with that *hithe'u* (the two verbs are found united in the Jeremiah passage and in the Psalm pass-

---

[1] Budde, *op. cit.*, p. 9.
[2] Cf. also Moritz, *Der Sinaikult in heidnischer Zeit* (1916), pp. 34ff.
[3] Galling, *Die Erwählungstraditionen Israels* (1928), p. 8.
[4] Cf. Ehrlich, *Randglossen*, i, 360.

age; for *tha'a*. cf. also Isaiah 53:6) with regard to himself: the divinity has caused him to wander away from his herd, from the Aramaean pack. And the remarkable beginning of the prayer, recognizable as a memory-verse by means of its wealth of alliteration, characterizes the historical provenance of the grandson according to that of the forefather: he belongs to that tribe of the 'strayed Aramaeans' in Canaan (the obvious fact that he moves *out of Canaan* to Egypt remains unsaid;—dare one *on this account* assume that the prayer is not acquainted with the sojourn of the patriarchs in the promised land?) The verse agrees completely with the Genesis-tradition as it is presented to us in Genesis 12:1 on the one hand and in 24:4, 7, 10 on the other hand (the connecting double-motif word is *erez-moledeth*); indeed it is based on the Genesis-tradition.[1]

I have discussed all that is important which, so far as I see, has been adduced in the literature for the view that at Sinai Israel was 'converted'[2] to the religion of the Kenites who had worshipped JHWH 'from times immemorial'.[3] (I have not treated the assertion that they had as roaming smiths[4] worshipped JHWH who 'was undoubtedly a fire-god',[5] from which alone the Jews' sabbatical prohibition of kindling a fire and their Sabbath as such is to be explained:[6] the *onus probandi* must remain on those who represent the opinion that for the biblical JHWH the fiery element is not a large sphere of power and manifestation, but the original and essence-determining principle.) Accordingly, the Kenite hypothesis dare not be regarded as exegetically justified.

To be sure, there remains the *religio-historical* problem at the basis

[1] Cf. Speiser, 'Ethnic Movements in the Near East' (*The Annual of the American Schools of Oriental Research*, viii, 1933), p. 43, which understands *obed* in terms of the Akkadian *abatu* as 'flighty'.

[2] Budde, *op. cit.*, p. 13.

[3] Lods, *Israel* (1930), 367ff.; Oesterley-Robinson, *Hebrew Religion* (1930), p. 114.

[4] Cf. especially Eisler, 'Das Qains-zeichen und die Qeniter', *Le Monde Oriental*, xxiii (1929), 48ff.; Budde, 'Sabbat und Woche' (*Die Christliche Welt*, xiii, 1929), pp. 266ff.

[5] Oesterley-Robinson, *A History of Israel* (1932), i, 92; cf. Eisler, *op. cit.*, 55ff., as well as, among others, Gershenson, *The Key to Faith* (1925), pp. 31ff.

[6] Budde, *Sabbat und Woche*, 268ff. In his explanation of the prohibition Budde has omitted the ethnological material which shows the diffusion of the fire-tabu valid for given days and times with the most different peoples, and also its original apotropäic character. Cf. Webster, *Rest Days* (1916), pp. 257ff.

of this hypothesis. I believe I ought still to indicate in this connection
how it presents itself to me.

Jethro's '*barukh JHWH asher* . . .' with which he praises the
Liberator of Israel belongs together with Melchizedek's '*barukh el
'elyon asher* . . .' (Genesis 14:19) which celebrates the Protector of
Abraham. In the Genesis-narrative, which is obviously supposed to
prove Jerusalem's primeval expectancy of the rank of the cultic centre
of the world,[1] Abraham borrows in his answer to the king of Sodom—
originally in an answer, presumably, to Melchizedek himself—the
designation of God with which the priest-king of Salem had greeted
him, but precedes it with the Tetragrammaton. In so doing he *identifies*
his God JHWH with the *el 'elyon* of Salem, the 'creator of heaven and
earth'. What is expressed here is not a late theological construction, but
a religio-historical genuine basic phenomenon which may be regarded
as the concretely accessible starting-point of the 'fusion of gods'.[2] The
devotee of a god comes upon, possibly in another region, the image and
worship of another numen which seem new and yet familiar to him:
this foreign god, in opposition to many another which he met with
on his travels, seems in the exact sense *real* to him, real in a way similar
to the way in which he knows it from his own divine lord,—in a similar way? No, in the same way; for he looks, he is astonished, finally *he
recognizes him*. The process is advanced and intensified if an extraordinary hour generates it, an event for example which brings to the
two partners, to the wanderer, and to the worshippers of the other god,
liberation, perhaps from a common enemy. Then they perceive the
divine deed so unitedly that they are overwhelmed together: it is the
same god! The fusion, into which also that which is different about
the image and worship enters, in so far as it does not resist the fusion
and must drop out, has consequently already begun. A more profound
resistance proceeds from the reservation of the *name*. It can perhaps
be overcome in such a way that the mysteriously more powerful of the
two names enters into the union as the name, the other only as the
epithet; such a union is expressed in the declaration of Abraham. It can
also happen, however, in such a way that perhaps with the similarity
or relatedness of the two names the one stronger in meaning absorbs
the other; a process of this kind appears to me to be what stands behind
Jethro's homage.

[1] Buber and Rosenzweig, *Die Schrift und ihre Verdeutschung*, p. 235.
[2] Cf. Bertholet, *Götterspaltung und Göttervereinigung* (1933), pp. 14ff.

The acceptable part of the Kenite hypothesis is that the Kenites worshipped the god of a mountain. With the experience of Moses who on this very mountain receives declaration and address of a God who makes Himself known to him as the God of his fathers and as JHWH—that is, probably as the one named with the Trigrammaton up to now, but from now on the one to be named with the Tetragrammaton—with this experience the process of identification would then, religio-historically speaking, begin: thus the God of whom they tell, who dwells on the mountain, was no other than our God! It may be stated as a religio-historical principle that experience of the divine begins with the apprehension of a single manifestation, knowledge of the divine, however, with the identification of two manifestations; thus knowledge begins with recognition. With the first communication of Moses to those related to him by marriage the identification would begin, from an identification proceeding in the soul of the experiencing person to an identification about to take place between the popular representatives of two religious traditions. Of course, this communication could not yet arouse an act of faith, but only fruitful astonishment. Only under the impress of the exodus—whose success the leader ascribes to the God of his covenant of the tribes, to the God who had indeed once, in calling him, made Himself known to him—, under the impress of the liberating power ('Yes, this is He, the one flashing down out of the cloud over the mountain; it can be no other!') the Kenites would complete the equation and acknowledge the name, which in its power-producing verbal meaning can be opened up to them in their language through 'translation': *'atha yad'athi*, now I have come to know! In the community of the extended covenant joined together under this divine name they would then go along and take part in the occupation, be devoted to the now common image and worship and yet preserving with a peculiar tenacious nomadic loyalty their own traditional life-customs, the alternative which can remain untouched by the fusion of divine forms and cults (Jeremiah 35).

Israel—thus it would follow—is not converted at Sinai to the God of the Kenites, but neither are the Kenites converted to the God of Israel. Israel observes that its folk-God also rules the earth-powers; the Kenites recognize that their mountain or mountain-fire God rescues and guides tribes. The divine image of both grows. Instead of one image which is only a god of nature and one which is only a god of history, there dawns the form of the One Who is the lord of nature and the lord of history.

In any case, even if the act of identification itself can proceed in a creative hour, fusion begins with it; the resistances of the uncommon have effect for a long time afterward. If the God of the Kenites was a mountain-god then one can explain the declaration of Exodus 33 against the idea of a God attaching to the mountain as directed against the after-effect of the Kenitic image which tended to be connected with the Canaanitic religion of local-gods, with the tendency toward Baalization.[1]

IV. Gerhard von Rad[2] regards my theses as 'constructive in so far as the attestation of Jahwe as the *melek* does not attain general theological significance in the Old Testament, as Buber assumes'. He substantiates this criticism with the following statements:

1. 'It is certain that in the Old Testament Jahwe is never characterized as *melek* before the time of the kings.'

2. 'It is without exegetical basis in the text if the Sinai covenant is expressly understood as a kingly covenant.'

3. 'On the whole the predication of Jahwe as king occurs rather in the hymnic exaggeration of elevated speech than in what one could regard as an especially meaningful exponent of a principally religious attitude.'

4. 'Buber confronts the *malk*, "the leader-divinity", most sharply with the *baal*. . . . But where in the stubborn struggling with the Baal-religion . . . is this battle waged with the theological motto that Jahwe is the *malk*?'

5. 'Buber adduces many passages which in some way declare that Jahwe has "led" Israel; but the theologumenon "*malk*" is not yet given in the alleged meaning in these passages. Rather the specific gravity is taken from those attestations to which the theologumenon really belongs (in the cultic or eschatological sense).'

To this one must answer:

On point 1. For the assertion that it is certain that JHWH, before the period of the kings, is not designated as *melekh*, no proof has up to now been offered either by von Rad or by any one else.

---

[1] I enter into other objections in Baumgartner's detailed critique in the notes. Cf. also Buber, *Moses*[2], 111ff.; *Der Glaube der Propheten*, 42ff. (Addendum to the third edition.)

[2] ThW, under the entry 'βασιλεύς', i, 568.

To be sure, if it were a matter of the positive datability of passages then Isaiah 6:5 would have to be regarded (with Eissfeldt[1]) as the oldest passage. But von Rad obviously does not mean positive datability; for otherwise the apodictic 'it is certain' would be meaningless. He would otherwise have written: 'before Isaiah', and not: 'before the time of the kings'. Accordingly he must wish to say that there is no passage which *may* belong to the pre-kingly period in which JHWH is designated as *melekh*. This, however, is not conclusive. One certainly dare not limit one's self to substantive designation: the kingly predicate can be attributed to JHWH in the most unequivocal way by means of the verb form in a proclamation like Exodus 15:18. We have here, in the Song of the Sea, a text whose foundation (cf. p. 132ff., and the literature listed in note 85 appended to p. 210) is to be regarded as prior to the period of the state. The same is true of the blessing of Moses, from the frame-song, which, looking back in verse 5, remembers the formation of that proclamation in connection with the substantive designation *melekh*. If accordingly it is inconclusive to say that it is certain that the designation does not occur in the early period, it is nevertheless an important fact that in the prophetic texts before Isaiah —except for the allusive Amos 5:26, to which my translation and p. 194, note 23 is to be compared—it does not occur at all, and in texts of all periods, those which narrate and those included in narrative, it occurs only seldom. Seldom, and then only in passages where it appears to be representatively important, even indispensable. The four passages of the Pentateuch—except for the two adduced, Numbers 23:21 and the quite relevant[2] Exodus 19:6—which I treat in the seventh chapter, emphatically have such a focal significance. After the successful liberation the people proclaims its king (Exodus 15:18); the King establishes His constituency with the marking out of His 'kingly domain' (Exodus 19:6); the mantic representative of universal man bows before the divine kingship in Israel (Numbers 23:21); Moses remembers before dying, before he blesses the people at parting, with the last words before the beginning of the blessing, the hour at Sinai when over the united tribes 'a king there was in Jeshurun' (Deuteronomy 33:5). One might investigate whether the designation *melekh* in any of the four passages was dispensable, but also whether it was indispensable in any other passages beside these four. Those respons-

---

[1] ZAW NF V (1928), p. 104: 'die älteste sicher datierbare Stelle'.
[2] Not adduced by Eissfeldt with the others, *op. cit.*, p. 91.

ible for the textual selection preserved what had to be preserved, no less, but also no more.

In the Book of Judges which swarms with *melekhs* (cf. the second chapter), in the decisive passage, 8:22ff., the application of the word, noun or verb, to JHWH is carefully avoided. Here it can be avoided because it is not yet a matter of the historical fact of the Israelitish kingship with which the divine kingship is to be confronted in the same linguistic expression, but only the first unrealized striving after it. It can no longer be avoided in the confrontation with the historically realized kingship: I Samuel 8:7; 12:12, 14 (on the latter passage cf. p. 222, note 89). Because here the vocable *melekh* is given for the human ruler, it must, in the confrontation, be applied to the divine ruler also.

Of pre-Isaiah prophetic passages, as has been said, only one comes into consideration if I interpret it rightly: Amos 5:26. If, in terms of my interpretation, one examines anew the peculiarly constructed verse in its context, one notices that here something otherwise held back seeks for expression and admittedly receives it only in veiled fashion.

Only with the mighty, absolute *ham-melekh* in Isaiah's report of his call does a new atitude break through, which, however, only gradually begins to have its consequences.

(I disregard the early Psalms in this context because of the special problem of liturgical language.)

It follows that the *melekh*-ship of JHWH, already in the pre-state period, was a reality of belief and of the theocratic constitutional tendency, but that its expression remained limited for a long time to that which was religio-politically necessary. The occurrence in representative passages, indeed exclusively in these, can be explained by an embarrassing reserve of the authors and redactors, this, however, primarily through the threat of the *malk* myths and cults of the neighbouring peoples, whose advance was feared until it had proceeded to the point that it had to be combatted directly, by opposition of *melekh* and *molekh*, of divine and idolatrous image and worship.[1]

With this the question (point 4) is also answered as to why the struggle of Hosea against the *baal* did not stand under the *melekh*-sign. The danger threatened that the *baal* would be driven out by means of *molekh*.

[1] Cf. below, p. 110ff., as well as Eichrodt, *Theologie des Alten Testaments*, i (1933), 96, with whom, however, I can agree only in part.

But this is also an explanation for the fact that (point 3) the assertion occurred more in hymnic exaggeration since the spiritual storm which expressed itself in this exaggeration conquered inhibition sooner. After all, for the knowledge of an elementary religion no other source is to be preferred to the hymn; one need only think of the Rigveda and the Gathas. 'Elevated speech' in this sphere is precisely the direct testimony.

Point 2. The exegetical basis upon which the Sinai covenant is to be understood as king's-covenant, consists of the following elements: first, as has been said, it is preceded by a kingly proclamation; second, the declaration begins with a kingly saying which is probably not early, literarily speaking, but obviously traditional; third, the covenant is developed into a constitutional or legal document; fourth, the promise given by God is the original kingly obligation (I Samuel 8:20): leadership (Exodus 23:20ff.) and subduing the enemy (v. 28ff.).

Point 5. *Malk* is the divine leader of the wandering and occupying tribe. That is a concreteness without which he would be *only* a theologumenon, not rooted in real folk-history. This concreteness of His enters into the cultic, above all in the form of the accompanying ark; only for that reason can a cultic *melekh*-passage like Psalm 24:7–10 be clearly understood, not from the procession itself, but from its prototype, the going-on-before of the *gibbor milchama* in the historical march. And this concreteness of His enters into prophecy, the proclaimed liberation appears in the picture of the wilderness-way; a *melekh*-promise like Micah 2:13, where JHWH leads the army, as it breaks forth, like a battering-ram, is illuminated by the tradition of such occurrences, and the context finds its completing expression in the proclamations of guidance of Deutero-Isaiah which, as already said, are not to be separated from his *melekh*-proclamations. The 'specific gravity' of purely cultic and purely eschatological testimonies would be a sham gravity. Out of the transmitted experience of divine *melekh*-ship, out of organic memory there develops for the cultic, and for the eschatological as well, the corporeality which hinders them from becoming apparatus and schema, and on the strength of which they exert influence down to our own day. If they had not attained this then they, like all the innumerable instances of the merely-religious in the history of ideas, would long ago have been buried in museums and libraries.

V. Jecheskel Kaufmann,[1] to be sure, regards a primitive theocracy in Israel as historical, but my interpretation of a theocratic tendency in the sense of the exclusion of a human kingship as far too venturesome, and substantiates this in essence with the following theses:

1. The Pentateuch, which countless times attacks the worship of idols, nowhere speaks against a worship of a king. The human kingship is never objected to, but rather exalted in several passages in the promise to Abraham (Genesis 17:6), in the promise to Jacob (35:11), in the narrative of Melchizedek, in the story of Joseph, in the prohibition of cursing a *nassi* (Exodus 22:28; cf. Leviticus 4:22), in the king's law (Deuteronomy 17:14-20), in the blessing of Jacob to Judah and to Asher (Genesis 49:10, 20).

2. Of all the scriptural prophets only Hosea takes a critical position on the kingship, and even he has only its decadence in view. No fundamental opposition existed between prophethood and kingship.

3. Messianism cannot be derived, even in the form of the Messiah, from the primitive theocracy.[2]

In particular points Kaufmann rightly expects a clarification from the following volumes. But already in the preface to the first edition of this volume I have characterized it as the task of the second 'to disclose how the conception of a human regent of God intersects with and transforms that primitive-theocratic tendency', and to 'show how the sacred character of the Israelitish king as an "anointed" of JHWH is related to it'. In other words: from the fact that the human kingship in the Samuelic crisis is *religiously received* and is sanctified in the sacrament of the annointing there results the relatively positive attitude of the prophets toward it which necessarily from time to time—if we disregard the special problem of Samuel-Saul: from Nathan to Jeremiah—changes suddenly into a critical one; and it is this critical attitude which finds its fundamental expression in Hosea. From here the origin of Messianism is to be derived; from here the great tensions arose within Messianism.

From the historical fact of the religious reception of the kingship, that is, of its regency character, which certainly is taken with crucial seriousness by the prophets and by the Biblical authors who stand near

---

[1] *Kirjath Sepher*, x (1933), 62–66.
[2] I enter into Kaufmann's objections to my interpretation of Numbers 23:21 and Judges 9:2 in the notes.

them, it is also to be understood that 'royalistic' Pentateuch texts like
Genesis 17:6 and 35:11 do not need to be perceived as anti-theocratic.
If it is correct (which I attempt to prove here and in further discussions) that in the pre-kingly period the principle of leadership which
again and again united the tribes was indissolubly bound up with the
tendency toward a direct theocracy, then such passages certainly
cannot belong to the pre-Davidic period, which for Genesis 49:10 is
quite out of the question. It is worthy of notice that all of the three
passages named belong to the 'shadday'-texts; except here, this divine
name occurs only three other times in Genesis, and of these twice in
the Joseph story. The idea suggests itself that here the pan-Israelitish
kingship is to be connected with promises whose genuineness is to be
attested by means of the archaic divine name. The fact that also the
Melchizedek-narrative with its bias toward the cultic primary claim of
Jerusalem attained its characteristic stamp in the period of Solomon I
have already indicated above; the whole of the fourteenth chapter,
which anticipates the future victories over the kings, sounds pan-
Israelitish. That which lies hidden in the Joseph-story as announce-
ment of later rulership over all the brothers can most easily be connected with Ephraimitic counter-aspirations which can quite well be
localized in the early period of the northern kingdom. The Deuteronomic kingly law finally seems to me, according to its nucleus
(17:14–17; verse 18ff., is a later addition of quite different style and
character), to refer back to a prophetic anti-Solomonic pronouncia-
mento. For the horses of verse 16, the wives of verse 17a, and the
treasures of verse 17b such marked evidences do not occur for a later
period as they do for this one (I Kings 5:6; 10:28ff.; 11:3ff.; 10:14ff.),
in which also commerce with Egypt begins (verse 16). With the *ish
nokhri* of verse 15, for which there is no explanation from the entire
history of Israel, the son of the daughter of the Pharaohs is quite possibly meant.[1] The kingly law which in verse 14 cites the popular demand of I Samuel 8:5, expresses clearly in verse 15a the theocratic
conditionality of the kingship: JHWH it is who chooses the king.

----

[1] 'The prohibition from choosing a foreign king is scarcely conceivable
before the exile', observes Eissfeldt (in Kautzsch-Bertholet) on the passage, who,
moreover, traces references to Solomon; but the verb 'to choose' is intentionally
avoided in this context; only JHWH appears here as the chooser. 'To set' can
refer to a definite hereditary succession which is feared and fought; *nokhri* can be
termed the son of a *nokhria*.

One detects the atmosphere of a period in which the dynastic principle has not yet become self-evident, that is, only breachable by means of revolutions. The limitations of the kingly authority introduced by the *raq*—later extended by means of 18ff. to all limitations which derive from 'this Torah'—point to the responsibility of the ruler toward the divine power in whose name he rules, and *implicite* to his possible deposition by that power. In connection with 15a there sounds throughout: what happened to Saul can also happen to you. The Pentateuch passages adduced by Kaufmann (I disregard Exodus 22:27 and Leviticus 4:22, since they on no account need to have reference to the king[1]) accordingly reflect the spirit of an epoch in which the fact of the religious reception of the kingship has consequences on a broad scale: from its glorification, for which the fact essentially means authorization, sanctioning, divine favour, all the way to admonition and warning, for which the sense of giving a charge for a strictly accountable regency inheres in the same fact of religious reception. For a radical rejection of the degenerated kingship, as we find it two centuries later with Hosea, the presuppositions at that time did not yet exist. A veneration of the king was also subsequently not attacked because the theocratic tradition, united with that inclination to freedom of the West Semites which had not died out and with which that tradition had a peculiar affinity, was also still strong enough in the age of decline to prevent its rise. That also Hosea's rejection, in spite of its fundamental character, is not an unconditioned one, is a point in which I agree with Kaufmann so much that I have expressed it myself in the first edition of this volume (now p. 82ff.). The kingship was so strongly built into the theocracy or theocratically undergirded that the criticism of the prophets could not reach to the foundation itself: it could only point to this foundation, confront the possessor of power with the origin and significance of his power.

VI. As an appendix I would call to mind a peculiar observation which I find in the recently published second volume of Elias Auerbach, *Wüste und Gelobtes Land*, on p. 231. It belongs to a section which deals with the Persian period and in which there is also a discussion of the idea of 'the divine rulership over Israel' as a 'genuine substitute form ("sublimation") for the kingship' originating in this period. 'This idea' is said to presuppose foreign rulership, 'if not intellectually, at

[1] Cf. Noth, *Das System der zwölf Stämme Israels* (1930), pp. 151ff., as well as Wendel, *Säkularisierung in Israels Kultur* (1934), pp. 184ff.

least with its entrance into the world of things'. From this point of view 'then the entire past history of Israel' is said to have been 'newly seen, evaluated, arranged and comprehensively portrayed anew; but to trace back the idea of theocracy itself into older or even the oldest strata of the Israelitish development signifies a misunderstanding of the actuality'. In addition to this the remark: 'This fundamental mistake is made by Martin Buber in his *Königtum Gottes*, 1932. The Biblical proofs there furnished cannot be accepted since they are taken without exception from less ancient literary strata'.

In the present phase of development of Old Testament scholarship such a dogmatic utterance is remarkable. Nearly everywhere people have begun to discover that the literary-critical methods which have flourished to a wonderful degree of skilfulness are not sufficient to distinguish the actual strata, that 'formal source criticism on the basis of quite insufficient linguistic characterizing marks and unevennesses of content' (Staerk, 1924) is not able to open up the way to the genetic history of the text; and it is precisely the younger generation which embraces the insight which one of its well-known representatives, himself productively familiar with all the niceties of that methodology, has expressed (von Rad, 1934[1]): 'In spite of all the literary criticism we know almost nothing about the nature of the Old Testament literature and about the laws of its growth, about its constitutive forces.' In all the fields of research the problems have surged up, the questions are being posed anew with new candour. The criteria of literary criticism are in the process of being re-examined; in addition, however, it has been recognized that a judgment concerning age or youth of a literary stratum by no means involves one concerning age or youth of the corresponding stratum of religious development, because it still remains to be investigated, for example, whether an early genuine tradition has reached us in a late form or transformation; it is recognized that without the co-operation of an investigation of tradition—to be sure, still in the process of becoming—or rather investigation of the compilations of tradition and of the forms of bias which determine them, the criticism of sources must miscalculate and lead astray. Elias Auerbach, however, *knows* with a knowledge which obviously perceives itself as identical with the knowledge of contem-

[1] *Die Priesterschrift im Hexateuch*, p. 37.

porary scholarship and therefore presumes to require no further argument: my Biblical proofs are not to be accepted because they are taken without exception from literary strata which are not ancient. I have given in this volume, in the text and in the apparatus, several contributions to the dating of my sources (see, for example, concerning the dating of Numbers 23:21b, pp. 211ff.),—but this is temporary; many a supplement will be necessary; still, there are contributions. One can accept them, weigh, discuss, challenge, oppose; one dare not make decrees above and beyond, from the cloudy throne of the school.[1] This is no longer to the point.

In any case, the self-evidence with which here the idea of the divine rulership over Israel is treated as a product of foreign rulership is only possible if one has concerned himself seriously with the problem of an original *melekh*-ship, that is, of a concrete leading of the federation of tribes by its God, and is so possessed by the idea of 'projection' current in the schools that one is not able to penetrate to the question of whether the theocratic idea of the Persian period does not perhaps possess merely a restorative character determined by a sacrally maintained tradition; if, in short, one protects himself from this question by dismissing it as 'retrogressive'.

For that which results from such a position I will only adduce one sentence of Auerbach: the idea of the divine rulership over Israel is said to be 'a completely different one from the powerful conception 'of Isaiah, Jeremiah, and Deutero-Isaiah' concerning God as the Lord of all peoples and Leader of history'. But whence this powerful conception? If one does not want to derive it from external influences (which Auerbach obviously does not have in mind), one will have to attempt to understand it in terms of the religious history of Israel. This, however, if with Auerbach one wants to know nothing of an original *melekh*-ship, is a futile labour. It is otherwise, however, if one takes that *melekh*-ship seriously. Then Amos 9:7 (cf. p. 99) makes itself known as a link of prime significance. The verse deals with God's

[1] Permit me in this connection by way of exception—especially also on behalf of the person of the speaker—to cite one of the voices which is not critical. John Wood Oman closes his review of this volume (JThSt, 1933) with the sentence: 'this is a work which, if it is wrong, will require a serious and circumstantial answer, and, if it is right, is very important for the history of religion as well as for the interpretation of the Old Testament, and even of the New'.

age-old activity in history: as Leader of the peoples moving from vassalage into freedom, from confinement into wide expanse. Just as JHWH once strode on before our procession out of Egypt (cf. 2:10) (this Israel learns here), as actual *melekh* also in the original sense of the word, as 'counseling' dispenser of the path and battle oracles (cf. pp. 86, 101, 170 note 4) just so did He command the wanderings and settlements of our neighbours—our neighbours often hostile to us![1] However each one of the peoples names its divine *melekh*, all the names are of One. He has brought each people into a good land and has helped it to occupy and to settle that land. Each people has erected for itself upon the new *adama* a political order, has chosen for itself men as *melakhim*, founded dynasties, has grown into a *mamlakha* into a king's domain, a kingdom. He, however, JHWH, the primeval Leader, primeval Founder, has remained the Overlord of these *mamlakhoth*, Who judges them and extirpates those who sin from the *adama* (v. 8). Here the decisive phase of clarification of the great religio-historical process is accessible, in which the Mosaic God-sheik of the wilderness wanderers makes Himself known as the Lord of all the peoples and the Leader of history. Whoever preserves for himself an unprejudiced vision or has regained it, sees how deeply and securely this mighty bridgepier is driven into the ground, but also that it is a genuine bridge which it supports: the shore of antiquity with which it connects is not a fiction sprung from the post-exilic hankering for foundation, but the remembered reality of early time, without perceiving which one cannot perceive Israel.

That which occurs in the notes by way of rejoinder to objections is to be found partly under a numeral furnished with an a or b, partly in angular brackets; likewise that which I have to reply to significant publications of this year which, without reference to my book, represent an opposed standpoint in the one or another question. My reply (printed for the first time in the September-October volume, 1936, of *Theologische Blätter*) to the most significant among them, Eissfeldt's 'Molk als Opferbegriff im Punischen und Hebräischen und das Ende

---

[1] It is from this point of view, then, that the above-mentioned proclamations of impending and future leading of the people, from *Micah* 2:13 to the accomplishment in Deutero-Isaiah, are to be understood: JHWH did not merely lead us at one time; He leads us and will lead us. The One recognized as world-king remained for Israel's entire historical course the *melekh* in the original sense.

des Gottes Moloch' (1935), I have appended to the notes for the fourth chapter.

For valuable references I have yet to thank Dr. David Hartwig Baneth, Dr. Max Eschelbacher, Prof. Michael Guttmann, Prof. Eugen Mittwoch, and especially Dr. Arthur Spanier.

Heppenheim on the Bergstrasse, in early autumn, 1936.

PREFACE TO THE THIRD EDITION

I

I HAVE left the text of the previous edition essentially unaltered because the literature which has appeared since that time gave me no occasion for important changes. The apparatus has been enlarged only so far as absolutely necessary (with the praiseworthy help of my student Meir Michaelis). Other discussions which supplement that which is given in this book are to be found in the books which have since appeared, *Moses* ([2]1952) and *Der Glaube der Propheten* (1950). Of the reviews which have come to my attention after the second edition I must enter briefly into the one by Albright (JBL 1938) because he condemns my distinction between *malk*-gods and *baal*-gods (in the fourth chapter) as an 'aprioristic approach to historical problems' and recommends that I evaluate more strongly the material from Ras Shamra for the acquisition of another position. Elsewhere (*From Stone Age to Christianity*[2] and *Archaeology and the Religion of Israel*) he appeals for his critical attitude toward a Canaanitic plurality of *beʿalim* especially to Eissfeldt's important essay, 'Baʿal-šamêm und Jahwe', (ZAW NF XVI, 1939) which ought also to be adduced here.[1] From another side it has been asserted against me that 'the *malk*-idea stands in indissoluble connection with the naturalistic myth of the ancient Orient',[2] that is, with 'kingly ideology' as, in our time, in particular the so-called Swedish School 'has exhibited' it 'in a nature-mythical schema', and thus is said to contradict the fundamental essence of the religion of Israel. The first group of objections is related consequently to the

---

[1] Cf., however, the strongly limiting remarks *From Stone Age*[2], 333, and *Religion*, 156ff.

[2] H. J. Kraus, 'Gespräch mit Martin Buber', *Evangelische Theologie* xii (1952/3) 69; cf. also, however, his work, *Die Königsherrschaft Gottes im Alten Testament* (1951) 91. On kingly ideology cf. particularly Engnell, *Studies in Divine Kingship* (1943) and Widengren, *Sakrales Königtum im AT und im Judentum* (1955).

baal-gods, the second to the *malk*-gods. I have to treat the former and the latter separately.

2

History of religion, like all of history, can only be carried on scientifically by connection of individualities and generalities. Historically considered every great religion arises before a background which more or less resembles it typologically, with which it, however, nevertheless contrasts decisively. In the concrete process of its origin it is once-for-all and individual, as well as in its concrete appearance; but the incomparable in it can be scientifically grasped only from the point of view of the comparable. This eminently historical approach would, however, not be scientifically possible unless the religious tradition of the events themselves, as visualized in faith, led thereunto. The transmitted event is transmitted as having happened in a historically determined medium; also that which is designated by religion with the religious concept of revelation is entirely related to the historically characterized receivers; it happens in their language, and that means under the presuppositions of their historically conditioned character. Magicians may indulge in combinations of sounds which are unintelligible to all others; that which in the primal depth of a religion enters the ear of the listening man as God's Word, wants to be understood by them; that is, it is directed upon the historically determined contexts of their remembering and associating, it enters into them.

I have discussed in the seventh chapter of this book the passages of the exodus story, which is only to be understood in terms of a conception of God which prevails in the story itself, a God who stands to the wandering host in the relationship of an absolute leader of its marches and battles, of a wisely and justly ruling lawgiver and lawguardian, of an arbitrator and giver of decisions; stands, indeed, to this multifarious crowd as to the crowd which He calls His *'am*, His people. In the four passages of which each one appears in an especially significant context, this relationship is designated by the noun and verb from the stem *malk*. If this word, related to the divinity, was to awaken in the spirit of the earliest hearers the correct associations, there had already to be living in them an idea which inhabited them and other related nomadic tribes in common; but now, however, had unfolded itself in an unexpectedly grand manner in their especially great experience, the idea of a *malk* in the original sense of the word, of a 'giver of decisions', coming down to them and going on before them, in this pre-nation-state tribal life daily in need of new decisions.

Eissfeldt, in his essay 'Jahwe als König (ZAW 46, 1928) 84 characterizes 'this idea and this naming' as 'primitive Semitic', and, indeed, precisely in the sense of a chieftain in that period, 'since the Semites as yet knew no kingship', therefore in the sense of a 'tribal god' (104). With this one ought perhaps to compare Nielsen, *Ras Šamra Mythologie und biblische Theologie* (1938) 44: 'He is the heavenly leader of the tribe, of the caravans and war-expeditions, and as such is called *malik*, an appellative which originally designates the "leader" '. I have referred (*Der Glaube der Propheten*, 51 ff.) to the fact that the God of the ancestral history is just such a 'leading God', venerated as protector of the clan and that these 'pictures of the wandering herdsmen with whom their God associates' are not 'the "projection" of a late, "nomadic ideal" ', but 'of genuine, original, undiscoverable nomadic belief' which, changing in terms of tribal and folk-history, flourishes to the full in Israel. With other clans and tribes the 'god of the way' has an astral character, but with the fathers of Israel He is no nature-god any longer (see on this point *Der Glaube der Propheten*, 56 and especially *Moses*[2], 148ff.). But in the exodus history for the first time those who undergo it become aware of His actuality as God of history; only now can they call Him *melekh*.

It was the representation of this at once historical and religio-historical situation[1] which gave me the impulse in the third chapter, in a simplifying manner made necessary by the insufficiency of the material at hand, to premise a reference to that which is situationally common in the west-Semitic *malk*-belief for the presentation of the uniqueness emerging from it of the faith of Israel in JHWH as its *melekh*.

The Israelitish tradition, as is well known, has, in different stages, brought to bear the conception of the divine leading of migration and occupation also upon other tribes and peoples, those related by blood as well as those completely foreign. Thus the political document, Judges 11:12–27, an elaborate, but presumably a literary product nurtured by tradition, presents the god of a neighbour-people, for

[1] Its historicity is connected with that of the 'covenant' for which especially Cazelles, *Études sur le Code de l'Alliance* (1946) is to be compared; I have portrayed its character as *malk*-covenant in the seventh chapter.

whose benefit the indigenous population is 'disinherited', just as
JHWH 'disinherits' them here and in so many other passages for the
benefit of Israel, precisely as Leader in the wandering and the settling.
Here first of all (v. 24) JHWH and Chemosh are spoken of as two
tribal gods of the same kind, whom the agreement about to be reached
between their peoples directly includes, as if a division of territory
were executed between them themselves. Nevertheless there breaks
through at the close an essentially different outlook in which suddenly,
in opposition to all the diplomatic language, JHWH is appealed to as
judge set over the two parties, thus corresponding with the epithet,
assigned to the primitive period, of a 'judge of the whole earth'
(Genesis 18:25). It is, however, not the attribute of the Kosmokrator
which is herewith referred to, but that of the Lord of history in a
special sense if we may follow (as I believe) the theological interpretation which we receive at the beginning of Scriptural prophecy.
The divine verdict, Amos 9:7, is certainly not to be understood otherwise than that JHWH is to be recognized as the leader of *all* the
migrations of the peoples, even the wanderings of peoples hostile to
Israel from earliest times. With exception of Israel, all, to be sure,
know virtually only caricatures and false names—some even suggest
(thus may well be limited in the apprehension of the prophets) in a
surname his character as *malk*. Israel alone, however, which at the
same time knows itself as standing in a special contact with Him, that
of 'becoming known' (3:2), has come to know His character in a
living way. This coming to know manifests itself (cf. the first chapter
of this book) in this, that the absolute Lord of the journey becomes
the absolute Lord of the settlement, Whom—as earthly leaders of
Israel know—man may only represent, not supplant. The word stem
mlk (over and above the hindering *molekh*-motif discussed above,
p. 38) must certainly be avoided as the designation for God as long
as the fact of the Canaanite petty-kings, concerning which the Book
of Judges has so much to tell and which are also so solemnly enumerated in Joshua 12, stands in the foreground of attention and strongly
determines the word-association. Only when the external-political pre-
conditions for the emergence of a sovereign political entity are to some
extent given, thus in the period designated by the name of Samuel,
does the *malk*-concept come to the fore: in the tradition which shows
through from behind I Samuel 8.[1]

[1] Cf. Buber, 'Das Volksbegehren', *In Memoriam Ernst Lohmeyer*, 53ff.

I believe that I can claim the name historical for the approach here outlined.

3

In its wandering the federation of tribes calling itself 'Israel', in spite of a fetish cult persisting in domestic living, seems as a whole to have found satisfaction in JHWH; it is indeed dependable leading from above which the land-seeking band of nomads vitally needed. But in the measure that the people comes into active contact with the fertility of the earth it no longer knows how to apprehend a central domain from the point of view of the relation to the God unverified as giver of water. It allows itself to be initiated by the indigenous population into Canaanitic Baal-customs, into sexual myths and sexual rites as into the standardized basis of blessed agriculture. The super-sexual sphere of JHWH now stands in opposition to divine copulation, fertilizing the land, open to the knowledge of men and capable of being influenced by their practice. To this process, which the narrative in Numbers 25 anticipates with symbolic vividness—a compressed style in which the prophet of the synthetic interpretation of history (Hosea 9:10) psalmists (Psalm 10:28), and preachers (Deuteronomy 4:3) have followed—and its presumably typical elements which I have emphasized in the third chapter, the trend of research culminating in the works of the school of Uppsala places in opposition a fundamentally different picture.[1]

According to this interpretation JHWH is 'the great west-Semitic sky-atmospheric high-god El' who was brought already by the first wave of Semitic immigrants to Canaan; in his late form Moses is said to have 'activated' him and made him into the Israelitish national god. However, since in the pantheon of Ras Shamra El and Baal appear as father and son, although sometimes standing in severe conflict with one another, one is inclined in place of the opposition of JHWH and Baal to see a more or less familiar relationship which was odious only to the prophetic zealots. The leading, choosing, rescuing, preceding, constitution-giving folk-*melekh*, the history-preparing, history-directing Lord who emerges from the *malk*-typology with the once-for-all character of his revelatory discourse, has here apparently disappeared from the history of religion until the reformatory painting-over by Moses of a sky-god who had become otiose.

[1] Engnell, *op. cit.*, p. 177.

In order to help clarify beforehand an essential point with regard to this interpretation whose detailed presentation has been announced,[1] one should emphatically be referred to an ambiguity of the concept of a divine king in the ancient orient through which the interpretation is made possible at all.

On the level of the migrations of west and south Semitic bands— appearing in the religions of Israel and several neighbours in principal, in old Arabic tradition in secondary function—the leading, preceding tribal god is designated with the appellative *malk*, possibly the decider, that is, certainly above all: the one who, from time to time decides concerning the path to be entered upon. The kingly title of a god within the pantheon belonging to a mature oriental state is fundamentally different from this pre-state surname of a divine solitary goer. If an Egyptian, Babylonian, Phoenician god is called 'king', he is called thus either as one of the princes of the gods or also as the highest lord of the state of the gods, in addition doubtless also as Kosmokrator, and then probably also as ruler of the state for which the human king represents him as his 'son'. In Israel in the sphere of the exodus history JHWH is designated as *melekh*, that is, as the one who goes on ahead of the wandering people; in the mature state He is venerated, to be sure, as the proclaimed world-ruler of heaven and earth and adopts the crown prince as His 'son' and designated regent in Jerusalem,[2] but still in eschatological promise (Micah 2:13) He strides, as formerly, along before the delivered bands as *malk*.

From the exodus narrative up until the early forms of Messianism the *malk*-idea proves to be separated according to origin and nature from ancient oriental nature mysticism, however many contacts it experienced with it in the course of its history and however many elements it assimilated into its phenomenal world from it in the course of its history.

---

[1] *Op. cit.*, 174ff.

[2] For the problems of the relationship of Israel to the ancient oriental ideology of kings, problems which do not belong any more in the context of this volume but in that concerning 'the annointed one', it is sufficient here to refer to Noth, 'Gott, König, Volk im Alten Testament', ZThK, xlvii (1950), 157ff. and Johnson, 'Divine Kingship and the Old Testament', *Expository Times*, lxii (1950), 36ff. For an *historical* understanding of Israelitish kingship the works of Albrecht Alt have not been made use of in a noteworthy manner in the countless discussions growing out of ancient oriental ritual.

4

Albrecht Alt[1] has expressly referred to the context of passages, actually in need of renewed investigation, in which JHWH resembles the lord of an ancient oriental state of the gods, except that possibly the gods have become 'sons of god'—whether they appear in the creation (Genesis 3:22) or in the prophetic vision surround the heavenly throne, here called 'host of heaven' (I Kings 22:19; cf. the seraphim Isaiah 6:2, 4; cf. also Job 1:6; 2:1; 38:7), whether in the primeval world they violate the daughters of men (Genesis 6:1ff.) or— a significant idea which ought to be added to the one adduced by Alt—misuse the delegated office of judge for the exercise of which they have been set over the lands of the earth and now themselves meet with the judgement of their lord (Psalm 82:16, 6).[2] But the Israelitish conception of God does not begin with this latter domain of images which certainly stem from ancient oriental myth. The circle of the sons of God belongs to the formative work of the process in which the *melekh*-concept is changed in such a way that from among the powers operating between heaven and earth the one in the Song of Deborah who goes before the host of warriors in the storm and leads them to victory over their enemies (Judges 5:31), the one en- throned above the clouds, becomes Lord of the worlds.

In the comprehensible beginning stage of this process the sacred form of the ark[3] stands as the movable seat of the One who comes down occasionally. The religio-historical peculiarity of Israel is mani- fested in this, that the circle of power surrounding the heavenly throne has no element of an individuation in common with the pantheons: in the multitude which here comes into view there are neither individual names, nor individual forms, nor individual myths—everything is collective-dynamic, periphery of activity. Personality in the real sense befits the *melekh* alone, and when on one occasion 'three men' appear active upon earth (Genesis 18:2) only He steps forth from their midst bearing a name (v. 17); otherwise we see only 'messengers' at work (19:1, 15). Not until under Persian influence, literally not until the Hellenistic environment (Book of Daniel) do they receive, as 'princes',

---

[1] 'Gedanken über das Königtum Jahwes' (*Kleine Schriften zur Geschichte des Volkes Israel*, 1953, i), 351ff.

[2] Cf. Buber, *Recht und Unrecht. Deutung einiger Psalmen* (1952), 27ff.

[3] Cf. Alt, *op. cit.*, 350.

individual forms, individual names and special domains; not until then does the separation between them change from a functional one into an individual one. Only now does one build in Israel the heavenly monarchy in accordance with the model of the occasional actual earthly one.

5

But there is also a distinction to be made within the Baal concept. Except that here one does not have to distinguish origins and natures, but only levels. Naturally these are not to be understood as following one another temporally. Thus the Tyrian Baal which Elijah attacks doubtless represents a more highly individuated level than the '*bᵉalim*' against which Hosea strives one hundred years later.

Eissfeldt (*Ba'alšamêm und Jahwe*, 15ff.) understands the plural form *bᵉalim*, which confronts us in Hoseanic and post-Hoseanic texts, as metaphoric language. This does not seem to me to be sufficiently established. To be sure, I regard the plural usage as a personal innovation of Hosea who probably wishes to call attention therewith to the apostasies of Israel to Baal cults in different cultural localities in different periods; from him it seems to me to have passed to Jeremiah as well as to sundry later texts. That, however, all the local cults are to be related to a single, individual numen, known to be such by their participants, seems to me unproved and improbable. Rather '*baal*' may not here throughout designate a divine figure, but a divine type, and may indeed be regarded as a genuinely undifferentiated one, probably like a crude pillar-idol clumsily springing from the block. On this lowest level scarcely more is to be understood with 'the *baal*' than the fertile-making power at separate places of the earth, to which the '*baal*' of higher cults and of the myths is not essentially differently related than the Manitu-god of the Algonquins to the magical power of the same name which possesses a thing or a living being. When, however, Hosea says 'the *baal*' in the collective sense (13:1) he probably means both together, the entire Baal nature.

Moreover, it is to be assumed that the difference of meteorological conditions here has not been without influence.[1] The inferior Baals appertain to the water coming out of the earth; in ascent they merge with rain gods, concentrate in their hands decision as to the vegetation and have the tendency to coalesce with the sky-gods.

[1] Cf. on this point Semple, *The Geography of the Mediterranean Region* (1922), 511, 572; for Israel, Buber, *Israel und Palästina* (1950), 44ff.

We have received an extensive description of the power-conflicts and power-increases of Baal from the texts of Ras Shamra. Baal, whose living, dying and rising 'meant life and death for tillers of the soil and cattle breeders and consequently for the entire society',[1] is, to be sure, the lord of the fertilizing water of the heavens, but he has yet no house of his own as do the other gods;[2] he must first overcome the resistance of the old god of the heavens, his father El who supports his rival against him, evidently the god of the lower water-expanse named 'sea' or 'stream', and also does not protect him from another enemy, like the former son of El, whose name means 'death'. We may assume that Baal does not belong to the oldest stratum of the pantheon; he is perceptibly a 'younger', supervening god, one having arrived at full individuation only in a longer process. In noteworthy manner there surrounds him a host of 'Baals' who here apparently occupy an inter-mediate position between undifferentiated and fully differentiated numinousness.

Baal is called 'king' as *king of the gods* or rather one of their kings, to whom according to nature a cosmic jurisdiction is assigned. Kings of the gods can very well exist alongside of one another even without encroaching upon one another, as, for example, Anu and Enlil or Indra and Varuna. Moreover, Baal is not king from time immemorial; he is installed as such, loses the throne, and wins it again. That, as some investigators assert, he finally rises above El cannot be deduced from the cries of the gods 'none above him'.

So far as I see, from the very beginning Baal is in no way a tribal god.

6

Of the publications of the nearly two decades elapsed since the previous edition, Alt's essay discussed above, 'Gedanken über das Königtum Jahwes', has stimulated me the most strongly because here one treads upon historical ground. Precisely on that account, however, it seems correct to me to append to this very essay an observation of a methodological sort necessary for supplementary clarification.

Alt expresses himself to the effect[3] that 'the idea of Jahwe's king-

[1] Kapelrud, *Baal in the Ras Shamra Texts* (1952), 25.
[2] I believe that the house-myth can be traced to the fact that Baal, originally dwelling everywhere where water springs up, after becoming the god of the water of the heavens, takes his seat in the heavens.
[3] Alt, *op. cit.*, 348.

ship appears to have had no constructive element in the original growth of the Israelitish religion'. As proof of the thesis he refers to the fact that in the Old Testament we possess no evidences for Israel's belief in the kingship of JHWH 'which definitely stem from the pre-state period of the people'. This formulation is certainly indisputable; but are we justified to conclude from this lack of definiteness that one 'dare not regard' the idea of the divine *melekh*-ship 'as a primary datum of Israelitish religion?'[1] One could certainly not regard it as such if the concept of a divine *melekh* had to be synonymous with this or that concept of king known to us from Semitic political history. What speaks against this is that the designations of political authority some-times emerge from pre-political ones, and when the latter have been employed as titles of gods, an analogous change of meaning must doubtless be carried out in the religious sphere also.

Alt himself speaks[2] of the 'extraordinary flexibility and versatility of the ideas concerning the kingship of Jahwe'. It is just this flexibility and versatility which lie at the base of the attempt here undertaken to point to a pre-political early state of these ideas. Against the background of the west and south Semitic early typology (showing through in the *malk*-concept) of a divine leader, of the way and of existence, for clan, tribe and confederation, we are confronted here by a religio-historical uniqueness in the strictest sense: the ever and again realized, but always intended relation of dialogical exclusiveness between the One who leads and those who are led. Unfolding in forms capable of exchange in folk-history, the relation reveals its intimate reality in the biography— historically valid or legendary—of mediating persons. Whether the man whom God, in His willing to lead, fetches 'from the home' or 'from the herd' in order to tell him 'to go' where He wills that he go, is a 'patriarch' in the twilight of the primeval period (Genesis 12:1) or a 'prophet' in mid-day glow of history (Amos 7:15), it is the same process, the same action. Here, to be sure, JHWH does not act as *melekh*, but as the divine dialogue-partner of the individual—however the one addressed by Him is called, whether as 'father', or as 'spokes-man': it always involves an Israel which worships the One here acting as its *melekh*, and that means: as its way-determiner.

Michaelis[3] explains that my 'direct theocracy' of the early period is 'no theocracy in the proper sense of the word'—he becomes right if the attribute 'proper' is replaced by 'customary', if theocracy accor-

[1] *Ibid.*, p. 345.   [2] *Ibid.*, p. 348.   [3] ThW III, 909.

dingly is equated with hierocracy; not, however, if we do not wish to withhold from so important a word its *proper*, and that means certainly: its most reality-containing sense. This can certainly not belie its special character. What is involved here is not just a simply constitutional-historical, but a religio-historical concept which tends to actualize itself as constitutional history: as that which attains expression in the beginnings of a people, in its subsequent history actualizes itself as effective striving for a real-earthly divine authority. To this concept does not belong belief in an established sacred character, but probably belief in a *charis* which, always in the right moment, grants to chosen men the genuine charisma.

Michaelis further declares that the 'combination' of direct theocracy with the kingdom of God p. 138 below) is 'questionable'. Certainly, the question does not remain small, but one may, I think, credit a fact of such primeval power as the messianic belief of Israel with such deep historical roots if the texts permit it. I have undertaken to prove that they do permit it in this book and other works.

Then Michaelis says that the proximity of my 'direct theocracy' to the concept 'theopolitics' (see below, p. 140) is 'dangerous'. The reproach is quite understandable to me. With theopolitics in Israel I mean, as I have explained elsewhere in an example from a far later phase,[1] action of a public nature from the point of view of the tendency toward the actualization of divine rulership. In the transition from an epoch of the simple charismatic fact (Moses) to one in which the charismatic leading begins to assume an institutional character, the theopolitical task is changed just as later it will be changed anew in the transition to the conception of the hereditary charisma, thus to 'Davidism'. I deal with the first of these two changes, the one, accordingly, which is completed within the direct theocracy, in the passage adduced by Michaelis. I am able, after minute reconsideration, to find nothing 'dangerous' in the fact that I see delineated, already in the early period which this book has as its subject, a theopolitics corresponding to it.[2]

Kraus[3] agrees with me in the decisive point, that the Book of

---

[1] *Der Glaube der Propheten*, chapter, 'Die theopolitische Stunde', p. 192ff.

[2] From another theological viewpoint Carl Dallago in his posthumous work 'Christentum als Theokratie' (*Neue Wege*, Zürich, Jahrg., 1955) has referred to this book.

[3] *Op. cit.*, p. 91.

Judges is in fact to be explained 'in terms of the situation of an absolute divine rulership': 'Jahwe alone is sovereign Lord over the people of Israel'. And he remarks: ' "Israel"—this means "May God manifest Himself as Lord, Ruler!" ' This is what it comes to: the realization of the all-embracing rulership of God is the Proton and Eschaton of Israel.

MARTIN BUBER

Jerusalem, the end of 1955.

CHAPTER ONE

THE GIDEON PASSAGE

As the leader Gideon-Jerubbaal returns home from the victorious war of liberation against Midian, the 'men of Israel' (Judges 8:22) offer to him the hereditary rulership. The extraordinary character of his answer does not lie in this, that he declined it. The chronicles of the nations, and not only the legendary ones, are acquainted with the act of a drawing back from proffered power. Sometimes, most clearly in Chinese tradition,[1] one can perceive how an original, secret renunciation turns into the rite of a pretended rejection, which only precedes the acceptance in order to appease the principle of a divine anger. In Gideon's refusal this is the remarkable thing, that it is not spoken for him and his descendants alone, but rather goes beyond all that is personal: not only is it intended to withhold the rulership over this people, whose representatives have just called upon him, from his own house, but from all people. His No, born out of the situation, is intended to count as an unconditional No for all times and historical conditions. For it leads on to an unconditioned Yes, that of a kingly proclamation *in aeternum*. 'I, Gideon, shall not rule over you, my son shall not rule over you'—in this is included: 'no man is to rule over you'; for there follows: 'JHWH, who is God himself, He it is who is to rule over you'. The saying dares to deal seriously with the rulership of God.

Since it does not occur eschatologically but historically, not as prophecy but as political declaration, this is a risk to be regarded as almost contary to history. For the 'theocracies' known to historical scholarship are—and the historian will be inclined to add 'according to nature'[2]—presentations of a form of rulership in which the power of men over men is fundamentally at its strongest, is, according to its constitution, unlimited, because it is derived from divine authority, or is itself believed to be divine.[3] For historical scholarship theocracy appears to have to be equated with hierocracy, with 'rulership of the consecrated ones', whether this expresses itself in the direct rule of the priestly cast or[4] in a kingship legitimized by a priestly oracle and partly dependent upon it, or also in the deification of the ruler. Therefore it is worthy of consideration that it is in this latter form, thus in utmost opposition to the Biblical notion, that the dynastic conception which Gideon opposes finds its unlimited guarantee.[5] A characteristic example in Islam is that persuasion of the Shia which, in opposition to the hereditary order introduced by the Omayyads, safeguarding on the one hand the legitimacy of the Aliites and on the other hand the purity of the theocratic principle, arrives at the deification of Ali and his descendants. 'The problem was this: How can it be made conceivable that the qualities of a prophet, since he must be believed to be at the head of a divine state, adhere to a certain family? The explanation is: This family itself is divine.'[6]

The paradox of the Gideon passage is so striking that several investigators[7] have attempted to take away its religious character and make it into an act of convenience with regard to the cumbersome office of king—as though out of such a thing the antithesis could be explained! Others[8] have attempted to interpret it in the sense of the current concept of theocracy. It is supposed to be simply the answer of a man who seizes the power while he in august manner avoids the title: 'So be it, but I shall not be the master; JHWH shall reign over you all.' This interpretation fails to recognize, however, the emphatic form of the sentence. Nowhere in the Scriptures does a plain and fervent opposition such as this leave a hiding-place for a 'So be it, but . . .'[9]

Modern scholarship has therefore, for the most part, taken another path with regard to the curious passage. It has moved it out of a time of historical contemplation near to the occurrence to a time of historical elaboration far from the occurrence, while conceiving of it perhaps as an interpolation[10] or also as a 'biased alteration of a wording which is no more to be ascertained',[11] which in any case reported the acceptance of the proffered rulership.

Beside the question of the stage of development in the history of religion from which the passage in the form known to us may descend (a question which is an essential subject of this discussion), an aspect of the textual continuity has determined the late-dating: the apparent disagreement with 9:2.[12]

After Gideon's death, his son Abimelech from a so-called matrilocal marriage[13] (in which the wife stays in the parental home, and the children, in compliance with the regulation of maternal law, belong to the clan) with a Shechemite, turns to the 'masters', that is, the lords, of his native town with the summons to aid him in winning sole rulership. This will be advantageous for them also; for: 'which serves you better, / that seventy men rule over you, all sons of Jerubbaal, / or that a single man rule over you?' This is almost universally understood to mean that Gideon had 'in no way disdained the office of king',[14] and had accordingly bequeathed it to his seventy sons.

It has been assumed[15] that what is involved here is a rulership of brothers which was established after Gideon's death. As proof[16] a few cases have been adduced in which *two* sons of a dead king share in the power. Yet, however historically widespread in manifold forms and however rich in significance dyarchy appears,[17] which indeed sometimes is traced back (as Herodotus did for Sparta) to a mythical or historical rulership of brothers, a dyarchy which rests upon a greater number of heads—for which 'seventy' is supposed to serve as a symbolic designation—would be completely without analogy and in conflict with political psychology.

If, however, as is to be assumed,[18] the expression 'sons of Jerubbaal' refers to the totality of the living descendants, there is disclosed another understanding of the circumstances referred to. Abimelech, in his speech to the citizens of Shechem, makes use of the same word *mashal*, translated by me as 'rule', with which 'the men of Israel' express their offer directed to Gideon. The word stem *malakh*, 'to be king', of which, as is yet to be discussed, the Book of Judges and in particular the narrative of Abimelech has much to say, occurs in neither of the two places. Both the non-mention of the king-concept in this place as well as in the other, where it nevertheless apparently is involved,[19] and the repetition of the 'ruler'-concept here as well as there—here twice, there four times—dare not be taken as incidental. Especially when one takes into consideration the fact that *mashal* occurs only two more times in the Book of Judges (14:4 and 15:11), and indeed not the *mashal* of a ruler's office, but the *mashal* of the power which the Philistines exercised over Israel. As such the word in Biblical language signifies not the formal possession, but rather the factual practice of a power[20] which can also be affirmed of a 'kingship' as predicate (Psalm 103:19). Thus Joseph 'rules' in Egypt (Genesis 45:8, 26); thus also Abraham's chief steward 'governs' his house (24:2).

The silent rule of sun and moon, for the author of the first chapter of Genesis certainly no princely rule, and the husband's 'ruling-over' the wife are designated by the same word. Accordingly Abimelech does not declare concerning the Jerubbaalites that they had taken possession of the rulership after the death of his father, but that they had grown up into a mighty generation whose hegemony the lords of Shechem would soon have occasion to notice if they did not take care.[21]

Repetition is, in the Biblical style, the great means for singling out or emphasizing inner connections.[22] The narrator wishes 8:23 and 9:2 to be known as related to one another. He causes the almost dramatically antagonistic figure of his Abimelech to disavow his father: 'The fanatic renounced power for himself and his sons because it allegedly belongs to God alone—what has now come of all this? This herd of sons has the power in its possession unless we anticipate them and inaugurate the wholesome monarchical principle in my person!' This tone is perhaps struck by the resumption of the verb *mashal*. No matter whether 8:22ff. and 9:2 spring from the same tradition or from two different ones, in the version which lies before us they form an intelligible and stylistic unity. There is no contradiction in content, and the stylistic connectedness is expressly brought to the fore.

More important than the calling into question of the inner connection is the other argument of critical scholarship against the originality of 8:23. We are said to have here before us a 'secondary product in which the original features are distorted according to later taste'.[23] The answer of Gideon is said to express an antithesis between human and divine rulership as it was conceived only in a far later epoch more capable of abstraction.[24] The ground of his declining is said to correspond to the high level of I Samuel 8, of 10:17ff., and of 12. These, however, are said to be no older than Hosea, upon whose condemnation of the kingdom they were based;[25] they are said to originate as a matter of fact, 'in the kingless time after the exile'.[26] The theocratic summons in the exclusiveness of its demand would be, then, not the naive utterance of an unproblematic early time, but the back-dating of the results of longer and unhappier experiences with monarchy—not action but reflection, not venture but 'dogma'.

First of all, a possible misunderstanding must be prevented. Wilhelm Vatke, who, 120 years ago[27] was the first to present the argument of developmental history against the dependability of the Gideon passage, formulates the question to this point: 'whether this speech and the motive are to be regarded as really historical'. When he continues: 'or as a view point of the reporter', this can be understood: whether Gideon really said this. It is not my purpose to maintain the historicity of the passage in this sense; indeed it appears to me to be extremely doubtful whether it can even be discussed scientifically at all. A narrative like this whose major part, the report of calling, combat, and victory (6:11–7:22) is determined throughout and beyond all source analyses primarily by a religious view of history, does not permit itself, if no other witness can be placed in relation to it, to be sifted down to its historical content. The 'divergences of the religious version from the natural'[28] are not really to be ascertained, since, for the essential elements, a 'natural' version is lacking. Here it is not as if saga had joined itself to history and accordingly had to be detached from it,[29] but the holy saga is for this reporter the immediate and single way of articulating his 'knowledge' about the events; moreover, this knowledge is itself a legendary knowledge, that is, one which represents the believed activity of God with His people, one which represents in the organic employment of a mythicizing memory. What is involved here actually is religious *viewing* of history: the wonder is beheld by a wonder-expecting person and imagined by the wonder-gripped person in narrative language.[30] It is not fantasy active here, but memory; but precisely that believing memory of individuals and generations of early times which, driven by the extraordinary occurrence, builds for it in a manner free of arbitrariness the extraordinary context—a poetizing memory, certainly, but one which poetizes believingly. In this connection one could apply Jacob Grimm's word[31] concerning 'objective inspiration'. How, with all its scarcely to be doubted historicity, can a historically tenable person, Gideon, be extracted, concerning which person one must decide whether his ascribed utterance fits him or not? Whoever defends his authenticity cannot characterize him as historically actual, but probably—and this is what is disputed just now—as historically possible in the significant sense. A time has been given, a saying has been given—can the saying, according to its nature, have been spoken in the time, according to its nature? That is all that I mean to affirm for the Gideon passage and for the epoch of the history of Israel between Joshua's death and Saul's ascension to the throne. It is the expression of a disposition; it seems to me to be a naive, non-reflecting disposition, an elementary, non-literary expression. The Gideon passage is not in itself of legendary character, like the narrative of Gideon's calling, conflict, and victory. Thus, what historical scholarship must inquire into is only whether it could be uttered in that time to which the Bible assigns it, according to its level in the history of religion, and according to its position in political history.

The proof of the historical possibility of the Gideon passage would be at the same time the proof of its historical truth. For the attribute 'possible' means here not just something that is not impossible, but an event corresponding with the character of a folk-epoch. The saying is not to be exhibited as a peculiarity on the margin of an epoch— that would be idle—but rather as something welling up out of its depths and thus something derivable out of its meaning. The thesis cannot be that an isolated genius or an isolated fool in the time between Israel's seizure of the land and Israel's formation of a government, without commission and without echo, proclaimed JHWH as the exclusive ruler. Only this can concern us, that a will of a religious and political kind in one, historically localizable in this its stage, a will toward constitution combined with faith, found here the straight-forward expression of its demand, as afterward in the Samuelic crisis it found the discordant expression of its defensive fight and its resignation.

Will toward constitution, I say, not constitution. Wellhausen[32] explains, in opposition to Josephus who invented the concept of theocracy, that in ancient Israel a theocracy never existed as a form of government. In so far as by 'theocracy' the direct sort is to be understood which the Gideon passage intends, and by 'form of government' is to be understood an institution of fixity and unequivocality like some democracies or aristocracies of history, no counter evidence can be brought. But the attached assertion of Wellhausen can and should be opposed, namely, that the rulership of God previous to the exile was consequently merely 'an ideal concept', which, moreover, appeared only with the prophets of the later state period. In addition to 'idea' and 'institution' in Wellhausen's sense there is a third possibility: namely, the real, struggling, religious-political will to fulfilment, wresting ever and again from the changing resistance of the times a fragment of realization, however altered; a will not just late-prophetic, but inseparable from the historical Israel. The kingship of God is a paradox, but an historical one: it consists in the historical conflict of the subjected person against the resisting one, a conflict which, without its naive, but on that very account most important, original form, cannot be grasped. It is the most visible appearance of that kingdom-dialectic which educated the Israelitish people to know history as the dialectic of an asking divinity and an answer-refusing, but nevertheless an answer-attempting humanity, the dialogue whose demand is an *eschaton*. That this dialectic has its quite earthly form, that it embodies itself not on theological heights, but in the midst of the whirl of political actualities, and that, robbed of these, the constant historical consciouness of a people, Israel, as bearer of the kingdom-message could not be understood—all this allows, yes commands, us to recognize the will toward constitution (that is, to actualization) as an original constant in the dynamic of this folk life, which functions in the historiography because it has functioned in history.

CHAPTER TWO

BOOKS OF JUDGES AND BOOK OF JUDGES

SINCE Wellhausen, in spite of all the divergences in the literary critical interpretation, the Book of Judges has been regarded as a late collection of legendary material the greater part of which—the main substance of chapters two to sixteen—is to be traced back for the most part to chieftains' histories of separate tribes, of which several, however, were collected in a compilation stemming from the time of the first Scriptural prophets, so that in them a more profane-historical original content is mixed with a theocraticizing legendary additive. In the redaction, furthermore, a 'uniform'[1] is said to have been put on over them; the narratives standing beside one another in disconnected fashion are said to have been squeezed into a frame which makes them into single instances of the same scheme: the people—which did not exist as a unity at all in that epoch, but for which the editorial bias had to weld together the tribes so that in the place of a juxtaposition of chieftains a succession of 'judges' of the whole community appeared— the people falls away from JHWH, it is punished by means of enemy invasion (whereby one neighbouring tribe after another dies); now it turns to its God, it 'cries' to Him, and He in turn summons for Himself a liberator, a *shophet*, a 'justifier':[2] for now, after the return, it again is in the right with respect to the enemy in relation to whom it was sinfully in the wrong, and this right is fought for and won.

That here a uniform framework has been drawn is obvious; but whether the traditional happening, literarily formed, was inserted in it or was observed in it in the glowing development of the tradition, whether accordingly four mouldings were placed around a finished picture, or a coloured window both encompasses the view of a landscape and uniformly tints it, appears to me not settled. When in a neo-Babylonian chronicle concerning the time of Sennacherib[3] his war against the country as the action of the God Marduk's anger is spoken of almost with the same words as in an old-Babylonian chronicle[4] about a famine nearly two thousand years earlier under Sargon of Akkad, the similarity is not founded in a subsequent schematizing, but in an original and—even if only in archaisizing formulae—self-maintaining manner of observing history as it is happening and of interpreting it already in the observing. And thus it was with an Israel touched in all its generations by the shuddering awe of a history experienced as dialogue! If one attempts to separate out the notion of a dynamic of reciprocity which is concealed in every event from the historical experience and historical narration of Israel, one will have no organic historical substance left over. 'The uncommon freshness and naturalness of their desires', which Wellhausen in the most significant passage of his 'Prolegomena'[5] rightly ascribes to Biblical personalities, is no argument against the originality and living actuality of the historical conceptions in which that notion realizes itself. 'The acting persons', thinks Wellhausen, 'behave throughout with such a necessity of their nature, the men of God no less than the murderers and adulterers'. That is a misstatement not just of a 'Deuteronomic' or even of a 'Jewish' but of all Biblical perspectives. First of all, the men of God are not so neatly to be distinguished from the murderers and adulterers. A profane David who belonged to the latter and not to the former would be an untenable construction. Furthermore, the necessity through which and in which a 'man of God' is, is in Biblical perspectives a completely different thing from that through which he or some other murderer and adulterer is; and the Biblical history has no meaning if it does not have that which allows the necessity of nature to be surrendered to the necessity of God and therein be elevated, genuine passion to genuine holiness, the creation to the Kingdom. 'In the ancient Israel', continues Wellhausen, 'the divine law was not in the institution, but in the Creator Spiritus, in the individuals'. I think it was indeed in these, not, however, in their structures but in their tension, in the dialectic of their existence between creation and redemption—and so also in the institutional will which was determined by this tension.

The 'schema' of the Book of Judges is, however literarily stiff, only a form of net with which the believing observer seeks to capture the history happening around him and to him. But does the lively opposing power of historical destiny allow itself to be mastered by a pragmatism? Only if in that pragmatism a deeper reality dwells, even if only deficiently. The schema, however, is in no way contrary to history.[6] Historical scholarship, if it replaces religious concepts with profane ones, that of the repetitive falling away from God with that of a repetitive falling to pieces of a unity of people into self-willed tribes, will recognize that the age of which the Book of Judges tells stood in a fluctuating movement between tearing-asunder multiplicity and a completion-desiring unity, and in addition probably this too, that here the principle of unity of a people and that of a faith were sustained by the same powers, by the same persons. The profane-historical transcription of the sequence 'apostasy-affliction-conversion-rest'[7] reads: 'apostasy-affliction-unification-rest'. But cannot it be assumed that just as at one time the believing experience of an event constituted the people, so the specific conversion to the believing experience of history again and again revived anew the power of unity in the people?[8] That it did not prove itself strong enough gives to the Book of Judges its melancholy character, to the whole, not just to the closing section. One ought to pay attention to this character, and one will embed in it many an episode which now appears to burst strangely out of the context. How Gideon sets up an 'ephod'[9] which then becomes the centre of a service of Baal, how Jephtha offers his daughter to the God whose interpreters rebel against nothing so much as against his 'Molochization', all this stands in its place with almost symbolic importance. The tradition supplied it, but he who knew how to impose selection and arrangement upon it in such a way was a great teacher.[10]

The view that the major part of the book consists of loosely-strung-together narratives which are only held together by the pragmatic schema imposed upon them after the event, fundamentally mistakes the construction of this particular literary work. No matter how the question of the chronological sequence or how that of the separability of sources[11] were to be answered, if one disregards smaller inserted passages, the work is composed of two books between which stand the two dissimilar Samson legends. Each of the two books is edited from a biased viewpoint, the first from an anti-monarchical, the second from a monarchical. We have in 'Judges' the result of a compositional balancing of two opposing editorial biasses, each of which had been represented in a complete book form. The manner of presentation of the bias is a different one in each book: in the second one its immediate expression can be distinguished from the narratives themselves; in the first one it appertains to these so organically that it will not do to ascribe it to the editor alone.[12]

If one eliminates from the first twelve chapters the sketchy sections, the general reflections and the speeches of the 'messenger' (2:1–5) and of the 'interpreter' (6:7–10), as well as the statements concerning the 'minor' judges of whom nothing is really related, then one obtains a succession of seven stories, some short and some longer, every one of which expresses the anti-monarchical bias, the one hidden, the others in univocal rendering. They all deal with kings and kingship, and all contemptuously or accusingly, or at least from the point of vantage of a kingless Israel. Probably one will not notice the purpose of the one or the other, if one considers it by itself; but once one has seen it together with what accompanies it, then it can appear to no one any longer as incidental.[13]

The first of the seven stories, the one which begins the 'introduction (1:1–7), is the one about the Canaanite ruler Adoni-Bezek, of the seventy 'kings' who had become subject to him, who, their thumbs and great toes cut off, gathered morsels beneath his table, and his defeat at Bezek by the tribes Judah and Simeon who prepare the same lot for him. It has been assumed, probably correctly, that the analogy-less name was corrupted from Adoni-Zedek.[14] Since with Zedek one would naturally think of 'righteousness' rather than of a strange divine name (if it was such),[15] this may seem to be legitimate, whereas *beẓek* presumably causes one to think of 'potsherd', 'fragment'.[16] Not less worthy of note is the fact that the conquered one is not characterized as king: thus the seventy petty kings enslaved to him stand forth all the more plainly in their nothingness. And he, the sovereign of the royal rabble, is now himself humiliated by Israel in the same manner as they all have been humiliated by him! It is the typical legend of derision, and the motif word is 'king'.

The second story (3:5–11) in any case corrupts the name of an enemy ruler, an Aramaic king, but in a far more drastic manner: as a rhyme on the name of his kingdom, of 'Two-streamland', Aram Naharayim, the dual Rishathayim, 'Double-sacrilege', was attached to his name Kushan as a nick-name, or, which is more probable, the second part of his name, perhaps Rishath,[17] is transformed in such a way. This king, too, is conquered by the first of the 'judges'.

The third story (3:12–30) narrates the murder by the judge Ehud of the Moabite king Eglon who holds Israel under yoke for eighteen years. Now whether Jerome and Luther translated the strange verse 22 correctly or not, the grotesque is eloquent enough even without this feature. What is at stake is to preserve of the fat tyrant a caricaturing picture of his downfall.[18]

Now follows the report of Deborah's and Barak's victory over Sisera, which precedes the older Song of Deborah. One of its most difficult and most discussed problems is that a Jabin 'king of Canaan' appears as the ruler of the hostile power—he himself apparently not taking the field—who is strange to the Song, but, since he resides in Chazor, is reminiscent of Jabin the king of Chazor whom we know from Joshua 11 as head of a coalition of Canaanite kings conquered at the waters of Merom. It has been assumed that Jabin and Sisera have been 'enabled to be contemporary with one another by a harmonistic trick'.[19] The editor is said to have united two different stories and to have made the king Sisera of Charosheth into the military leader, king Jabin of Chazor. The motives for such a fusion are not to be grasped.[20] If, however, Sisera's kingship was not transmitted to the redactor,[21] then in terms of his anti-monarchical bias it is doubtless easily to be understood that he for whom, for this decisive event, as leader of the allied 'kings of Canaan' (5:19) only a 'king of Canaan', thus an historical nonentity, could suffice, extracted this name from a blurred tradition of the Jabin alliance.[22] His purpose expresses itself at the close of the report in almost paean-like manner in three-fold repetition of the contrast of the sons of Israel with the representative of heathen monarchism, grown to symbolic greatness: 'So God subdued on that day Jabin the king of Canaan before the sons of Israel. / And down went the hand of the sons of Israel, coming down and pressing upon Jabin the king of Canaan, / until they had exterminated Jabin the king of Canaan.' Exterminated: this is the only place where that frequent verb is related to a single, named person; the person stands, of course, for more than a person.

The next judge is Gideon. Here the bias is conspicuous no longer in the ironic or triumphant treatment of the opposing heathen king— the 'kings' of 8:4–21 are just as much untouched by it as the 'princes' of 7:24–8:3—for here appears the man who expresses it himself, straight out and unconditionally. The anti-monarchical book centres plainly in him and his house's, after the Yes and after the No, equally meaningful history. He is the genuine hero of the primitive-theocratic legend and is not for nothing named in Samuel's great speech to the

people as foremost among the liberators called by God (I Samuel
12:11). Of his two names Jerubbaal stands here. However the etymological and the historical problem of this name is interpreted,[23] the
redactor, for whom both did not exist, sees in Jerubbaal a nick-name
for which he, evidently on the basis of popular opinion, wishes to have
suggested the analogy of the nick-name Israel as it was interpreted by
the tradition whose intensive vitality the Hosea passage (12:4) attests.
Both are constituted from a verb which means 'to strive', 'to fight',[24]
and a substantive which designates a divine being, and this substantive
not, as scholarship commonly construes it, subject, but object of the
sentence.[25] Beside the former who fought the El, the redactor places
the latter who fought the Baal; thus, beside the wrestler for the blessing
of the genuine numen he places the annihilator of the anti-God and
false God—both 'fighters of God'.[26] Certainly the new name is not
bestowed upon Gideon, as upon the first and the third of the patriarchs, from the upper sphere and in a process which the Haggadic
tradition could understand as new creation,[27] but from the people,
and even, according to the interpretation cited in 6:32 (but obviously
intended by the author as anecdotal beside the interpretation represented and brought forward by him) from popular humour. And
therefore contrast is preserved for the redactor as he sees the spheres of
time together, and he can let the bias of the legend come to pathetic
expression in the manner in which the nick-name here appears joined
with the narrative of the act of god-fighting. In addition there is the
fact that Gideon is the only one among the pre-Samuelic judges whose
call is actually narrated. This vocation story stands out in relief from
all other prophetic ones by means of the angel's greeting, without
analogy in the Old Testament, to which greeting he, hailed as hero,
answers in such a direct and resolute manner as would be unthinkable
in a later theological-literary legend. In so doing Gideon connects the
term (6:13) of 'being-actually at hand' (*yesh*) with the name of God
interrogatively in a manner similar to that in which Jacob (Genesis
28:16) connects them declaratively. And one must ponder the fact that
the only other interrogative connection, that of the people's doubt
(Exodus 17:7), is punished, whereas Gideon to his doubting question,
again an untheological and unliterary feature of legendary antiquity,
receives the reply of God (v. 14): 'Go in *this* thy strength!' which
clears away the doubt, but confirms its author. Verse 22 joins him again
with Jacob: concerning both (cf. Genesis 32:31) we discover that they

are allowed to look at the numen 'face to face'. It is consistent when
Gideon, like Jacob and Moses, pronounces over the constructed altar
a name-like assertion about God. And, like the calling, so the battle is
narrated in a naive-theocratic manner. It begins with the descent of the
Spirit, in a description characterized by unheard of boldness whose
primitive powerfulness dare not be confused with a late trivialization
(I Chronicles 12:18 where *ruach* stands alone; in a different way, the
archaicizing passage II Chronicles 24:20): the Spirit clothes itself with
Gideon. In the same style of the primitive legend is the account of the
selection of the shock-troop, of the three hundred who, only in order
to be able to rush onward, in all haste lapped up a little of the down-
gushing spring water while all the others allowed themselves time to
kneel down and to drink slowly from the pool.[28] In the same style is
Gideon's dream and the strange attack[29] which undoubtedly is to be
understood only as the beginning of an action (the main force stands
ready to pursue in the camp, which is what is meant by the term 'tents'
in 7:8; the core troop is certainly also in the forefront of the pursuit,
8:4), and its unclear description throughout cannot simply be traced
back to an awkward interlocking of two sources—the undifferen-
tiatedness of early battle reports is just as typical as the early cavalry
battle frescoes. The following episodes, presented in the fashion of
profane history even unto secondary details, are a material example of
how in a heroic legend those parts of the historical material are narrated which the point of view and manner of presentation are not able
to fit into the context of miracle. In one of them a detail comes to
notice which, considered in the context of the whole, dare not be taken
as incidental. The captured kings answer Gideon (8:18), as to the
question about the appearance of his cousins slain by them, that they
resembled him, king's sons in form. It is the last episode which immediately precedes the warrior-people's offer of rulership. Here, as it
were, the voice of the nations attributes to the Israelitish leader kingly
nature, equality of birth; and the redactor by means of the speech in
verse 23 causes this attribution to be answered.[30]

It is now probably sufficiently clarified how the theocratic saga of
Gideon, who serves his Lord as leader of the victorious military expedition, and the theocratic speech of Gideon condition one another.
There is told the story of a hero, but of a Biblical hero who, like all
these 'workers of righteousness', stands as one who has received a
commission, like them all a completely personal and wholly once-for-

all commission which can neither be continued, handed over nor dynastically exploited. Every attempt to do this, as well as every step into an authority-less self-rule, would be betrayal of the giver of the authority, the one ruling Lord. In Gideon's speech the mute saga has its banderole; in the saga Gideon's speech has the biographical foundation and authorization without which, notwithstanding its concreteness, it would only be a splendid aphorism.

What follows next is the story of the betrayal. The redactor knew what he was doing (no matter whether he welded together different traditions in the process or not) when, at the last, he told of the ephod which Gideon erected as sanctuary of his Lord and which the people made into the centre of a Baal cult,[31] thus of the very cult with whose annihilation the commissioning and the deed had begun. The short narrative introduces the motif of renunciation and conversion[32] which is set forth in the long narrative about Abimelech; people and son frustrate in like manner the intention of the dead hero. In Abimelech there arises the demonically intended adversary of the thought of the exclusive kingship of God. That his story is narrated in profane style— Wellhausen calls it: 'without gilding by means of supernatural nimbus'[33]—is more than a question of sources. The redactor sees in him, the enemy of the theocratic bias, the man who wishes—expressed in our language—to politicize history, rather, to make it into an arena of *merely* political interests. The style of the legend *must* give way here to that of the profane chronicle: God allows the adversary to set the tone—until the moment of annihilation. With the report of divine punishment the legendary style could resume again. But the punishment which in this developmental stage of the saga is consummated mostly in forms of natural events, has to do that here for a special reason: the political curse of Jotham is to come to fulfilment politically. Yet this fulfilment occurs expressly from above, and indeed characteristically through that very divine sending forth of an 'evil spirit' (thus *ruach* is to be understood kinetically in such cases) between Abimelech and the lords of Shechem (9:23) the like of which we meet with only in Saul's punishment (I Samuel 16:14ff).

The theophoric name Abimelech was taken over from the Canaanites with whom it probably had the characteristic function of connecting with one another two different orders of divine denotation, the father-order and the king-order, thus the biological (the god as primeval father of the tribe) and the political conception (the god as overlord of the tribe). In the adoption, the name's constituent parts referring to the divinity were here as well as on other occasions applied to JHWH.[34] In the Bible this is the first Israelitish name formed with the divine designation *melekh*, and it has been correctly observed[35] that this is no coincidence; but not because Gideon was the first 'upon whom the title of king was bestowed'—I have shown that the text does not entitle us to such an assumption—but because that very Abimelech was the first who bestowed upon himself the title of king. In other words, Abimelech is obviously not at all the original name of the usurper. 'His concubine', it says in 8:31 concerning Gideon, 'who was in Shechem, she also bore him a son; he appointed unto him the name Abimelech'. But the expression 'to appoint a name' is never used concerning the name-giving at the birth of a child, which is much more consistently reported with the verb 'to call'. 'To appoint a name', otherwise occurring only in late texts, means 'to give a new name'— as in the divine granting of a name to Abraham (Nehemiah 9:7) or to Jacob (II Kings 17:34)[36]. Here it would accordingly mean that Gideon granted to a son who perhaps like his grandfather was called Abiezer, possibly on the occasion of his rejection of the kingly office, and furthermore as a declaration, the altered theophoric name. One can, however, translate either 'they appointed him' or 'he appointed for himself'. I assume that the redactor wished it to be understood in the latter sense, perhaps not without a certain irony which would probably suit his fundamental attitude: the usurper, the 'son of the maid servant' (9:18) assumed a proud name ('my father before me was—really—a king') which, however, basically refers to the divine king, a name accordingly which judges him. That the expression stands here and not as one might expect at a later place, is to be explained on the ground that the redactor did not light upon another name in the tradition which he could have introduced in order to report the change of name later in chapter 9, presumably because the acquired name had suppressed the original one.

The meaning which the name has for the author or redactor emerges especially clearly from 9:16 where the name is employed to juxtapose the root *malakh* three times and thus to make the failure of the Shechemites phonetically noticeable: *wa-yamlikhu eth abimelekh l^e-melekh*—'and they kinged father-king as king'—in connection with which it is to be noted that the pleonasm 'to king as king' (the simple expression 'to king' occurs in verses 16 and 18; 'to anoint as king' in verse 15) occurs otherwise only in I Samuel 15:11 in a passage determined by the same bias, only in a far advanced stage of its crisis. Here too the stylistic medium of repetition has the function of a sensuous emphasis of the purpose.

The Jotham fable, the strongest anti-monarchical poem of world literature, is the counterpart of the Gideon passage. Independently of the latter it could be understood anarchistically. Fitted into the strict context it functions as a keenly realistic illustration of that fundamental manifesto. The kingship, so teaches the poem which is to be compared in content and presentation only with certain Taoistic figurative sayings,[37] is not a productive calling. It is vain, but also bewildering and seditious, that men rule over men. Every one is to pursue his own proper business, and the manifold fruitfulnesses will constitute a community over which, in order that it endure, no one needs to rule—no one except God alone (so the Gideon speech interprets the doctrine which, without it, appears to embody a primitive belief in freedom). The 'commonwealth without government'[38] is thought of by the author or the redactor of the antimonarchical Book of Judges as a commonwealth for which an invisible government is sufficient.

Sellin[39], who draws far-reaching conclusions from the opposition of the 'political point' of the fable to the reputed kingdom of Gideon (as a matter of fact Jotham, if that kingdom had existed, would be marked as the father 'of a lazy, useless person') at the same time nevertheless observes in it that it is 'born out of a situation in which the question of the kingship had real, actual meaning'. This is precisely my view, and not for the Jotham fable alone.

The antimonarchical chronicle of Judges closes with the story of Jephtha, apparently derived from another East Jordanian tradition and joined with the preceding narratives.[40] It is told as an antitype to the story of Abimelech. Like Abimelech Jephtha does not stem from a principal marriage, but rather from a fleeting connection; yet he becomes not a destroyer but a liberator. He too gathers about himself a corps of 'reckless men', but his corps apparently supplies the nucleus of the army with which he conquers Ammon. He has himself appointed 'chief', but he thereby becomes only the highest commander in the war, judge in the peace. He does not strive for the kingship. For the bias of the book he has the special significance that he champions that bias once again at the book's conclusion, and, what is more, to

the outside world, in his message to the 'king of the sons of Ammon'—
a message which is certainly obviously strange to the original tradition
and attached to it later according to the redactor's purpose—a message
which treats of the happenings between Israel and the heathen kings
on the journey from Egypt to Canaan: none of them was able to get
the better of the kingless Israel. And like an allusion to the judgeship
as the representation of the divine Lord appropriate for Israel there
sounds the challenge at the end: 'Let JHWH the judge judge today /
between the sons of Israel and the sons of Ammon!' Only in this one
place in the canon is God plainly characterized as *the* judge; not even
Genesis 18:25 has this absolute form.

It is to be noted that Jephtha has only one daughter and also that
he sacrifices her. The dynastic problem is not again posed. It remains
at rest from the tragedy of the house of Gideon up until the delinquency of Samuel himself in relation to the anti-dynastic temper of the
judgeship (I Samuel 8:1–5), a delinquency not yet sufficiently recognized in its significance for the Samuelic crisis.

Proceeding from what has been presented, the question which was
only touched upon at the beginning is now answered, namely, why in
the narrative concerning the offer of rulership to Gideon the concept
of king is avoided. It was precisely a question of devaluing the concept,
and therefore it dared not be employed in a positive sense. Where
otherwise God is always characterized as king, here it was not allow-
able. Association with the term which had been made contemptible had
to be withheld from the divine rulership in the proximity of the
Jotham fable (Cf., however, p. 38 above).

I now summarize the most important findings concerning the
antimonarchical book:

1. The opposition between Israel and the neighbouring nations is
understood as one between a theocratically intended judgeship and a
kingship peculiar to the heathen (with respect to *goyim* in I Samuel
8:5, 20, it is to be noted that as a variation from the linguistic usage
elsewhere Israel is not characterized as *goy* either in Judges or in
I Samuel).

2. The primitive conception of Israel in the epoch between the
occupation and the installation of a king is understood in its minimum
of institutions of rule and in its complete lack of assurance of continuity as, so to speak, the negative of direct theocracy. The office of
the *shophtim* on that account is understood not as a form of govern-

ment (like that of its namesake, the Carthaginian *suffeten*), but as a mandatory vocation conditioned and limited by the situation—an exclusively charismatic office whose interruptions of tenure thus ultimately belong to its essence.

3. The bias wrests from the historical material a gradual and, where possible, a complete declaration. The story of Samson singles itself out for our consideration. It is first of all included in a compositional balancing, different in species from all else. A prologue and epilogue furnish in their utmost brevity that which is indispensable for joining it with the two books between which it is imbedded (the last sentence in 13:5 is presumably secondary—it seems to me more original if in the promise it is not stated *for what purpose* the boy is called). On the other hand, the prologue and epilogue in the antimonarchical book do not belong in essence to the stage of the compositional balancing, but to the stage of development previous to this, from whose unified structure they cannot be spared. They are, as I have stated, according to their 'pragmatic' content early, and their 'abstract' form is to be explained in terms of the redactory task. The extent to which single features (viewed from the point of view of the narrative leading over to Jephtha, which is of independent origin) were worked out subsequently does not need to be investigated here. That the 'generalizing to all Israel' is no argument against originality results from a comparison of all passages of the Book of Judges in which 'Israel' stands for a part of the people.[41] The historical question concerning the existence of an actual folk unity in the time of the judges will confront us later.

In chapters 17–21 a monarchical book appears at the side of the antimonarchical Book of Judges, or rather, in opposition to it, a book which in its entire appearance, just like the other one, can be comprehended only as a political declaration. The theocratic chronicle was wont, indeed, to tell of ever-returning periods of cultic defection on the part of the people which were also at the same time periods of collapse and of weakness toward the outside world; but it nevertheless permits one to assume in the very loose political structure a sufficient security for internal order, and in the 'judges' dependable and superior guardians. The opposing chronicle undertakes a rectification. Outside of the chronological time sequence, in two temporally undetermined examples, they want to show what a mischief and outrage the famed kinglessness had produced. This bias is expressly carried forward. It, too, has its slogan that gives it a frame. It is a complete closing verse: 'In those days there was (simply) no king in Israel', or, as it reads the first and the last time in expanded version: 'In those days there was no king in Israel, / every one did what was right in his own eyes'. One cannot say more plainly: 'That which you pass off as theocracy has become anarchy,' and: 'Only since this people, as is fitting for human beings, took unto itself a human being for a king, has it known order and civilization.'

The two stories which are utilized in such a manner are in every other concern utterly different. The first doubtless consists of material formed from of old which only in the recasting somehow met with an accident. The second is put together from a baroque, overspread elaboration of a legendary theme (with the use of a legend of the patriarchs) in a loquacious style reminiscent of the strange second half of the narrative of the Judaic prophets in Bethel (I Kings 13:11-32), and an accumulation of happenings reported circumstantially and unclearly, though apparently, in essence, authentically.[42] Nevertheless, on the one hand, the first story also distinguishes itself from the legends of the antimonarchical book and from the Samson epic poem not only through its lack of contour, of simplicity, of grandeur, but also—in rhythm and sentence structure—through the unmistakable literariness of its rendering, in contrast with which the book and poem prove themselves to have been born and reared rhapsodically. On the other hand, probably even the most stringent critic has felt that the kidnapping of the women in 21:19-23 is an old popular tale and not simply an old topic. Nevertheless it is plain that the monarchical book followed after the antimonarchical book just as a disputation follows the disputed thesis. Oral form and written form, compactness and confusion, but also information and correction, religious-political theory and its 'purely political' counterpart, in any case thesis and counterthesis, thus the two books stand beside one another, books which a remarkable spirit of balancing has linked together, the same spirit in which, then, the canon originated.

In one important point the Gibea narrative certainly seems to contradict the picture of general anarchy which the appended chronicle depicts. The antimonarchical book, which presupposes an organic folk unity, nevertheless in no way conceals the laziness and obstinacy of the tribes where an active community of interests is involved. The monarchical book, which wishes to exhibit the disorder and helplessness of the pre-royal age, reports how at the news of an act of outrage the entire people arises as one man and prepares the punitive expedition. But it was certainly not the intention to deny to the pre-royal Israel the function of unity, but to concede to it the capacity for actual unity only in the moment of extraordinary arousal and only for the purpose of the subduing of a tribe which is breaking the primary law of inter-tribal loyalty—against all of which the enduring safeguarding of unity and inner pacification through the kingship stood out in contrast all the more clearly. The tradition which furnished the story of such a moment was welcome, and the fact that it reported concerning an acting community, an 'eda,[43] did not need to disturb any one. By 'kingship', however, only the Davidic is to be understood throughout. The Gibea-tradition had obviously experienced already in the time of the Davidic opposition to the Saul-ites[44] a re-working directed against Saul. 'You praise', such was its bias, 'the man from the tribe of Benjamin who divided the yoke of oxen[45] and sent the pieces by messengers into all the borders of Israel in order to summon, with the most pointed threat, for a campaign against Ammon. We want to tell you now how the corpse of a woman ravished to death by Benjamin was divided in order to summon the people for a punitive expedition against the criminal tribe'. Also the report concerning the insubordination of Jabesh in Gilead (21:8ff.) seems to have been influenced thereby in such a way that people wished to reduce Saul's famed rescuer's act at Jabesh (I Samuel 11) to an ignoble debt of gratitude.[46]

Against the late datings it has been pointed out here that the exaggerated portrayal of the united action in chapter 20:1ff. points in all its essential elements to the linguistic usage of early historiography, of the period of the complete kingdom. There is the Israel 'from Dan to Beersheba', which stands here for the first time in the canon; there is for the last time 'all the days of Solomon' (I Kings 5:5) and the Books of Chronicles have the expression no more. Otherwise only the story of Saul knows the 'corner-pillars of the people' (I Samuel 14:38), and otherwise only the Absolom story knows the 'people of God' (II Samuel 14:13).[47] Only the pallid 'all the tribes of Israel' and 'as one man' have persisted still in later historical texts.

The monarchical bias of the appended chronicle appears to emerge in a still more peculiar way in the narrative of the journey of the Danites if in the passage 18:7, apparently become obscure through repeated reworking in word choice and sentence structure, we take the

Massoretic text seriously, in spite of everything, precisely as result of such a process and trouble ourselves anew for its interpretation, as well as for the meaning which it had for that redactor who has handed it down to us. Then we discover concerning the inhabitants of the city-state Laish, obviously a daughter settlement of Sidon, three circumstances which caused them to appear to the Danites as easy booty, and which appear to be correct: their distance from the mother city which is able to grant them no help; their lack of allies with whom they could perhaps have arranged signals for an emergency;[48] and—adduced first—that there was no one among them who, as inheritor of the 'fencing-in' power of rulership in the land, had the strength of 're-proof', could accordingly attempt to ward off the attack by means of ruthless allocation, having to face no opposition, of all forces. If we dare understand the passage thus as it has come down to us, then we have in it, in any case from the point of view of the reviser who granted it this form, an example of the helplessness of a king-less commonwealth. Certainly the Danites too are masterless people. A people without a king plunders; a people without a king is plundered—that is the opinion.

Consequently we have in the two books which have been embodied in the Book of Judges the productions of two opposing biasses: a naive-theocratic which narrates piously, and a reflective-monarchical which wishes to refute a representation of history which it fancies to be illusory with samples of a more dependable kind. The one begins its declaration with the very inception of the formation of tradition. It is active in the formative work of remembrance; it is there when the rhapsodic word awakens. The other has no pre-literary existence. Out of polemical impulse in opposition to something already found to be formed it undertakes its gathering, combining, interpreting activity with a material which had been rejected, as only a *chronique scandaleuse* can be, by any one who was a genuine and ardent historiographer.

We must keep this generic difference in view as we approach the difficult question concerning the 'when': When was such declaration, when such counter-declaration possible and appropriate? When could the one, when the other redaction take place? The question does not have the same meaning for the two instances, since the concept of a redaction is not the same in both. For the appended chronicle redaction means a setting in order, but for the original Book of Judges a creation.

The former can be differentiated from the material in which it occurs, the latter not. In the former one asks about the epoch in which a book —a book almost according to our conception—was produced; in the latter one seeks after the epoch in which the substance of a book, a closed cycle of history with binding and supporting bias, originated, and also when it was subsequently written down, when reworked, when brought into its final form. The declaration was an actual speaking or even chanting; the counter-declaration was already a writing. This stems presumably out of the time in which the declaration circulated for the first time as document and thus issued a challenge for a counter-document. But the important thing for us here is not when, approximately, this was, but when the stories of the judges of Israel were narrated, not, to be sure, in the elaboration which lies before us, but already cyclically with the very same bias inhabiting and linking them with which we are acquainted from the elaboration. The imprint of this bias, as old as the original shaping of the stories themselves, is that which I should like to call the 'original' redaction of the theocratic Book of Judges: redaction accordingly before its becoming a book in the literary sense, redaction of a cyclical tradition at an early stage of formation.

Scholarship frequently produces a well-motivated hesitation to include in the subject of research a tradition about whose origin and development no documentation has been obtained, which we consequently are directed to infer from nothing else than its literary final condition, a vague and philologically inaccessible-appearing element, accordingly. But this most understandable precaution could bring it about that a stratum of development was dated according to 'sources', that is, in any case according to precipitates of a centuries-long process of tradition formation, and thus sometimes dated falsely, ages off. In Biblical scholarship the method of *Formgeschichte* has had a wholesome influence, but in Old Testament scholarship, really, only with regard to single motifs and configurations, not large contexts. We could profit from a useful rendering of aid in the still unfinished posing of problems in the history of bias.

The decisive formation of the original Judges-cycle in the straightforwardness of its intention was 'born out of a situation in which the question of the kingship had a real, actual meaning'. Since the expression of bias, as shown, does not here attach to the surface of the stories, but has penetrated their basic structure, this cannot be so late a situation as that in which Hosea does not perhaps, as has been opined, condemn the human kingship as such, but only exercises prophetic criticism upon the rulers unfaithful to God.[49] There is only *one* epoch in which the antimonarchical bias could operate in the decisive formation of the Judges-tradition: that in which the pro and con with regard to the kingdom had immediate political importance, that of the Samuelic crisis. In regard to this, certainly, a presupposition must be made which is still to be confirmed[50]: that the Samuelic struggle against the installation of a king possesses historical importance, and not that of an individual, but that of a group attitude. The narrative of Samuel's resistance must be understood as the individualizing expression for the real dialectic of the theocratic problem at the close of the period of the judges.

Determining the time for the monarchical text is a more difficult matter, since this involves the dating, not of a formation of tradition, but of a literary work. I assume that its first redaction and publication[51]—presumably emanating in court circles—was forthcoming as a reply to the writing down, and perhaps the putting into circulation pamphlet-wise, of the antimonarchical Book of Judges (until then transmitted only by word of mouth), as rejection of a 'romantic' error. Neither the one nor the other seems to me to belong to a time of political decline or even of collapse. The opposition which here manifests itself is obviously one between those politically malcontent and those content in a time which does not yet allow the malcontents to depend on anything but ideas, and which still allows the contented to depend on actualities. I have already emphasized that the terminology of the act of unity at the beginning of the twentieth chapter in no way justifies the conception that what is involved here is a 'churchly' unity[52] which was projected back from the post-exilic situation into the early period; and this argument has surely been the strongest for the late dating.

The bias-refrain speaks the language of a time in which for by far the overwhelming majority of the people there still existed a connection felt as self-evident between the idea of the kingship and the idea of order and civilization. One sees the shrugging of shoulders, hears the superior, regretful tone: 'At that time they simply didn't have a king yet in Israel!'

The late compositional balancing found the document of five chapters for that very reason suitable for establishing the transition from the book which coalesced from the antimonarchical chronicle and the Samson saga to the Samuel-Saul story, because the Micha-narrative was associated thus through the tribe of Dan with the immediately preceding Samson saga, and the Gibea-narrative through the tribe of Benjamin with the following Saul-story. More important by far than this formal one was another moving cause. The story of the origin of the kingship in the context of the Book of Samuel was not assimilated in a unified report and also not in one simply put together from different sources or individual fragments, but, as will be discussed in the course of these investigations, in a balancing of two literarily worked-out traditions determined, in turn, by opposing biasses, a monarchical and an antimonarchical. With this peculiar composition there must have been associated a preparatory one for the preceding epoch, since otherwise the disharmony would have made itself all too palpable.

But how could two literary works, produced by such opposing purposes, be joined to one another without nullifying not only the unity but also the credibility of the resulting book by reason of the contradiction between its parts? The balancing did not need to fear this result; rather, despite that opposition, it had to succeed and did succeed because it depended upon an historical perspective which would be accepted by the readers of the book in so far as it was not already their own. This implicit view of history, which preserved the unity of the book while it enabled its two antithetical parts to be true simultaneously, one can perhaps formulate thus: Something has been attempted—about which the first part reports; but it has failed—as the last part shows. This 'something' is that which I call *the primitive theocracy*. The readers received in the totality of the book, in various gradations between dimness and clarity, an aspect of history, or were strengthened and instructed in one, which perhaps corresponded to the assertion of modern historiography that a people in a given epoch was not 'ripe' to actualize a structure intended for it, that is, empirically speaking, intended for it by its spiritual leaders. This aspect was supported or corroborated by the fact of the pause, for a time, beteeen *shophet* and *shophet*, thus of a *normal* 'interregnum'; a fact which was inseparable from the institution of the judgeship, as an institution again and again in an extraordinary period of emergency resulting, only in such a time, in vocation of the liberator and unification of the tribes. Continuity of the union was not guaranteed; without judges, thus without unified and superior earthly government, the people was not able to maintain order and civilization. The primitive theocracy therefore was plunged again and again into anarchy, as is demonstrated for us in the five closing chapters in two examples. In this view of history which caused the compositional balancing to succeed, post-exilic Judaism read the Book of Judges. Out of the book, thus understood, it could draw instruction and admonition.

The Book of Samuel has been called the Biblical *Politeia*.[53] The Book of Judges deserves the same designation. Together they are a Biblical, i.e. certainly not philosophical but historical, not ideally pure but concretely fragmentary, *Politeia* by virtue of the view of history which, matured in the course of many generations, both allowed and implemented the compositional balancing of so many kinds of historical traditions.

CHAPTER THREE

THE KINGSHIP OF GOD IN THE
ANCIENT ORIENT

IN order to demonstrate the historicity of the Gideon passage, and of the theocratic disposition in pre-royal Israel as well, I have tried to show first of all how this disposition operates in early historical reflection. An original history-cycle, that of the judges, presented itself to us as decisively informed by that very tendency. Now, however, the objection will be renewed against this whole train of thought that it is invalid, since the notion of unconditional divine rulership does not correspond to the religio-historical level of that epoch, but to that of a far later period. With respect to this objection it is necessary, in view of the disputed dating of the most important of the pertaining Biblical passages, to extend the field of vision to the entire contemporary Orient so far as it could be of importance for the early religion of Israel.[1] We know indeed that we shall nowhere encounter the notion of an immediate and exclusive divine rulership in the sense of the Gideon passage and of its Samuelic expansion. But even the discovery of notions of a god as king of the people, notions which lack immediacy and exclusiveness, will advance our inquiry substantially.

In so doing, however, we cannot be satisfied with hearing,[2] as a result of the investigation, that all Semitic peoples conceive of their gods as kings.

Namely, we must above all eliminate those images and concepts as irrelevant for our task in which there appears a kingship of God understood not politically but cosmically—however closely the two are joined together with one another, and even flourishing in the history of faith in Israel. Ancestral gods of heaven such as Anu, sun gods prone to annexation such as Re, are naturally rendered homage as the rulers of a cosmic kingdom which one construes as prototype and model of the earthly kingdom. Thus in the change of hegemonies a king's title falls to other numina, a title which, to begin with, evidences a lordship in the political sense only, in contradistinction to the heavenly powers or spheres, and not to the human community.[3] Even if a more historical god, a so-called 'bringer of salvation', supplants the preponderantly natural one, if, for example, in the Babylonian creation epic the gods proclaim Marduk as king before he enters the fight against the powers of the abyss, just as a council of earthly princes may elevate the chosen leader of the campaign as the overlord of them all—this does not as such make known how the Babylonian is related to the 'king of heaven and earth', to the 'lord of the gods'. Only when it is shown that in the designation of king there is contained the proclamation 'our king' or there is nevertheless the suggestion that here was expressed not simply reverence for a lord of heaven on the part of those cultically bound to him, but also for the heavenly lord of an earthly community of his people, only then have we grasped a fact which can be helpful to our investigation in this point.

We must first of all, however, have eliminated that sphere of phenomena of the Semitic history of religion where a god is named or characterized as 'king' without our being able to detect with certainty a relation between state and sovereign, because from its inception a strictly political meaning is not inherent in the Semitic root *malk*. Primarily the *melekh*, as is yet to be shown, does not have to be 'king', but may be 'leader',[4] *rex* in the original sense, 'prince', from the point of view of the original Semitic meaning of the word, one who renders counsel, thus one who guides by means of oracular speech; because, indeed, from the beginning on this designation is applied to one who is lord; lord, however, not necessarily of a community, but perhaps of a major clan, a band, a tribe. We will dare approach unto the problem of the Semitic tribal god, one of central importance for the object of this essay, only when we have secured a knowledge of that which existed in the way of a state-political conception of the gods in the historical world in which the people Israel was established and formed. From there on we shall be able to grasp everything more closely in its connection with this conception and in its contrast to it.

The ancient oriental notion of a mediated theocracy, and indeed without exception not as demand or promise, but either as the official theological interpretation of political actuality, or even as the firm foundation of a constitution, appears in three great spheres of culture: in the Egyptian, in the Babylonian, and in the South Arabian. In this sequence is demonstrated, even in the very attempt to determine the peculiarities, so far as is still possible today, a plausible gradation of completeness, of maturity of the concept. Of course, no kind of dependence can be pointed out here, in spite of the great age of a part of the Egyptian and Babylonian sources and the relative youth of the South Arabian. Nevertheless the perceptible juxtaposition of the three spheres of ideas affords us the picture of an increasing illumination of the horizon.

To characterize that interesting episode of the late Egyptian period which is known as the Theban theocracy, and which is perhaps paralleled temporally by the inception of the kingship in Israel, as 'the *erection of divine lordship* and along with it the rulership of priest's,[5] does not appear to be quite justified in the light of the religio-historical context. The rulership over the land of the sun god called Amun-Re, which is used by his high priests for the founding of a hierocracy, is an age-old notion of faith which the priestly authority sanctioned just as the kingly authority had done formerly. This priestly authority, too, wanted it to be understood in terms of a divine rulership sending forth the king as 'son', and the rites which connected the king with his 'father', which included a dialogue between the two,[6] were in connection with extra-ritualistic revelations only with respect to their form, not with respect to their content, something other than the Theban oracle. If the latter 'was introduced in the church-state at every opportunity sensibly before the eyes of the faithful', the former were scarcely less active through their secret ceremonial. Here as as well there the god is the 'king who really possesses kingship',[7] as is asserted in the creed of the religion of Amun. Its formula 'king of upper and lower Egypt' seizes upon early notions from the period of the unification of upper and lower Egypt on the basis of which the sun god, who in Heliopolis has the name Re-Atum as 'lord of the two countries', wears on his head the united kingly crown and thus appears 'exactly like an Egyptian king of the historical period'.[8] From this was achieved that characteristic historicizing of the cosmic divinity which made a primeval king out of the one who once reigned over the awakening Egypt[9] 'at a time when men and gods were still completely one'.[10] Grown old and despised by men he moves back into the heavens; the dynasty of gods is followed by one of humans; the Pharaoh as the son conceived by Re is regarded as his heir and successor in the rulership.[11] But Re remains as father of the ruling king with whom he regularly communicates, 'the protector and guide of the nation, at the same time an ideal king'.[12] In a time of grave emergency and confusion he is the one whom the wise man, answering the Pharaoh, who seeks information, in speeches of lamentation and admonition, remembers reverently[13]—not as the god who in his bark travels through the two realms of the bright sky and the dark underworld, but as the just king of earthlings in the first generation, the 'shepherd of all men in whose hearts there is no evil'. He is also besought by the poor, the oppressed, the unjustly persecuted for righteousness' sake,[14] he 'who was king at the first' and even now 'directs the earth with his fingers'.[15] He, 'the lord of law',[16] remains the overlord to whom one appeals from the partisan decisions of earthly misuse of power; certainly for the reason that he rules *the world*.[17] But into this knowing about the rule of the world the notion of the primeval king of the Nile-land seems inextricably to be mixed, the one who even now yet, the enduring father over the changing Pharaohs, reigns over it.

The kingship of Osiris, that of Horus frequently connected with Re, and of other divinities, although bearing political features too,[18] is for us less important.

In the Babylonian-Assyrian world[19] the concept of the god-ruler appears solidified and grown to a specifically political validity and binding force.

Priestly regents of the god of the city or of the empire, always according to their sphere of power, are known as regents of the 'genuine king'[20] with a seriousness which visibly projects above the continuity of the ceremonial formula, at least in the early period. It signifies primitive realistic consistency, when, before 3000, in a border settlement between two city-states[21] it is not their kings at all, only the gods, who alone are concerned with the holy law of drawing boundaries, who appear as partners. In the first half of the third millennium Lugal-zaggisi characterizes himself simultaneously as 'king of the countries' and as great-regent of the god Enlil.[22] But still at the end of the eighth century Sargon of Assyria[23] is not called king of subjugated Babylon, but wishes only to be known as the representative of Marduk as of the only king. The god as the true king 'chooses in his righteous heart'[24] the man of his mission and 'invests' him[25] with the sovereignty as his 'legitimate shepherd.'[26] He calls the chosen one, still in his mother's body, even in the first days of creation, by name and thus founds, in accordance with the popular belief in the secret of the called name,[27] a union of power between god and man which is to endure. Tiglath Pileser I proclaims: 'In order that I become the shepherd of the four regions Ashur pronounced my name for the cosmic age.'[28] Of divine origin, divine nature, are kingly power and kingly insignia.

As in Egypt so also in Babylon the prince is looked upon as son of the god, except that here where the office is the holy thing, the idea of adoption, there where the person is the holy thing,[29] the idea of a bodily generation predominates. At stake are the two great religio-historical categories of adoptionism and nativism, or better incarnationism, which will find their history-shaping conflict in the Christological controversy.[30] And, as in Egypt, in Babylon also, the king himself is divinized,[31] not, however, as in Egypt as the embodiment of the miraculous, the superman immune against the fate of life and death, the heir of the divine name, but as the possessor of divine splendour, the earth-bound bearer of the heavenly dignity, a mortal container of the immortal kingly essence.[32] To this corresponds, in spite of all the grandeur of apotheosis, the recurrently impinging feeling that the mystery of power is conditioned in its existence by the fulfilment of the commission, which fulfilment is placed into the human freedom of the authorized man, that thus no vested favour prevails. A 'righteous scepter' is granted the prince;[33] but it is up to him himself to preserve that righteousness. He is called, as Hammurabi proclaims in the introduction of his book of law,[34] 'in order to establish the right in the land'. The hosts are given over to him 'for a protection in order that the strong might not harm the weak'. As the sun-god he is to 'illuminate the earth'.[35] The gods whose counsel in the chamber of fate determines each year the wellbeing and misfortune of the year, watch over his deeds. From the ruler who is unworthy of the office they withdraw the power (just as according to the Iranian belief the royal glory forsakes the dishonest one[36]). 'If he does not attend to the justice of his land Ea the king of fates will alter his fate'.[37] How greatly, in the same way as in Egypt, the divine-human nature of the prince weakens the theocratic tendency. We hear here in Egypt only the outcry of the oppressed ascending above the throne of the Pharaoh up to his father in heaven. In Babylon, however, we hear the word of law, the will of the gods standing above the head of the ruler, as over the one who is bound by an oath and is therewith held responsible, if only in view of that word, and can therefore be tried, judged, and condemned. There we are able to discover only a plasmatic arrangement; here, however, a preliminary form of that which will manifest itself in the relationship between God and the receiver of His mandate in Israel.

I do not wish with this preliminary sketch to refer to influence, to borrowing. In the early contact between peoples everything flows together and yet marks itself off from everything else again, since form always originates because there follows upon surrender a resistance, a new independence. I attach great importance to showing in what mental world-atmosphere the early Israel grew, against the background of which great phenomena of intellectual history one must see the theocratic will to actuality in relief, in order to recognize, on this account, the way in which it fits into ancient oriental existence and ideals, but to recognize its elementary particularity not to be grasped by means of content analysis.

With the consideration of the South Arabian theocracy the viewpoint of the investigation of dependence must be completely separated, because our knowledge about the historical relationships is all too scanty and because the manuscript material known to us does not refer back behind the first pre-Christian miliennium. Nevertheless it discloses vistas into ancient key ideas.[38] But for the consideration of analogies Main, Saba and their brother kingdoms have an extraordinary importance. To be sure we cannot here, as in Egypt and Babylon, get behind the annals, epics and reports, the hymns, dirges and aphorisms to the blood-flow of the inner life. We cannot come to know how the king perceives the god, how the poet, whether the sacred or the courtly, secretly representing the heart of the people, perceived both. Nevertheless it is granted to us to fashion from the inscriptions a knowledge which, in its quite different value, is incomparable, that of an object of a scanty, skeletal sort, but for our inquiry not less meaningful than that corporality of a living subject: namely, the knowledge of a theocratic *constitution of society*.

Let us begin with the opening formula of an ancient Sabaic source[39] concerning a great cultic action of the head of state, of the Makrab, a title apparently analogous to the Babylonian-Assyrian of that priest-kingly 'god's regent'.[40]

The 'cultic and political sacred action'[41] which the prince performs (he is the mighty Kariba-ilu-Watar, reigning about 700, thus, a contemporary of Hezekiah of Judah) indeed contains a once-for-all, extraordinary act of state which is to be understood historically through-out; but this act is apparently connected with a periodically recurring feast, in the centre of which stands the renewal of the covenant between god, ruler, and people. All that has plainly to do with the state is always at the same time in every recurring consecration at a festival a fulfilment of this covenant[42] between the god and his people, a covenant whose mediator is the priest-prince.[43] A two-fold historical action goes together with this renewal of the covenant and the 'covenant community'. Its one side is the surrender of the lands, conquered in a series of vitorious campaigns concerning which the document reports, *to the god and to the people*. ' "God, king (as god-representative) and people" is the legal formula for the state; the ground is their property; the king rules over that ground as earthly agent of the divinity'.[44] Therefore the solemn surrender of the lands signifies their change into the property of the theocratic unity of god and people established through the covenant, or, since the tribe itself belongs to the tribal god,[45] into his property. The god is 'owner of the properties'.[46] The other side of the action, however, is historical in a still more exact sense. It is a remarkable proceeding. The prince, who mediates in priestly fashion, the 'regent in the name of the national god and supreme lord of the soil',[47] explains that he has become *malik*, king; that is, he assumes the secular title of ruler. Herein is expressed the very fact that Kariba-ilu 'at the end of his campaigns had become the lord over all South Arabia':[48] the empire creates the emperor, and the traditional sacred designation for the time being still stands beside the new profane one. But with this process certainly 'a new era is opened', and it has presumably been assumed with justice[49] that with the secularization of the office of ruler a transfer of the territorial domain to the secular power began. In other words, the theocratic principle begins to lose its comprehensive power and to be limited to the merely-religious in order finally merely to provide the intangible shielding of autocracy, as in Egypt and Babylon. Moreover, this process had already begun as the act of the conqueror lent it expression: 'the image of society had certainly already been altered as the theocratic form of state was secularized in the title also'.[50]

We have received out of the Sabaic document the image of a peculiar form of society, apparently in the moment of its highest triumph, which at the same time proclaims its downfall. The actual unity of god, prince and people, the social validity of the covenant, is

confirmed as probably never before through the solemn surrender of
the lands, and is at the same time weaknened through the acceptance
of the 'kingship'. If anywhere, there is world-history in such an event,
in which the problematics of the relation between religion and politics
assumes its climactic manifestation.

The analogical value of the South Arabian constitution for our
problem centres in the principle of the divine ownership of the soil.
The Biblical passage, 'Mine is the land, for you are guests and
sojourners with Me' (Leviticus 25:23), which is usually regarded as a
theological utopia, here finds its strictly historical counterpart; private
ownership is feudal tenure. Significantly the political cast of covenant
and covenant community are further represented. Although there are
agreements between god and king elsewhere in the ancient Orient,[51]
nevertheless we find only here and in Israel the concept of a divine
covenant as an enduring and encompassing institution fundamental to
the public life. Here as well as there the human leader is only the
mediator of this covenant.[52] The ancient Arabian culture also provides
us with the concise political formula for a religious idea which has its
high representations in Israel's history of faith, from the negotiating
of Moses between God and people to that purest word form where in
the designation of Deutero-Isaiah (Isaiah 42:6; 49:8) the 'servant' himself is viewed as 'people's covenant', as the very man, through whom
the streams of covenant fulfilment move from above downward, from
below upward, who must become the living symbol of the covenant.
The conception of a festive observance of the renewal of the covenant
is also worthy of attention in this connection. Yet here the material
on both sides is not so clarified that the attempt of a comparison could
be hazarded.[53] But Saba is to be thought of in yet another respect.
In relation to the ruling conception of a progressive 'theocratization
of the Israelitish social order'[54] it apparently manifests the example of
a development in the opposite direction[55] which must prove to be
fruitful for the understanding of the pre-exilic history of Israel.

We have reached the conclusion that the kingship of God in the
ancient orient is more than an idea and designation of a general sort.
Out of a vague world-lord's countenance the features of the supreme
ruler of an earthly commonwealth stand forth ever more plainly. In
Egypt he is first only the primeval king who, withdrawn into heaven,
holds his protecting and guiding hand over his human followers. In
Babylon he looks down upon his regent as though examining the

guardian of his law and, if it must be, as ready to judge him. In South Arabia, he is, constitutionally related to his people, founder and partner of the covenant on whose fulfilment the preservation of the commonwealth hangs. From the point of view of this tendency of the cosmic continually being changed into the political, the question ought to be renewed as to whether there can have been a primitive will to theocracy in Israel. The Biblical reports concerning the early contact of the Hebrews with Egyptian, Babylonian, Arabian life have yielded, through historical research, confirmations of varying degrees of certainty. It cannot be disputed that the fortunes of Israel's early period caused it to breathe in, over and beyond the mere original being-immersed in early Semitic character, Oriental spirit in the Canaan[56] 'strongly coloured in its culture by Babylon and permeated by Egyptian influences'. The kingship of God is not to be derived from this influence.

But in our inquiry we are not concerned about theocracy in this general sense, but about that immediate, unmetaphorical, unlimitedly real theocracy which is demanded in the Gideon passage. This requisite conditionality remains in every case, however we have to date it, peculiar to Israel; we have met nowhere else anything comparable to it. The inquiry breaks down into two parts:

1. What is the unconditionedness of the theocratic will to actualization in relation to the general oriental idea of the divine kingship in its constitutive form? As of what nature is the new, the supervening, to be understood?

2. How exactly, from the viewpoint of the answer to this question, is the process or the result of this alteration to be thought of, and how accordingly is its historical locale to be determined?

The way to the answer leads first of all to the previously postponed consideration of that divine designation, *malk*, as a title of the Semitic tribal god.

CHAPTER FOUR

THE WEST-SEMITIC TRIBAL GOD

I AM limiting myself here to the West-Semitic material since the question cannot yet be decided as to whether, as I consider probable, the divine epithet '*malk*' or '*milk*' points back into the early Semitic period[1] or whether, originating with the Phoenicians, it was adopted by the Aramaeans, Ammonites, Moabites, Israelites, and arose independently of these with the South Arabians.[2] The latter view would certainly be difficult to maintain in terms of the history of religion, particularly with respect to the Babylonian divine designation 'malik',[3] probably signifying only counsellor, but nevertheless scarcely to be regarded as unrelated. In any case the differences in meaning are so great that they alone justify the restriction to the West Semitic.[4]

'*Malk*' is, like '*baal*', a relational concept, whereas the most universal Semitic designation of a numen, '*el*', is a phenomenal concept. All three are concepts, not proper names; all three have the tendency to distinguish themselves in relation to the individuality named, perhaps through ever closer connection with a determinative word: an attribute or an objective genitive. But '*el*'[5] is the naked, appearing, potency which appears efficaceous, divine, finally personal; '*baal*' and '*malk*' are personal potency in relation to something; they indicate in which respect a potency is potent and in which way.[6] A still deeper difference, however, is that of the sphere of origin. '*El*' has his source in the non-historical, regular experience of the world; the two others in an experience which, although also primeval, is nevertheless characterized as historical in nature by the emphatic uniqueness of its events and the participation of the entire tribal unity. In the course of the surprizes through which the power of natural occurrences meet him a thousand-fold, in the horrified or enraptured perception of energies springing forth like lightning, but also in the long, wondering, view of a very high mountain (Psalm 36:7), of a spreading tree (80:11), of a very strong or mysteriously authoritative human being (Ezekiel 31:11), yes perhaps even in the ever-recurring strangely-happy impression of the power of one's own hand (Genesis 31:29) the individual Semite, close to nature, experiences that there are *el*'s, that there is *el*. But that an *el* is *baal* of something, that an *el* is *malk* over someone, that the Semitic tribe discovers in the destiny-determining events of his primeval history. And the first of the two is specifically different from the second.

A band, a tribe, a union of tribes emigrates from a countryside hitherto a homeland, now economically or politically forbidding, into the unknown. The orderly departure takes place. As though one possessed ancient trail lore one strides ahead without a mistake: there is one who leads. A demonic plague is compelled to vanish on the third day: there is one who overcomes it. Innumerable enemy hordes are put to flight: there is one in the front rank who wields the sword. Persons in whom no one would ever put any confidence display unforseeable wisdom and heroism: there is one who imparts both. The subjugation of the aimed-for land succeeds piece by piece; *malk*, the *el* of the tribe, has accomplished this. '*Malk*' means the *accompanying* god.[7]

But already on the journey blessing happened to the wanderers which they were not able to ascribe to the tribal god. For weeks they moved through nothing but desert. In vain they called upon the lord through sacrifice. Plainly he was no longer able to help here. They doubted. Then the oasis sprang up before them with its spring and palmy shade. And in settling a region they discovered the wonder again and again. A hidden potency rippled and flowed. From secret springs and streams grew the luxuriance of the meadow. *Baal* and *baalath* are *encountered* divinity.

Malk is one, the leader of his adherents; in his oneness they discover their own. Another people may have another deity. This does not concern them. *Baal* is manifold, ever and again this *baal* here, the pair of *baals* of this region of heaven and this region of earth in the mystery of their fruitfulness. In particular places the *baals* receive the victorious warriors as though these were their favourites from time immemorial.

For the *baal* duality and mating are essential. A secondary consort who remains without function[8] can always be placed beside the *malk*; as *malk* he is separate and alone.

Malk is—in a sense from which the later state-political meaning will develop—the 'king'; to him a tribe is subject. *Baal* is the 'master', the 'possessor', the 'owner'.[9] To him belongs a locality, originally always a locality of fertilization and fruitfulness. For early man the great cosmic process of fertilization was to be found even in the out-pourings of flowing waters—rain from the sky, head-water from the mountain, ground water out of the depths–upon a conceiving, now impregnated soil.[10] The head-water is the *baal*, but also the mountain from which it comes, also the tree which it reclaims from the parched earth and in which her fulness is delivered forth most luxuriantly; and also the sky, whose rain is marriage, becomes *baal's*, to begin with certainly not the 'entire' sky—a conception of later conspection of the phenomena of nature as developed in Phoenician, and then in Syrian, Palmyrian, and Nabataean culture[11]—but merely the sky of this place, the sky which brings moisture here while a neighbouring region remains dry.[12] The human settlement of a divinely blessed place also becomes *baal's*.

If, however, out of the settlement which was first a camp on the waterway,[13] then a village of log-and-mud huts, in the growth of agriculture and crafts the walled city arises, its founder is not the *baal* but the *malk*. The consecration of a city is not earth-magic, but social-magic; not the power of earth and also not that of the sky, only that of the people's destiny, is represented. The god who led the band through the trackless wilderness bequeaths it representation in space; the 'king' of the tribe, enthroned in the temple of the city, becomes king of the state. That is what Melqarth, 'king of the city', signifies; and with legitimate sense did myth ascribe the founding of Tyre to him.[14] It is not to be concluded from his name that he was 'not the king of a people, but of a city and its outskirts'.[15] But it does not do justice to his uniqueness either if one sees in him only the *malk* honoured in Tyre:[16] he becomes founder and ruler of the city by virtue of his nature and office.[17] Now, as so frequently, he merges as the god brought-along with the one encountered, with the *baal* of the place.[18] 'Our lord Melqarth the *baal* of Tyre' he is called; and also the Carthaginians, who maintain his worship,[19] collect taxes for the Tyrian sanctuary. From this it is not to be concluded that the *baals* were originally tribal gods.[20] That they never were. Probably, however, they were swallowed up by many a tribal god.[21] It is a process worthy of note in the history of religion, when the band which gazes with astonishment at the miracle of fruitfulness of the localized demon, seized by an ecstatic passion for identity, breaks out into the cry: 'the *baal* is indeed the *malk*!'[22]

Baalism is encountered divinity, encountered by land-occupying nomad-warriors. One may understand the being encountered historically. It has been assumed, probably correctly,[23] that these local genie already in the ancient Semitic period 'were lords in the land and were adopted by the Canaanites and named with the common Semitic word *baal*'. A much discussed image of Hittite art,[24] the god at Ivriz at the foot of the Taurus, above a fruitful valley which looks forth out of a broad swamp and salt-marsh terrain, the god carved out of the rock near a down-plunging mountain torrent, on his head the helmet trimmed with steer horns, in his right hand the vine branch heavy with grapes, a sheaf of grain in the left hand, a ploughshare apparently at his feet, opposite him the adoring king—he is a genuine *baal*,[25] a dispenser of corn and wine (Hosea 2, 7, 10).

On the other hand *malk* is throughout the primeval god of the tribe. The ancient-historical competence in action of a biological group is beheld in his form. He is, however, not, as the French school of the sociology of religion wishes to conceive of this sort of thing,[26] the personified spirit of the community, but he represents the power which transcends it, happens to it, which *changes* it, even historicizes it; a power which in a formative hour drives it on to do the unaccustomed and untraditional, in a feud-overcoming gathering together of all clans as a single tribe, of all tribes as a single people, to travel the unbeaten path into the land of a hope or promise. He can coalesce with an ancestral spirit, a 'primeval father', as well as he can coalesce with a *baal*. But he is from the very beginning definitely not an ancestor, but, at the turning point, the one obviously becoming the leader in whom the future supreme king of the empire is announced— the giver of history. The Semites encounter in the conquered land local gods, nature-gods, gaze at them in wonder, admire them, fall down before them. But their own gods which are 'with them', the ones coming with them, fighting for them, are gods of the tribe, national, historical gods, 'kings'.

The blessing of the *malk* is different from that of the *baal*. The *baal* bestows the fruit of the soil; the Ashtarte probably especially the fruit of the herd-animal. The *malk* increases the power of the tribe, increases its quantity; he grants the fruit of the human bosom.[27]

People give to the god what they wish to receive from him—primarily not in a process of exchange, but also not because they thought that they had to compel the higher movement, but because they believe that they must begin it. The 'imitative' rites are also initiative. They earnestly desire of the *baal* that he complete the holy copulation on which the future of the field hangs. Thus people themselves celebrate holy copulation in the field. They solicit children, however, from the *malk*, and children are sacrificed and dedicated to him.

It is a much discussed question whether the rite which is mentioned in the Scripture: to present a child through the fire to the *melekh* or, pronounced with the so-called 'pejorative vocalization'[28] *molekh*, signifies sacrifice or dedication.[29] That the latter designation is exclusively correct, that what is involved is simply a rite of lustration or dedication[30] of the sort thoroughly presented especially by Mannhardt,[31] is certainly rendered impossible by the fact that in one passage (Ezekiel 23:37) the goal of the presentation is described unequivocally all the way through 'to the eating' (see also 16:21),[32] and that in other passages[33] burning-up rather than presentation is spoken of. But also the view that the presentation signifies nothing else than a sacrifice, seems to me to lend force to the word which indeed does not have the sense of leading-into, but that of leading-through.[34] We may have here one of those developments where the rite wavers between actual and imitative-symbolic killing, whether the original sacrifice of a living thing is replaced by a symbolic one,[35] or whether dedications which represent a dying and rising again lead to actual death,[36] or whether, as here, they are enhanced to the point of sacrifice.[37] That this is the case here is evidenced by the term which cannot well be taken in a secondary sense.[38] The child is thus carried 'through the fire' into the domain of the god. But when it is a matter of entreating him more strongly—not just for the sake of increasing the tribe, but in order to ward off a catastrophe which threatens it[39]—the child is left in the fire, slaughtered, as is done with the sacrificial animal.[40] [41]

CHAPTER FIVE

JHWH THE MELEKH

SINCE Amos has to say that the God of Israel is the only God, that there is no other, he says it in this speech of JHWH (9:7): 'Did I not bring Israel out of the land of Egypt— / and the Philistines from Caphtor / and the Syrians from Kir?' Thus it is stated that JHWH is the God of the peoples; and, to be sure, not the one who is worshipped by them, but the one who has *led* every wandering people, like Israel, into a 'good' land.[1] Thus, even then when Israel was prone to adopt the delusion that it had a monopoly on its God—it has one, and thus no more is implied than that the Ethiopians have one—even then, if it is to be explained unmistakably that JHWH is not the God of a tribe, even then, and precisely then, is He proclaimed as tribal God; for ever and ever God of the tribe just as it might name the liberator whose deeds it experienced in its own history. So strong, so central is JHWH's manifestation is the character of the God walking-on-before, the leading God, the *melekh*.

Where, in the narratives, stemming from the period before JHWH places his throne on the temple-mountain, He is connected more closely with a single place, it is at the same time reported or announced that He is not as *baal* attached to that place; that rather He searches out the people of his choice in far-off regions, fetches, accompanies, guides them. I wish here to refer only to the two most eminent examples: Bethel and Sinai.

Jacob dreams (Genesis 28) at the 'awe-full' place at which, as he experiences in the dream, 'JHWH dwells'. His head rests on the stone which he, awakened, will call 'a house of God' because in the dream God stood above it. He speaks to him: He promises him three things: this land into which one day his descendants are to be led by the divine leader; the increase and expansion of the tribe as these are incumbent upon the tribal God; and thirdly, His assistance on the way which Jacob has yet to go: 'For I am with you, / I will protect you wherever you go, / and I will cause you to return home to this ground, / yes, I forsake you not, / until I have done what I have told you'. God is not bound to the spot at which He appears; He lingers at it, to be sure, but only as at a place of manifestation. And also the sky out of which His 'messengers' descend and, ready for His signal, pass in review before Him, does not hold Him fast. He wanders with His creature, He remains near it, He stands by it wherever it stands. He follows Jacob into the foreign land; He comes back with him into the home land.[2] When it is time He calls to him (31:3): 'Return to the land of your fathers, to your kindred! / I will be with you there'. But the whole process is determined to repeat itself on a wider scale. Invited by his son Joseph to Egypt where, as (15:13) God had announced to his ancestor, his descendants are to be enslaved and oppressed for four hundred years, the old Jacob-Israel hears again, in a night-vision as formerly at Bethel, the voice of *el* (46:2ff.): 'I Myself / go down with you to Egypt / and I Myself bring you up here again / yes up here!' The 'bringing-back-up-here' obviously does not merely pertain to the corpse which will be carried out of Egypt into Canaan to the hereditary grave (chapter 50). Rather the phrase points forward to the 'great tribe' which is to grow in Egypt and whose one-time journey home was already announced to Abraham (15:14, 16). Therefore the words 'there I will cause you to become a great tribe' are not, as is usually assumed, to be regarded as a gloss which interrupts the context; it is through them that what follows becomes intelligible.

Of the three speeches of God to Jacob which I have adduced the first two are ascribed to the Jahwist and the third to the Elohist source. In spite of the difference of the divine designations they are of the same spirit, the same character. The one responsible for their context was concerned to exhibit in the life-course of the last of the patriarchs the ruling of the One-Who-goes along, of the Leader-God.

Just as in the history of the patriarchs one must come to the point of detaching JHWH from the Canaanite cult-places, so in the history of Exodus one must get to the point of causing His connection with Sinai not to appear as a being-bound to it. Never is He called the God of this mountain; never is an altar erected to Him there.[3] It dare not happen that the mountain, which is the place of His dwelling and revealing, be understood as His sphere in the *baal*-sense. In a decisive passage (Exodus 19:11, 18) it is reported how God came

down upon it in the fire. In the first proclamation to Moses the manifestation at the holy place had been explained with the same word
(3:8). But this is as little sufficient here to counteract Baalization as
the open heaven was with Jacob. As there with the patriarch, so here,
JHWH goes to Egypt with Moses. The threefold (3:12; 4:12, 15)
promise of abiding presence is here as spacially-real as the same expression addressed to Jacob. During his dealings with the Pharaoh Moses
does not need to wait for a proclamation of God or to seek Him out.
He turns to Him (5:22) and converses with Him. And in the last
night JHWH moves 'through the midst of Egypt' (11:4) and 'passes
through' it (12:12, 23) in order to strike the first-born. His might
prevails in the land subservient to strange gods no more restrictedly
than at the places of His manifestation. In this consists His 'judgment'
on them comparable with no action of any god of the history of
religion (12:12; Numbers 33:4). And now He, a genuine *melekh*-god,
leads 'His armies, His people' (Exodus 7:4)[4] out of the land in which
it was enslaved. He guides the people (13:17ff.). He 'goes on before
them, / in a pillar of cloud by day to lead them the way, / by night
in a pillar of fire to give them light, / to go by day and night'. (v. 21)
'Upright', a proud army, He causes them to walk in His footsteps
(Leviticus 26:13), causes them to go 'through the eddying waters' as
a horse through the wilderness (Isaiah 63:13; Psalm 106:9). At the
right hand of Moses He strides on before them through the sea
(Isaiah 63:12). Thus He leads them to His mountain. From the place
where He set out with Moses, there He brings them now as those
purchased out of the 'service' of Egypt into His 'service' (this double
meaning of the word '*aboda* goes significantly through the entire
narrative) to serve Him here (Exodus 3:12). With the great reference
to this leading He now opens the series of speeches from the mountain
with a word (19:4) which in meaning and language seems to me
completely original; which, however, if it were secondary, would be
sufficient to demonstrate the religious genius of the redactor in having
put it in this place: 'You yourselves have seen what I did in Egypt, /
I carried you on eagles' wings and had you come to Me.' This 'I carried
you' and this 'to Me' furnish together with one another the picture of
the tribal numen Whose abiding is contained in His wandering;
Whose natural potency is contained in His historical potency.

From this point on it must be grasped why, after the sinning of the
people, it is the subject of such an intensive dialogue between Moses

and JHWH, such a forceful pleading and granting, whether from here on 'the countenance'[5] of God is to move along with them and before them. What Moses implores: that JHWH on the continuation of the wanderings may not lead them merely through an emissary as He has done with other peoples (that could, in any case, from the viewpoint of the redactor, be the background of 33:16b—the word of God with Amos concerning this matter seems to express the immediate leadership of the others too), but that He Himself might lead, means: that He remain Israel's *'melekh'*—*melekh* also in the original sense of the word, the 'Counsellor', the 'Decision-maker'.

But there has already appeared, too, in the narrative the cultic-sacramental presentation of that wandering and abiding in one, the tent of divine 'meeting' or presence whose archetype JHWH Himself appears to have created under the covering of the clouds in six days, as He once created the world, in order to reveal it on the seventh day (24:16), the *movable place* to which now, as formerly to the mountain (24:15ff.),[6] the divine cloud 'indwelling', taking-up-dwelling (this is what *shakhan* means here: action, not condition),[7] is let down. The tent whose mid-point,[8] the ark as the throne of the 'Sitting One', moving out and in before the army, already in the wilderness period 'expression of the local unboundedness of God',[9] even in Canaan after the replacement of the tent by a fixed cult-building, remains fundamentally movable—therefore the carrying poles dare never be drawn out (Exodus 25:15 is supported by I Kings 8:8)—the tent is the corporeal sign against that Baalization of the God Who does not allow Himself to be attached to any natural spot, not even to Zion, the original spot of His habitation. The leading of the One-who-goes-on-before remained so much the central idea of Israelitish faith that the wilderness-wandering reported by the narrator as the punishment of an entire generation of people and also remembered as such in song (Psalm 95:10ff.), appeared to many singers and story-tellers as an abundant mercy. After 'He who brought us up out of the land of Egypt', 'He who caused us to go (*molikh*) through the wilderness' ranks next in importance as JHWH's title of glory[10] for the prophet (Jeremiah 2:6; cf. Amos 2:10) as well as for the Psalmist (136:16).

Also the much discussed characterization *ṣᵉbaoth* might well be investigated from this point of view. If in this task one starts not, as usually happens, with the prophet, but with the writer of history, a remarkable statistic results. If one subtracts from the fifteen passages

the three in which Elijah's and Elisha's divine warfare are discussed
and the one from Isaiah's message of divine warfare to Sennacherib
(II Kings 19:31 in the form expanded by the Massora based on Isaiah
37:32), there remain four passages from the history of the Samuelic
crisis and seven from the history of the Davidic early period, and,
indeed, exclusively such as fit together with God's commission to
David, and thus with the theopolitical meaning of the kingship. Thus,
what is involved here throughout,[11] mediately or immediately, is the
concept of the *melekh*-God empowering His human regent. But one
can probably go still further. If it may be in itself impossible to decide
whether in the *ṣᵉbaoth*-idea the earthly or the heavenly 'hosts' are the
original element,[12] still it seems to me in the characteristic word-
formation 'JHWH *ṣᵉbaoth*', that the first are involved, whether or not
the designation is regarded as primary or as a shortened form of
JHWH *elohe ṣᵉbaoth*, 'JHWH God of hosts'.[13] Since the plural
ṣᵉbaoth does not, like the singularized plural *elohim*,[14] lend itself to
being understood as apposition, and since, as for example follows from
Isaiah 13:4, 'JHWH of hosts marshals the battle-host Himself', the
plural was not congealed into a name hiding the plurality, we must
think of a genitive construction perceived as such.[15] But what sort
of meaning can it perhaps have had for Isaiah? As long as we hold
fast to the opaque nomenclature of JHWH we obtain nothing from
the construction. But passages like Amos 5:8 and 9:6, Isaiah 42:8,
Jeremiah 16:21 and 33:2, also Exodus 15:3 (as is apparent to everyone who substitutes experimentally for JHWH any divine name, Indra
or Enlil, Zeus or Odin) become absurd if we hold fast to the strict
nomenclature of JHWH. It becomes 'meaningful only if we somehow
it makes no difference how, whether with "Lord" or with "Eternal"
or some other way, interprets the name as bearer of meaning'.[16] But
of what meaning could the name be bearer for a person of the Biblical
Israel—at least so long as it could be pronounced? No other meaning
than that contained in the dialogue of the thorn-bush[17]: He who is
here is He who is present. This is probably also how that generally
misunderstood passage of Deutero-Isaiah (52:6) is to be explained:
'Therefore shall My people / know My name, / therefore in that day /
that I am He Who says: / here am I.' In any case this is the way in
which it seems to me that the genitive construction is to be explained.
In I Samuel 17:45 the young David characterizes the God with Whose
name he confronts the Philistine as JHWH *ṣᵉbaoth* and as *elohe*

maar^ekhoth yissraeι in one. The pathetic parallelism has the most genuine sound; moreover each is indispensable, the epithet which like a refrain completes the movement begun in verses 10 and 36, and then, properly, the *shem* which is invoked against the adversary. If, however, the former means that the battle ranks of Israel have in God an *elohim*, then the latter probably means that the hosts (Israel's) have in Him a JHWH (one thinks here of the term *elohe ẓ^ebaoth* which is far and away preponderantly without an article). And as the concept *elohim* here, as in many another passage, has a transparence into the original meaning of the fulness of power, so it seems to me that the name JHWH is here transparent in this its fundamental meaning. Behind the cry 'JHWH is His name' of the sea-song, which without this giving of meaning would seem empty, stands the certainty—in the narrative context probably anticipating the later disclosure—that the name itself hides the presence of God: in 'JHWH' there is here suggested a *yihye immanu*; the hosts glorify Him 'Who is with us'. (cf. Numbers 14:43; 14:9; Deuteronomy 20:1) Thus there may stand behind the designation JHWH *ẓ^ebaoth* the ancient confidence which knows courageously about the Sinaitic disclosure of the name: He is called JHWH; JHWH is the One Who is with them, the One Who remains present to them, thus the One Who comes-along with them (Exodus 33:16; Deuteronomy 20:4; 31:6), the One Who goes-on-ahead (Exodus 13:21; Numbers 14:14; Deuteronomy 1:30, 33), the Leader, the *melekh*. In the first passage of the canon where JHWH is spoken of simply as 'the King', Isaiah 6:5, the prophet calls Him JHWH *ẓ^ebaoth*. And whoever composed the 'apocalyptic' twenty-fourth chapter of Isaiah, he has remained faithful to the tradition of Isaiah when he proclaims (verse 23): 'JHWH of hosts comes into the kingship / upon mount Zion and in Jerusalem.'

When the Psalmist (24:9ff.) bids the gates, probably those of the citadel rather than those of heaven, to lift up their knobs in order that JHWH *ẓ^ebaoth* as 'the King of power'[18] come in, it is not to be forgotten that another Psalm, in its essential structure perhaps Solomonic,[19] the sixty-eighth, names the princes of the peoples put to flight by God *malkhe ẓ^ebaoth*[20]: in relation to the 'hosts' *melekh* still means 'the leader', even in the royal period.

The resisting Moses asks the One Who speaks to him out of the burning thorn-bush, Who sends him with the unheard-of task to Egypt (Exodus 3:13): 'When I come then to the sons of Israel, /

I say to them: the God of your fathers sends me to you, / they will say to me: what is His name?— / what shall I say to them then?' It has been rightly assumed that with the question 'what is His name?'[21] the primitive belief in names is to be thought of: 'people were at that time confident of having the god in their power through the knowledge of his name'.[22] It must be added that the belief in names was as powerful with no people of antiquity as in that very Egypt,[23] where through knowledge of a hidden divine name one could himself become a god. Moses does not assume that the people, if he names the God of the fathers as his task-giver, will ask him: 'Well, what is He called?'[24] Such nonsense is not thinkable with any people, much less with one whose consciousness of tradition the author of the thorn-bush dialogue certainly did not call into question.[25] And if he, as some think, did not know what is contained in our Genesis concerning the invocation of the name JHWH by Abraham, still it could not be unknown to the redactor and could not, in a subject of such importance, remain without influence on his textual selection.[26] The question which Moses expects from the people does not have to do with the sound of the name, but with its secret, with its 'genuine' pronunciation, its magic applicability. The tormented ones will want to discover (thus they have learned from Egypt) how they can powerfully conjure God to appear forthwith and help. His message will not satisfy them; they will want to take possession of Him—how, then, are they to be answered? *To this* JHWH replies with His '*ehye asher ehye*', which discloses in the first person what the name in the third person hides—hides, to be sure, since it was out of the original 'God-cry'[27] *yah* or *yahu* as the primeval name of invocation (Genesis 4:26; 12:8; 13:4; 21:33; 26:25)[28], that the Tetragrammaton grew in which 'the name-like and the nickname-like completely coincide.'[29] Thus not 'I am Who I am' or the like; for *haya, hawa* means Biblically 'to be', admittedly (secondarily) in the copulative, but not in the existential sense—for which the Biblical language still does not yet have a concept—but rather 'to become, to happen, to become present, to be there (here)'. In our passage *ehye* means the very same thing that it means before (v. 12) and after (4:12, 15) in the narrative: to be there with some one, to be present to him, to stand by him, except that here the verb is used as an absolute without having added to it *with whom* the Present One is there.[30] God thereby makes no theological statements about His eternity or even His 'aseity',[31] but He speaks to His creature, His man, His people the assurance which they need and which frustrates every magic undertaking, but also makes it superfluous. The first *ehye* simply gives the assurance: I shall be there (ever and ever with My host, with My people, with you)—thus you do not need to conjure me. And the following *asher ehye*, according to all parallels,[32] can only mean: as I Who will always be there, as I ever and ever will be there, that is, as I ever and ever will want to appear. I Myself do not anticipate My forms of appearance; and here you think to be able to conjure Me with some means, to appear here and not elsewhere, now and not some other time, thus and not otherwise! In short: you do not need to conjure Me, but you cannot conjure Me either. What is here reported is, considered in terms of the history of religion, the 'de-magicizing' of faith: in the self-proclamation of the God Who is with His own, remaining present to them, going-along-with them. The liberation, the journey through the sea, pillars of cloud and fire, the tent and the ark, wilderness passage and occupation of the land, everything is already herein contained. This is a God Who chooses places for Himself, but belongs to none of them because even the heavens do not contain Him (I Kings 8:27); Who stands by the world which He has created; Who leads His hosts, those above and those below, through the battles and saving acts of history; Who goes His 'way' (Exodus 33:13)[33] and wills that man follow Him upon it, that he 'go in it', 'go behind Him'.[34] 'This is the living God,' the '*melekh* of the peoples', the '*melekh* for the cosmic period' (Jeremiah 10:7, 10). Even in His relation to nature He does not appear as without history like the *baals*, but as the Lord of history, the 'King'. With my observations concerning the dialogue of the thorn-bush I have wished to treat only the meaning and purpose of the text, thus also its view of the tradition of the JHWH-faith of Israel; not, however, the historical question, only just touched upon here, of this faith, which belongs in another context. Here I was concerned to point out one thing: that for the Biblical tradition, which there is no reason not to trust in this matter, the Mosaic 'becoming known' of JHWH (Exodus 6:3) thus signifies the revelation of His nature from His name, the revelation of His nature as *melekh*-God.

For the characterization of Israelitish theism I have joined to texts which undoubtedly refer to the pre-state early period and are meant to express its tradition, words of the late, state period, of the period before the collapse, words of Jeremiah, in order to demonstrate how

the maturity of knowledge manifesting itself in them really only completes what was already there germinating in obvious vitality. Jeremiah,
while he decided in one expression the way which leads over the Amos
passage concerning the equating of Israel with Philistines and Aramaeans and the Isaiah passage (19:25)—which sounds thoroughly
genuine to me[35]—concerning the equating of Israel with Egypt and
Assyria, could call JHWH the 'King of the peoples' because He had
appeared in the early period of the people as the 'King' of Israel—not
yet, of course, in the sense of the head of a state, which didn't exist
as yet, but in the sense of the head of a land-seeking confederation of
tribes, thus, in the original meaning of the West-Semitic *melekh*-God.[36]
Because He had appeared so genuinely as the kingly leader of the
historical period of this very people, Jeremiah could proclaim Him
as the universal King of the aëon, the King of the cosmic age. In the
meantime there had grown out of Israel one kingdom, then two.
Then one of the two collapsed. Now the collapse of the other was
announced, but the one who announced it knew even now for his
God, the universal God, no higher title than that of King.

CHAPTER SIX

THE FAITH OF ISRAEL

THE process which leads from the theism of the period of the Exodus to that of the period of the Exile is usually regarded as a change to something different which is commonly understood as a supervening of new values of the spirit and of morality; sometimes, however, also as a loss in reality-content. All this does not hold good if one means the faith-relationship of those who actually believe and not the religious activity of the pseudo-believers and misbelievers. What we find in unmistakably authentic lines in the picture of the 'JHWH-servant' Moses is related to the songs of the nameless prophet about the 'JHWH-servant' as the folded-up leaf is related to the unfolded leaf.[1] Thus also the I-sentence of the beginning of the decalogue,[2] in which the speaking God pledges Himself to the liberation and leading of the addressed Israel which is to have no God beside Him, is related to those I-sentences of the speech to Cyrus, the receiver of a mission, who did not know Him up to then, in which He acknowledges the creation of good and evil, since there is no God except Him (Isaiah 45:4–7). There is nothing added nor left out; an unconditionedness which at first was only there and kept silent now bears witness to itself in word. The God of Whom it is known that His kingship rules over all (Psalm 103:19) is neither more spiritual nor is He less real than He of whom it is only known that He 'was King in Jeshurun' (Deuteronomy 33:5)[3]. For this very One comes forward with the unconditional claim of the genuine kingship which admittedly in its implicit form only demands *that one concern oneself about no other kingships*, and only in its explicit form decrees *that there are no others*. As soon as the truth of his faith had so overpoweringly unfolded itself before any man in 'Jeshurun' that not only *while* he said, 'my King and my God!' (Psalm 5:3), but also afterwards, he was no longer able to invest the plural of king-gods of the peoples with reality and thus to conceive seriously concerning his divine Thou that it have only *more* power and not *the* power—as soon as one thus became aware of the unconditionedness of his God, at that point JHWH was attested to this believing person as the Lord of all reality. As the Lord Who not only had no rivals, Who also had no partners, none but the believing or not-believing, rather (since the concept 'to believe in someone' is not Israelitish) trusting or not-trusting man. This process in and with the person and its militant effect in and with the community are what made possible the attestation of the unconditionedness in the prophetic word, and with it the eschatological proclamation. Certainly Amos declared first that the leader-god of the Philistines and that of the Aramaeans is identical with JHWH; but that does not mean that no one knew it before him.[4]

Lagarde's remark[5] to the effect that the monotheism of the Jews stands 'on the same level as the report of a junior officer attached to the commissariat who reports the existence of only one exemplar of any object' proceeds from a remarkable confusion of faith-relation and 'Weltanschauung'. The doctrine of uniqueness has its vital ground certainly not in this, that one formulated thoughts about how many gods there are and perhaps also sought to establish this, but in the exclusiveness which rules over the faith-relation as it rules over the true love between man and man; more precisely: in the total validity and the total effect of the exclusiveness. The theism of Israel is characterized finally in this, that the faith-relation according to its nature wishes to be valid for, and to bear upon, all of life. It will not do to turn back from the prayer to JHWH to a life in which one reveres, or only acknowledges '*weltanschaulich*', other powers. Whoever to his King and God speaks this ardently singular Thou, cannot in the meantime remain in domains for which He is not pertinent; he must subject them all to the One. The uniqueness in 'monotheism' is accordingly not that of an 'exemplar', but it is that of the Thou in the I-Thou relation[6] so far as this is not denied in the totality of the lived life. The 'polytheist' makes out of every divine manifestation—thus out of every secret of the world and of existence with which he has to do—a divine being; the 'monotheist' recognizes in all things the God Whom he experienced in confrontation. That *asher ehye*, the vastness and unexpectedness of the forms of manifestation in which the uniqueness is wont to be recognized ever anew, leads him on to discover and to conquer realm after realm for Him. In this gradual,

believing discovery of all the realms of the world and existence, the
unfolding of the rolled-up leaf takes place—not as an unfolding of
the human psyche, but as the unfolding of its real relationship to being,
of the real relationship which the Biblical Hebraic characterizes with
the vitality-filled, not until later cognitively narrowed, concept of
da'ath elohim,[7] of the 'knowledge'-connection with God. Since the
entire faith relationship is in its actuality exclusive, in Israel there
arises the aspiration to deal seriously with the exclusiveness in vital
fashion far beyond the actuality of the faith relationship, even to the
entire fulness of existence. This wanting to deal seriously is the
dynamic actuality which drove Israel beyond the status of the ancient
Oriental spirit and into its own history of faith. I say 'actuality' and
not 'peculiarity' or the like because it is manifested—and most clearly
precisely in the most religiously vital periods—not in a steady movement of the generality of the people, but in a virtually polar-seeming
confrontation of seriousness and 'obstinacy', so that the inner fight
for JHWH, for exclusiveness, and for dealing seriously is to be regarded as the genuine form of movement in the history of faith of
Israel. In this fight the doctrine of uniqueness is perfected as doctrine:
the idea of the King of Israel unfolds itself, without being emptied
of meaning, to that of King of the universe; and, in dealing seriously,
the painfully experienced tension between the perfection of representation of such lordship and the actual condition of the world finds its
eschatological language.

Naturally the battle, like every genuine battle of faith, must be
directed with special intensity against the juxtaposition and inter-
action of true worship and idolatry: against the attempt to make the
service of truth and the service of error compatible with one another.
The 'obstinate', indeed, do not for the most part think of renouncing
the tribal God.[8] They simply do not follow after Him upon His
'paths', but wish to have and manipulate Him upon theirs.[9] Wherever
they encounter the secret of an unknown power, instead of recognizing
in JHWH that which corresponds to this power, commands it, dis-
patches it, and of enlarging the picture of their God in the process,
they are immediately set upon gaining control of the roving demon
of the new power, consequently of his myth and of his ritual, and
amalgamating their JHWH with him. On the other hand, however,
they refuse to accept in JHWH's message that whereby He stands out
from the Semitic *melekh*-dom in that He completes it and declares

Himself as the holy Leader for salvation, as the King of the kingdom, consequently, His person. They want to have a God, as do all the peoples, according to kind and fitting service a consistent *melekh*-god without peculiar characteristics, Who is precisely theirs. One can call the first of these two forms of an apostasy invested with all the gestures of faithfulness 'Baalization'; the second—according to that transformation of vowels which makes out of 'king' a 'pseudo-king'[10]—'Molechization'. The commandment (Exodus 20:7; Deuteronomy 5:11) which bids that the name of JHWH not be taken in vain, that it not be attached to a phantom,[11] is directed against both forms of loyalty-simulating betrayal just as the preceding 'Thou shalt have no other gods before My face' is directed against the half apostasy which divides up the world between JHWH and Baal or someone else and, as Elijah says (I Kings 18:21), is like the bird which wants to hop on two boughs at the same time.[12] Yet many a word about 'other gods' may also have that syncretism in view. For example, the two central apostasy-narratives (Exodus 32 and I King 12), which report concerning the service of the golden 'calf'—as the Baalic young bull[13] is called,[14] whether in the style of mockery or on the basis of the original wider scope of meaning of the word[15]—have a Baalization of JHWH as their object,[16] probably not in the purpose of the author, which may only have envisioned a pedestal for the invisible-remaining JHWH, but in the conception diffusing itself among the people. The strange divine animal has here expressly no other god to embody than the One Who 'has led out of Egypt'.[17] Whether or not the animal is originally Baal's it is now placed under the historical formula of the Israelitish *melekh* by Whom it is supposed to be possessed. And even if, especially in the first narrative, the Baalic sexual rites are celebrated (Exodus 32:6b; compare the 'dances' in verse 19), one obviously dare not associate a *paredros* with God as was a matter of course with the local Baal cults, also for the Israelites who inherited them.[18] Besides, as emerges from the name-forms with *baal* in thoroughly faithful circles,[19] and as is confirmed, for example, by the marvellous explanation of place-names, II Samuel 5:20,[20] JHWH also was certainly characterized, without any tendency toward Baalization, as '*baal*', 'Master', apparently up until the great Hoseanic settlement (2:18ff.) forbade it in this sense. On the other hand, in spite of all the considerations adduced against it,[21] the passages concerning a fire-dedication or fire-offering of children for the '*molekh*' must be brought to bear upon a Molechization of JHWH. 'The *molekh*' or rather 'the *melekh*' is no divine name, but a divine designation,[22] and in Israel no other than the tribal God could be so designated. The tribal God has, however, self-evidently, *as such* no rivals;[23] including Melqarth of Tyre, the only one whom one might like to designate episodically as a rival, who, however, came to Israel as a mighty, super-territorial missionizing *baal*, not as *melekh*. Certainly no Israelite, unless he was Phoenicianized, ever granted him the title of 'the' King. And the solemn assurance of Jeremiah (32:35; 7:31; 19:5) that it never came into JHWH's mind to command the sacrifice of children becomes unintelligible if one regards the rite as intended for another god.[24]

One detects here in extraordinary force the hard immediacy of the struggle against amalgamation. Thus, says JHWH, you pray to an ogre under my name and throw your children to him in the fiery jaws. So long as God contends against the idols there prevails for the people a clear demarcation: one's own and that which is alien stand in opposition to one another. It is a matter of withstanding the allurements of the alien and to keep one's vows to one's own. But where God rises against the idolization of Himself the demarcation is clouded and complicated. No longer do two camps stretch out opposite to one another: here JHWH, there Astarte!, but on every little spot of ground the truth is mixed with the lie. The struggle of exclusiveness is directed toward unmixing, and this is a hard, an awesome work. Gideon demolishes the altar of a simple tribal *baal* (certainly no Baalized JHWH!) together with his Ashera, and it is done. With the 'golden calves' it happens otherwise: annihilation happens or will happen—and the prophets undertake to smash not a statue but a ghostly caricature in which whoever of the people takes a fancy to it perceives JHWH as 'Moloch'.

There is, however, between the two formulas of idolatry an important difference. With Baalic orgiasticism JHWH, according to His nature, has nothing at all to do.[25] To be sure, He appears in Canaan as the protector of the field upon which He bestows fruitfulness. The function of the *baals* is absorbed in His great care;[26] He 'calls the corn', and it springs up (Ezekiel 36:29). A necessary discovery and conquest has taken place. But the Near-Eastern pathos of sexuality is and remains alien in kind to JHWH; every one of His activities is basically non-sexual,[27] and the author of the first, of the cosmic report of creation is profoundly consistent when he concludes his narrative, in contrast to sexualistic cosmogonies[28] which have it that all things were sprung from a marriage between heaven and earth, with the passage (Genesis 2:4a): 'These are the generations[29] of the heaven and the earth when they were created', that is: what others interpret as the marriage between heaven and earth, the birth of the universe, is in truth its being created. Therefore the conflict occurs here, as we know it at its most violent from the Elijah-history, in sharpest contrast: the natural versus the monstrous. With *molekh*-ism, however, which demands not sexual devotion, but that of life, JHWH is brought into association, by virtue of the very fact that He is a *melekh*-God, and the child-sacrifice, apparently that of the first-born, is the fitting offering to the King as to the augmenter of the tribe. This connection comes to expression, indeed somewhat clarified, in the JHWH-commandments themselves, when, immediately before the flight out Egypt (Exodus 13:2, 11ff.) the dedication of every firstling—with quite another accent than elsewhere that of the vegetable first-fruits, the *baals*'-tribute—and the redemption of the human is ordained. If Ezekiel (20:25ff.), in the exact usage of the phrase 'to cause to pass through every one that opens the womb', which occurs only in these two passages,[30] has JHWH characterize this law as 'not-good', as one which, if adhered to, would not suffice a man to have life, and has Him explain that he allowed the rebellious sons to 'become blemished through their gifts', then this 'enigmatic expression'[31] in connection with its citation and the resumption of the themes 'blemished', 'gifts', 'pass through' in the following proclamation of punishment (v. 31) can really mean nothing else but: JHWH has allowed an 'un-good' ambiguity of this commandment[32] to exist, although the *molekh*-ists appealed to it in order to perform their child-sacrifices to the 'filthy-blocks'—that is, the JHWH-*molekh*-images in the valley of Hinnom[33]—as the allegedly more complete fulfilment of the law (without redemption).[34] It cannot very well mean anything else because, however one may think concerning the Biblical-theological problem of the 'hardening', JHWH certainly cannot, in the same speech and with the same choice of words (which it will not do to regard as casual), proclaim punishment to the people with a great oath for that which He has just claimed to have brought about *Himself*.[35] 'I have caused it to happen', says JHWH, 'in order to bring the testing and refining to the innermost heart, that a man could behave as one keeping my commandment while he served *molekh*'. The following proclamation of punishment makes known completely the profound purpose of the elucidation. To assign its main portion (v. 33–38) to another context opposes, in the first place, the strong evidence of belongingness which lies in the central word of the declaration of punishment: 'I will establish Myself over you as *melekh*'.[36] It is the only sentence of Scripture in which the deity Himself utters the predicate *malakh*, to have kingship, to act as king, about Himself. If one does not think of the relatedness of molekh-ism—the genuine *melekh* against the caricature—the word at first appears strange; for the idea of command one would rather expect here a direct, non-denominative verb like *shalat* or *mashal*. Inserted, however, into the context of the speech against the desecrators of the kingship of God, it manifests its meaningful necessity. In what follows the relationship is expanded further, as the addressed multitude for the speaker expands to the entire imagined Israel in full dispersion.[37] JHWH says now what he means with the *emlokh*, I will establish myself as *melekh*: As I led you once as *melekh* out of Egypt 'with strong hand, with outstretched arm', so will I lead you out of the dispersion of peoples as *melekh*. As I guided you at that time through the Egyptian wilderness in order to complete purging and refining in you, so I will guide you through the Syrian-Arabian 'wilderness of peoples'[38] and there purge out from among you the rebels and the deserters. Then you will know—with this the section closes while it refers back like a refrain to the closing words of verses 12 and 20 on the one hand, of verse 26 on the other, and points forward to the final refrain in verse 44—that I am JHWH the present one, standing by, punishing and delivering. Thus to the first exiles at Babylon, four years before the destruction of Jerusalem,[39] is proclaimed the judgment upon those who in a prophetic speech forty years older, were accurately described as 'they who worship while they swear allegiance to JHWH and (at the same time) swear allegiance to their pseudo-king' (Zephaniah 1:5).[40]

This judgment of the genuine *melekh* upon the *molekh* points to depths which the problematics of such 'syncretism' reaches. The service of *molekh* demonizes an actual and characteristic essential demand of JHWH. The demand, posed by the nature of JHWH Himself as the unconditional king of existence, for unconditioned surrender, for that 'with all your heart, with all your soul, with all your might', finds its ritual response in the usage of the s͑mikha which we scarcely meet with outside Israel.[41] He for whose benefit an animal sacrifice is offered puts his hand on the head of the animal, thus performs the same gesture with which Moses (Numbers 27:18, 23)[42] appoints Joshua as his successor. It is the gesture of identification:[43] You there are now (functionally) I. The animal is now in its intended function identical with him for whose benefit the sacrifice is brought. So also the high priest on the Day of Atonement places his hands on the head of the goat which is burdened with all the guilt of the people. Now the goat carries the sinful and expiation-owing self of the community into the wilderness.[44] There is more involved here than representation[45]; rather functional identity. He for whose benefit the sacrifice is brought is counted as willing to offer himself. Now it is granted to him to do this *in* the being with which he functionally identifies himself[46] and whose offering is 'reckoned to the account' of his own person (Leviticus 1:4). The intention of self-presentation in which the beliefs of the various regligions concerning sacrifice condense,[47] is accordingly in Israel the genuine basis of the sacrificial cult: man feels guilty before God.[48] While this intention did not find a verbal formulation here[49] as it did in Babylonian and Phoenician sacrificial texts, and later in the liturgical dicta in later Judaism and in genuine prayer occasionally in Islam[50] it nevertheless has a univocal embodiment in the s͑mikha. Certainly its real value depends completely on the intention accompanying its use, that is, on whether the action is an essential action: whether the person *really* means himself. The concept of *opus operatum* can here find admittance neither in the primitive or Vedic-magical nor in the Christian sacramental sense, nor as an objective action of power, nor as an objective action of grace. The situation of the active confrontation of person to person (in the magical view the divine, in the sacramental the human, has become passive) in which the self-presentation is based, forbids both. While the growth of the intention was obscured by the outward appearance, the sacrificial cult in Israel had to forfeit its religious reality, to become ghostly, and ghostly moreover in the domain of real, reciprocal happenings between God and man. What was involved was certainly not, as in the Dromena of the Greek mysteries, a holy performance which even the impious was not able to desecrate because it had its symbolic existence in itself, but between mortal and eternal being a most real happening which, having become a performance became a lie, and having become

a lie transformed itself into a monstrous caricature. The great Protestantism[51] of the prophets, their protest against the ghostly farce of a
sacrificial cult empty of intention in the house of JHWH, is to be
understood from this point of view. But from this point of view also
the narrative[52] which humanity will never be able to read composedly,
unless it had no humanity left, the narrative of the child-sacrifice
commanded by JHWH. The 'son', the 'only one', he whom one
'loves' (Genesis 22:2) is that creature which the loving man, who
presents it as himself, simply was not able to offer with lessened
reality of intention. Indeed the essential action is even more final than
if one had only to offer his own body. Therefore JHWH demands of
Abraham just this. And what happens must happen in utmost seriousness until the intention has attained its complete actuality. Only then
does the compromise come; but then it must come. In actuality nothing
but the intention was demanded, but the intention could only then
become actual if the deed itself was demanded in utmost seriousness.[53]
This is what Old Testament piety, which, like no other, took the
confrontation of God and man seriously, called 'temptation'. It is
the reality of the 'molokh' in JHWH.

JHWH acts therefore as *melekh*, but in such a way that in His
acting the West-Semitic concept of the tribal God is at once realized
and personalized, at once fulfilled and overcome. The *melekh*—for
example Kamosh, the King of the Moabites (cf. II Kings 3:26ff.)—
misses the child-sacrifice proper for him[54] and demands it, while he
leaves his war-raging people in the lurch. He receives the first-born
of the king and restores his favour to him again. JHWH demands the
child-sacrifice, and when he receives it He sets it aside. He does not
will that the living be surrendered to Him in death, but that it surrender itself to Him in all of life (Genesis 17:1).[55] The gruesome title
which the peoples grant to their divine lord is for Him Who is, to
be sure, in special covenant with the Abrahamites (17:4), but still the
judge of the whole earth (18:25), not just too tyrannical but also too
narrow. He wants to be the genuine *melekh*, the leader, of the community as well as of the person. Abraham is to 'go before His face'
(17:11) and let himself be led by Him (Joshua 24:3), loving and loved
(Isaiah 41:8), 'known' (Genesis 18:19) and knowing (v. 17). Thus
the various epochs inferred the personal unconditioned-ness of the
tribal God JHWH from His relationship to the ancestor of His tribe.
But one cannot wring from the text quite so primitive a conception

of the Genesis histories concerning the beginnings of this tribe, into
which the unconditioned-ness had not yet been brought, and with it
that totality of consequence and totality of effect of exclusiveness in
Israel, that living will to deal seriously with the actuality of the faith-
relation. And yet that beginning and undisputed, early 'Go out of
your land! ... and Abram went" (12:1, 4) expresses it all, in the
history of the individual's call as leader and the people's call to follow.
In forty of its fifty chapters the book has the God of the universe
acting in the first ten as the God of the tribe, Who forms the tribe
out of the substance of the human race created by Him, through
election, elimination, and selection, But, as in genuine folk-history,
here also the *melekh*-ship is undetachable from the characteristic demand by JHWH, among all *melakhim*, of unconditionedness, immediacy, and unreserved completeness. No matter to which and to
how various textual layers one ascribes this 'Be whole' to the forefather, and the 'Whole shalt thou be with JHWH thy God' (Deuteronomy 18:13) to the people, they correspond to one another, supplement one another, and together express the essential thing without
whose knowledge one is not able to approach unto the problem
of the once-for-all-ness of the Biblical faith. The pre-state history of
Israel in spite of all attempts to extract from it the pure, 'profanely
historical'—as it simply is there, now, as history: history experienced
by believing persons with believing senses, formed in believing
remembrance, described by the believing word—this history of what
is happening between the King JHWH and His people exists by virtue
of the original possibility of this command and of 'obedience' as the
human response to it , a stammering, denying, recommencing response,
but a response nevertheless of frail human nature. I say: the pre-state
history; for while one may not ascribe it to an intention of the
narrator, it is nevertheless worthy of note that Solomon, in the passage
with which he concludes his temple oration (I Kings 8:61) does not
proclaim that the person or the people are to be whole with JHWH,
but the *heart* is to be un-antagonistic, 'satisfied' with JHWH. Although
he continues: 'to walk in his laws', nevertheless there already blows
here the air of a political life in which the *ruach* of God no longer
reigns through those unforeseeably touched by it for the time being,
but the dynasty reigns, although on the basis of annointing, and at a
time when the temple-mount and the citadel-mount, religion and
politics, are separated. It sounds to our ears like irony when shortly

afterward (11:4) the syncretistic faithlessness of Solomon who, as hospitable as a Roman emperor, allotted holy high-places to the *melakhim* of the neighbouring peoples, is summed up in the remark that his heart was not un-antagonistic with JHWH.

The patriarchal narrative of Genesis is not 'religious', but religio-political. It has, to be sure, not the life of a nation, but that of a clan as its object. Yet it is concerned with the politics—outer and inner—of the clan, and it reports concerning this politics as concerning that which is religiously determined. There is as yet no tribe, and thus there is yet no 'king', but the relationship between people and *melekh* is contained germinally in the relationship between the individuals, out of whom the tribe is to issue forth, and their Lord: the covenant, leadership and increase, command, testing and promise. Just as now, after the passage of those 'four hundred years' the action between JHWH and Israel, now however the people Israel, begins again, no longer on the level of biography, but on that of history, as soon as JHWH and Israel encounter one another in history, the kingship of God as such emerges. It dares to embody historically a tendency toward actualization which can be no other than a political one. When the divine kingship brings its unconditioned claim against the entire existence of the people, the answer can come only from the entire existence of the people.

The exodus from Egypt which places Israel as people into history makes preparation for its decisive divine encounter: a process which faith calls a revelation, and the science of religion, without wishing thereby to embrace its essence, calls a collective (or an individual, but collectively effective) act of faith. The exclusiveness in which this and every genuine act of faith stands is experienced by Israel as one with which it wants to deal seriously, in vital fashion throughout, with the actuality of the faith-relation, indeed with the entire fullness of existence.

We may characterize the domain, in which the individual as such seeks to deal seriously in vital fashion with exclusiveness, as the ethical, if we are only able to grasp ethics throughout, no longer in theoretical or practical isolation, but simply as the personal domain of action of that exclusiveness. The same is valid for the people with respect to politics. The striving to have the entirety of its life constructed out of its relation to the divine can be actualized by a *people* in no other way than that, while it opens its political being and doing to the influence of this relationship, it thus does not fundamentally mark the limits of this influence in advance, but only in the course of realization experiences or rather endures these limits again and again.

The unconditioned claim of the divine Kingship is recognized at the point when the people proclaims JHWH Himself as King, Him alone and directly (Exodus 15:18), and JHWH Himself enters upon the kingly reign (19:6). He is not content to be 'God' in the religious sense. He does not want to surrender to a man that which is not 'God's', the rule over the entire actuality of worldly life: this very rule He lays claim to and enters upon it; for there is nothing which is not God's. He will apportion to the one, for ever and ever chosen by Him, his tasks, but naked power without a situationally related task He does not wish to bestow. He makes known His will first of all as constitution—not constitution of cult and custom only, also of economy and society—He will proclaim it again and again to the changing generations, certainly but simply as reply to a question, institutionally through priestly mouth, above all, however, in the freedom of His surging spirit, through every one whom His spirit seizes. *The separation of religion and politics which stretches through history is here overcome in real paradox.*

Is this—which takes its place beside the oriental conception of the divine kingship—only a doctrine, or is its core an experience? Is it historicizing theology or is it history that a confederation of half-nomadic Semitic tribes at some time, undoubtedly more than three thousand years ago, on their wanderings from Egypt to Canaan, instead, perhaps, as other Semitic peoples did in such an hour of unification and high-spirited onward advance, of elevating its human leader as *melekh* (although under divine authority with the same title), proclaimed its God, JHWH, as *melekh?* That, accordingly, this confederation of tribes which called itself Israel, dared as a people, first and once-for-all in the history of peoples, to deal seriously with exclusive divine rulership?[56] As people—to be sure, in the unceasing dialectic of the divine conflict between subjects and rebels, between Gideons and Abimelechs, yet, even so, acting as people: proclaiming, obeying, following?

For scientific consideration the question, by its very nature, can be put only in this way: whether texts whose direct or indirect subject is the proclamation, consummated between Egypt and Canaan, of JHWH as King of Israel, are to be regarded as close to history or as far from it; that is, whether they belong to a genuine historical tradition, accordingly, to a tradition—however, much additionally mythicizing—sprung from the report of an event, or a fictional tradition of theological-literary origin.

CHAPTER SEVEN

THE KINGLY COVENANT

In presenting the great sacrifice at the foot of Sinai, Moses causes the blood of the animals to be divided into two parts. One half he sprinkles upon the altar, the other, temporarily preserved in a basin, upon the people, after he has obligated the people to the 'record of the covenant'[1] (Exodus 24:7), and thereby speaks the sacramental formula: 'Here the blood of the covenant, / which JHWH establishes with you upon all these words'.[2]

None of the parallels adduced by the comparative science of religion[3] offers a real correspondence to this ritual between God and people. It is, in its strict reciprocity,[4] not to be viewed as a variant of the usual: namely, 'that the people', in order to 'place themselves in intimate connection' with the deity, 'employ the mediation of an animal, whose blood they pour out on the altar, while they themselves devour the flesh'.[5] The deciding factor is here, that both partners, the altar as representative of the deity, and the people, are treated in the same way[6] as the two parties of a *sacral-legal act of reciprocity*. Far more applicable for purposes of explanation is the Arabian usage, according to which two clans establish a covenant unto death, in the process of which they dip their hands into a bowl of blood;[7] and thus 'both parties are simultaneously brought into contact with the same substance, without its belonging to the one or the other of them'. Therefore, as in actual blood-mingling, the drinking of one another's blood, 'a union of spheres'[8] takes place. However, I know of no witness, except the Sinaitic, for such a ceremony *between God and man*.[9]

There is also no analogy to be found in the Old Testament itself. The frequently adduced 'walking between the pieces of an animal' (Genesis 15:17); Jeremiah 34:18),[10] which the redactors of the canon, perhaps deliberately, have permitted to stand only in two places, at the beginning of the tribal history and at the final turning point in the fortunes of the state—this belongs to another order.[11] The view that the thought lying at the base of this rite is 'that all those establishing the agreement are represented by the sacrificial animal and become identical with it, and thereby call down its fate upon themselves if they break the agreement'[12] is supported by neither of the two texts.[13] For Jeremiah 34 is not concerned with a mutual obligation, but only with an obligation of the people through the king,[14] who thus has no cause to allow himself to be comprehended by the sacrificial animal and to call down its fate upon himself. In the Genesis narrative, which certainly reports no two-sided obligation, only one walks through, the assuring partner, and even He only in the form of a mighty fire which is able to leave behind it scarcely an undamaged residue of animal, so that the conception of a being comprehended cannot be introduced here. In addition, no matter to which period one ascribes this chapter it is nevertheless not to be assumed that the rite had by that time become so 'faded'[15] that the author caused JHWH Himself to call down upon Himself the fate of the sacrificial animal. The ceremony[16] is rather to be understood as a sacrificial action in which the walking-through-the-midst augments the 'inviolable power' of the obligation. But it appears to me that the ceremony has to do with a quite special kind of sacrifice. In both places the rite appears to be bound up with a present or future menacing disaster which is either to be warded off (Jeremiah)[17] or to be limited (Genesis 15:13ff.). In like manner the clearest and most important parallel, the Phedu-sacrifice of the Arabs in Moab,[18] is offered when a deadly danger threatens, when perhaps drought or pestilence rages. Then every clan slaughters a sheep, divides it in half, and all members walk through between the bloody pieces. The little children are carried through. That which lives issues forth from that which is dead. Life has conquered death. To this sacrificial ceremonial, which extends significantly beyond that which is generally apotropaic, is added, Biblically speaking, self-obligation. In Jeremiah it is the obligation of the people to appease the anger through fulfilment of the divine Law (the emancipation of bondsmen, moreover, may be connected with the notion of having, one's self, to fall into the slavery of the Chaldaeans). In the Genesis narrative it is the obligation on the part of God to put an end to the decreed servitude at an appointed time. As self-obligation, self-limitation, this event is called the establishing of a *b^erith*. For *b^erith*, which we translate as 'covenant' only out of necessity, means originally a relationship that 'confines'[19] and thus connects both parties, secondarily one which 'restricts' both or at least one. Certainly the cleaving of the sacrificial animal for the walking-through seems to have given the establishing of the covenant its peculiar designation, and yet one that is reminiscent of Greek and Latin terminology;[20] one does not 'establish' the covenant here; one 'slashes' it. (The pathetic juxtaposition of the calf-slashing and of covenant-'slashing' (Jeremiah 34:18), in spite of its somewhat difficult syntax, sounds original enough, and then, too, there is something here other than a mere play on words[21]). Therefore the fusion of a sacrifice of walking-through and of establishing a covenant might be very old. Nevertheless, only in the Sinai covenant is a holy action performed which *institutes sacramentally a reciprocity between the One above and one below.*

That is to say, the event at Sinai maintains its uniqueness also in contradistinction to the post-Sinaitic 'covenant-establishings' between God and people. In connection with none of them is a similar rite reported, and through that very circumstance they appear beside the Exodus narrative as repetitions, corroborations, renewals—and indeed, as distinct from periodic festival celebrations, as historically once-for-all renewals, especially in a new situation which requires a new expression of the covenant, perhaps also a supplementation of its statutes.[22] It is certainly not fitting to attribute historicity[23] only to the Joshua-covenant (Joshua 24), according to which the leader is not, like Moses,[24] a mediator, but a partner of the covenant (v. 25).[25] The rite accompanying it, the erection of the memorial stone, lacks the typical characteristics of a sealing of an original and decisive moment of history. It is, moreover, only accessory; for it signifies only the attestation and preservation of an event, and not, like the other, its sacramental consummation. We have here not 'a solemn covenant-ceremony',[26] but a solemn dialogue with mnemonic punctuation marks. Certainly the two reports compare with one another almost as one by Herodotus, shot through with legend, and one by Thucydides, historically conscious; but the 'Herodotic' account has, in its fashion, clearly preserved the older historical event. And if anything is to be inferred from the fact that Joshua set the people at liberty to choose a God, then it dare also not go unnoticed that the people[27] thereupon replied it did not want to *forsake* JHWH, that it knew itself as already belonging to Him in a covenant to which another, ostensibly later report (23:16) of Joshua himself makes reference.[28] The strange gods which this people, nevertheless—like the Jacob-clan—had kept in its midst, estranged it now as it had that clan (Genesis 35:2ff.).[29] This is an argument against the Sinai covenant or against its folk-embracing character[30] just as little as that Joshua set forth 'statute and law' for the people (24, 25), although, 'according to the traditional conception' the people 'must have received it long before at Sinai'. For a 'giving of the law' is described with the same term in a report (Exodus 15:25)[31] belonging to the same textual stratum. Thus, it signifies for the narrator not 'the Law' as such, but a complex of ordinances—here probably a new institutional fortification of the tribal alliance and its cultic-territorial centralization[32] connected with the renewal of the covenant.

In the Sinai covenant the concept of the *b*^e*rith* is realized according to its maximal meaning: as a confining of both partners to a community which permits the difference and separateness of both to remain throughout; brings them, however, into a relationship of unconditional super-ordination and sub-ordination, each of which has its own, its characteristic binding form in the reciprocal connection. The rite expresses the confining of the partners in their equal and simultaneous participation in the sacrificial blood in which is the life-soul (Leviticus 17:11).[33] The unimpaired difference and separateness, as well as the relationship of unconditional super-ordination and sub-ordination, have their expression in the representing altar and in the position of the mediator which the Deuteronomic retrospect (Deuteronomy 5:5) calls his standing-in-between. The covenant of God with the patriarchs which lacks this rite certainly signifies a reciprocal connection, but not, like the Sinai covenant, a joining and confining to a community which embraces a duty of God to the people and a duty of the people to God. On the other hand, all later covenant-establishing between JHWH and Israel represent, as said, only confirmations, renewals, re-establishments, as, especially after a convulsion or after an important alteration in the situation, the hour requires.

The Sinai covenant is for the most part understood as a purely 'religious' event: the people accepts JHWH as God. From this it is usually inferred that before Moses He could not be the God of Israel;[34] for otherwise the covenant-establishing would be superfluous. It would follow 'with compelling necessity from the covenant idea that up to that time Israel and Jahwe were strangers to one another';[35]

for it would lie 'in the concept of that covenant that it bind together two who fundamentally do not belong together'.[36] In the Sinai covenant Israel is said to 'receive' therewith 'with a solemn *b^erith*' a 'God until then strange' to it.[37] But this conception does not merely stand in opposition to the fact till now diminished in its significance by no textual analysis, that Moses promises the deed of liberation by JHWH to the people in Egypt as the action of the God of their fathers,[38] but also to the real significance of the *b^erith*-concept, from which is derived that which it does not contain, merely because it is wrongly identified with the current covenant-concept. *B^erith* is not limited to an agreement which establishes a 'community of interest' between two partners until then strange to one another.[39] Generally it does not only establish a relationship, but it can also alter an existing one in its character, compress, clarify, occasionally just sanction it, grant it sacred protection, re-establish one that has been broken, consecrate anew one that has been called into question. 'When those who belong together are joined in a new, common decision the Israelite expresses this by making a covenant concerning it'.[40] Solomon and Hiram already stand in a friend-neighbour association as they establish a *b^erith* with one another (I Kings 5:26). Jacob and Laban are not strange to one another, but have become estranged, as they swear the *b^erith* to one another (Genesis 31:44). Thus the Jehoiadan restoration is carried out in a covenant-establishing (II Kings 11:17) which is reported quite as though Israel and JHWH had been strange to one another up till then: 'that they should become JHWH's people'.

The Sinai covenant may according to this be so conceived as the context of the narrative[41] wants to see it conceived: it does not bring JHWH and Israel into a relation to one another as such, between whom until now none has existed, but it brings them into a *kind* of relation to one another which until now could not yet exist between them and which corresponds to the essentially new situation upon which the covenant is based. The new situation is characterized by the fact that there is by this time a people Israel, enabled to be partner of a sacral-legal reciprocal act. A people can, however, be partner of such an act only if it already has the power to act and to operate as a unity, in other words: if it is national-politically constituted. The liberation, the fearful flight of liberated wandering, the destruction of the pursuers, promise and leadership, welded together the shepherd

tribes into a people. It experienced this being constituted politically
in the order and division (Exodus, chapter 18) which made it into a
wandering community.[42] It is able only then to become partner of
an act of covenant which can be consummated between a God and a
people—no purely religious, but only a religio-political, a theopolitical, act.[43]

Johannes Pedersen has shown[44] that the *bᵉrith* between JHWH
and Israel corresponds to the Arabian *baia*-covenant as a relationship
in which 'the one stands higher, the other lower, or differently
expressed, in which there is giving and receiving', and that this
covenant is of the very same kind as the *bᵉrith* which the people,
through its elders in Hebron, established with David when they
annointed him (II Samuel 5:3): '*the position of the superior partner in
this covenant is designated with the same word-stem mlk*'. The Sinai
covenant is a kingly covenant[45] if one wishes to translate *melekh* in
its original folk-political meaning in the same way as in the later
state-political meaning. JHWH is not just the exclusive 'Protector-
God of the group';[46] He is its exclusive, political Head. One would
be robbing this insight of its essential worth if one were to visualize
in the report concerning the covenant-establishing simply the 'historicizing' of a cultic drama, the description of festival rites celebrated
every year,[47] 'presented in a historical and mythological form and
adapted to the historical and mythological framework of the Exodus
narrative', so that these rites function as renewal of a covenant whose
image in actuality was 'projected' from them into the legendary past.[48]
The spirit of an historical religion' does not, as Mowinckel[49] thinks,
express itself in such an historicizing; *this spirit would not be, if there
were no experience and memory to which it bears witness*. Aetiological
back-transfers of ritual contents into a primeval history are to be
found in almost all religions, and their formative power of projection
is sometimes a mighty one; but it is a peculiarity of historical religion
that it knows how to keep such things away from the central narrative
of its historical faith. It can do this precisely because these central
narratives are born from experience and memory. Certainly religious
memory—I have already referred to this—transforms the experience,
but it does not create it. The spirit of an historical religion is nothing
else but the passion of transmitting decisively awakened by experience.
If there really was in Israel, as people think themselves able to conclude
from Biblical texts,[50] as in Babylon, a festival of the divine ascension

to the throne, it did not on that account have in addition to the common character of cosmic renewal, also that of an historical renewal, because the spirit of the religion of Israel was the spirit of an historical religion, but because something had happened to Israel which in the cycle of the seasons became the core of its life of faith to think of again and again; because Israel could only come to understand its God as King of the world when it had proclaimed Him as King of the people. Whatever kind of nature festivals there may have been in Israel, there was of course no festival for ascension to the throne before there was a divine ascension to the throne, and this there was here, precisely not as that of a world-king, but as that of a folk-king, and not in timeless, unlimited mythical fantasy, but in time-bound, although mythicised, history. For here not nature but history has primacy—by which I do not mean historical reflection, but really history. In Babylon the cultic calendar undisturbedly could complete its eternal cycle over the vicissitudes of history; in Israel history transcribes it with its own hand in the tremendous signs of the once-for-all. It is a fundamental error to think that cult has everywhere caused myth to spring forth in the same way: their succession is determined by what *happens*. Where event and memory govern, cult follows their command; where they do not govern it bids myth to replace them with a timeless image. To be sure, every cult is founded; but only where event and memory govern does one know, in the mythically formed tradition, about the foundation as about a secret of history.

'Nothing hinders us' says Mowinckel,[51] 'from assuming that the ceremony of blood-sprinkling described in Exodus 24:6–8 was borrowed directly from a rite used in congregational worship in Jerusalem.' What hinders us is first of all this, that nothing is known to us about such a rite used in Jerusalem. But if something were known to us and if one wanted to attempt to make it the original actuality and the Sinai-report the projected reflection, then one would be forsaking the secure ground of the concrete history of religion and would be soaring into the aerial region of a merely-universal analytic of religion in which everything is everywhere and nothing is anywhere. 'Nevertheless, take heed, take heed exceedingly of your own soul, / let you forget the things which your eyes saw, / and lest they depart out of your heart—/ all the days of your life. / Give them to your sons to know, and to the sons of your sons!' This is spoken, even though it stands in the Book of Deuteronomy, not out of reformatory zeal, but out of the passion of imparting tradition.

However, a tradition of details, Mowinckel thinks,[52] is here inconceivable. For the Sinai covenant is to be regarded as founded according to the traditional rites of every covenant-establishing, and on that account it could have occurred to no one's mind to preserve in writing for posterity the forms known to everyone. On the other hand it is indubitable that neither the Jahwist nor the Elohist, so many centuries after Moses, could preserve an exact historical tradition concerning the manner in which the covenant was established. But there is nothing to adduce for Mowinckel's assertion that the Sinai covenant is to be regarded as founded according to the traditional rites of every covenant-establishing. It corresponds rather to natural feeling that so oustanding a procedure, among all others—related in kind, as this covenant-establishing *between God and people*, did not simply take over familiar rites, but modified them uniquely.[53] And if perhaps these consisted, and there is much to say for this,[54] if not in communal drinking of blood, nevertheless in communal contact with blood, the modification resulted automatically. At any rate it was commanded to preserve the report concerning the modified rite. On the other hand Mowinckel fails to recognize the vitality and the carefulness of which early oral tradition is capable.[55] Consider, for example, that the entire older literature of the Hindus originated orally and was preserved orally for centuries in a method which 'gives a greater guarantee for the preservation of the original text than the writing and copying of manuscripts',[56] that likewise the oldest works of Arabian poetry were preserved for the most part through oral tradition within a clan, sometimes within an entire tribe, until they were written down under the Abbasids.[57] Even with a high development of literary culture the sacred word quite often remains reserved to oral transmission.[58]

Disengaged from the purely religious narrative of ascent, divine vision and holy meal of the seventy, the report of the covenant appears as that of a communication, taken from a genuine historical tradition, concerning a sacral-legal, reciprocal act of theopolitical character: 'political-legal throughout, nothing merely theoretical'.[59] A people and its God, through a sacred reciprocal rite, the sprinkling of the 'blood of the covenant', are confined to a political unity within which both partners are related to one another as a primitive, wandering community and its more leader-like than ruler-like *melekh*. Between that agreement with the god Ningirsu[60] in which the 'first historically detectable lawgiver',[61] Urukagina of Lagash, in the first half of the third millennium, formulates his great social reform which is to liberate the working folk from servitude to officials and priests as 'the word which his king Ningirsu has proclaimed',[62] and the agreement with the people of Saba and the god Almakah in which Karibailu Watar, at the beginning of the seventh century, surrenders ownership of the newly-acquired land to the community of people and god, in which he serves as mediator—between these two agreements stands the Sinai covenant as one with no less politically real intent, produced by the strong and 'submissive'[63] mediatorship of a man who—in contrast to those other two who first bore the title of priest-prince and then called themselves king[64]—did not wish to be lord, since JHWH is 'the Lord' (Exodus 23:17; 34:23).[65] The fact that in our texts a social legislation, and also with it the conception of a divine ownership of the soil,[66] appears to be connected with the Sinai covenant, may well give scholarship something more to think about.

The kingly covenant is proclaimed by JHWH Himself immediately after the arrival of the people at Sinai in that first mountain-speech (19:3b–6) which to ascribe to a 'Deuteronomic' redactor means only to postpone the problem of where such power of word and such feeling for manner and style of the message belonging at the beginning of the report of revelation may originate.[67] 'Speak thus to the house of Jacob / tell the sons of Israel: / you yourselves have seen what I did in Egypt, / I bore you on eagles' wings and brought you unto Me. / And now, listen to My voice and keep my covenant, / then shall you be to Me / out of all peoples a precious treasure. / For all the earth is Mine, / but you shall be to Me / a kingdom of priests, / a holy tribe. / This is the saying which you are to tell unto the sons of Israel.' Significantly here for the first time two fundamental concepts appear together: that of the *b*ᵉ*rith* of JHWH with the people which is to supersede His *b*ᵉ*rith* with the fathers (2:24; 6:4ff.), and that of the *melekh*-ship of JHWH, in the form of the *mamlakha*, of the domain of the kingly rule.[68] A God speaks Who calls the entire world His, but within this His possession, wills to make of the Israel chosen from among the peoples, if it only keeps the covenant which He will establish with it, *a mere proprium*, an *allodium*: it is to become His exclusive kingly domain.[69] The being-exclusive is expressed with special fullness of meaning in the adjective *qadosh* which means originally 'segregated', 'separated', 'withdrawn' (in contrast to *chol*; 'exposed to the public'), and only by extension, 'holy'.[70] The character of the kingly domain is still more exactly described by the fact that it is to consist of *kohanim*, of 'priests'.[71] If one takes the word only from the point of view of cultic functions, the context of meaning must escape one. In early Arabian literature the *kahin* is the vessel which a demon, sometimes also a god, uses for his utterance. The character of a profane courtly office of the same name, in undeniably ancient texts[72] (II Samuel 8:18b compared with I Chronicles 18:17; I Kings 4:5; also II Samuel 20:26 with its characterizing postscript 'by David' obviously belongs here), whose incumbent is known as 'companion' of the king, as 'first at the hand of the king',[73] yields the fundamental meaning of a direct service, which meaning is confirmed in another connection by the report concerning the rebellion of Korah (Numbers 16), which treats of the priesthood as that which may draw near, as that which has direct relation to JHWH (in contrast to the indirect service of the Levites). 'Kingly domain of priests' and 'holy tribe' complement one another therefore like 'inside' and 'outside'; detached from the other peoples a covenant-fulfilling Israel with all its members stands in direct relation to its King.[74] It is from this point of view that Hosea (4:6) will proclaim to the covenant-breaking Israel that JHWH rejects His priesthood; it is, however, from this point of view also that a prophet who announes the new aeonic *b*ᶜ*rith* (Isaiah 61:8) will promise: 'You will be called priests of JHWH' (v. 6). The same direct relation of everyone to God, so strong that no one needs to instruct another in the knowledge of God, Jeremiah (31:33), before him, attributes to the new covenant, which is to accomplish what the breaking of the Sinai covenant had thwarted (v. 32).

That much-disputed verse (Deuteronomy 33:5) in the opening to the 'Blessing of Moses' should be understood as an echo of the Sinai covenant: 'Thus there was in Jᶜshurun[75] a king, / when the heads of the people gathered together, / the branches of Israel into one.'[76] The interpretation[77] which brings the verse into connection with the Joshua covenant (Joshua 24) cannot hold good. For this verse lacks precisely the essential thing which makes the Sinai covenant into a kingly covenant: the reciprocity of the speeches of commitment which are exchanged (Exodus 19:5–8) between the Lord and those who swear allegiance to Him (the speech of God in Joshua 24:2–13 cannot replace any speech of commitment), and the rites in which this reciprocal commitment is presented sacramentally. The laws which Joshua gives to the people with which *he* establishes the covenant, and which he writes into the 'book of divine instruction' (here actually a book like II Kings 22), are of another order than the constitution which has emerged from revelation. Nothing is spoken here about a 'kingly domain'; everything remains purely-religious. For the expression of the theocratic idea the book of Joshua is indeed only a trough between Moses and Judges-Samuel.

The meaning of the kingly verse in the 'Blessing' becomes still more unambiguous if we remind ourselves that the frame-song views an historical action, from the exodus up until the successful occupation of the land, as a constant theophany whose stages it celebrates in the sequence of events. However great the difficulties which the beginning sentence of the poem offers, this much clarity of situation is to be wrested from it anyway, namely that one dare not understand it to the effect that[78] JHWH brought His community from Sinai, etc., and out of the wilderness to Palestine: here He does not move *with* the community, but *against* it. He 'beams' upon those who receive Him; the dative is indisputable: JHWH shows, reveals Himself to them. However one may interpret the shifting of the manifestation of light from peak to peak, it remains a manifestation—different in kind and movement from the accompanying pillar of cloud and pillar of fire— and intended for those to whom it appears. It is just as unmistakable that verses 3 and 4 have in mind a stage of theophany following upon this one, which is characterized by 'sayings' and 'instruction'. And the first part of the frame psalm ends with the next-following stage: with the kingly covenant. The second part celebrates the battles for Canaan, the assistance of God from heaven (v. 26ff.), the present care-free settling of the land under His blessing (v. 28), and closes with the promise of salvation to the people which needs to fear no foe, since JHWH Himself has become its 'shield', as once He was the 'shield' of their forefather. In the entirety of the frame-song a unified chronological sequence prevails.[79] Therefore it will not do to relate verse 5 to the Joshua covenant which does not belong temporally in this place.

The insight appears to grow[80] that in this song[81] we possess a very old poetic source for which 'only the period after Moses and before Saul can come into consideration, when the tribes already dwell in Palestine but do not yet form a unified state'.[82] Nevertheless it is misleading to conclude further from verse 5 that we are able to date the song still more exactly because it could not have originated before Gideon,[83] since people 'first sang about a kingship of the divinity only then when Israel possessed an earthly kingdom'; Gideon, however, 'was the first to whom the kingly title was ascribed'. First of all, there is no need, as I have shown, to deviate from the text of the Book of Judges which reports that Gideon was indeed offered the office of ruler (not actually 'the kingly title'), but that it was declined by him. Furthermore, as I have demonstrated in the same place, it is not to the point to say what is intended in the somewhat imprecise sentence, 'a heavenly king cannot exist as long as people here on earth are not acquainted with such a thing'. For in ancient oriental cultural circles, which could have influenced the pre-state Israel, there were plenty of divine kingships in manifold variations.

The concluding stanza of the Hymn of the Sea (Exodus 15) has the kingly covenant at Sinai preceded by a proclamation of JHWH as King by the rescued people at the 'Sea of Reeds'. The investigators who regard the Blessing of Moses as having originated in the period of the judges ascribe the Hymn of the Sea in its canonical form to this period also.[84] I am inclined, however, assuming the primary character of verse 1b, to regard verses 2–11 and 18 as an older construction than 12–17. Verse 18 fits in with the warlike pathos of verse 11 far better than with the glorification of the cult centre in verse 17.

It has recently[85] been counted against an early dating of the hymn that it 'indeed deals with the event of the Sea of Reeds, but scarcely otherwise than in other Pslams and in connection with other deeds of Jahwe in history'. If, however, one places it beside Psalms 135 and 78, which are adduced for comparison, one sees that the Hymn, in complete contrast with the event-litanies of those two, tells of a completed historical action, and moreover, in direct actuality: the earlier song portraying the deed of liberation at the Sea of Reeds, which song extended to the leading to Canaan and the settlement, as furthermore the frame-song of the Blessing of Moses, portrays an historical action from the Exodus up until the successful occupation of the land as a constant theophany. Of course, one may understand the poem as a liturgy[86] and even as a hymnic liturgy; but like the divine paean into which the Blessing of Moses is inserted and whose 'no one is like unto God, O Jeshurun' corresponds so strangely to its 'Who is like unto Thee among the gods, O JHWH' that one might think of a common origin (certainly in a quite different sense than

Lagarde[87]), the hymnic liturgy also, essentially different from the Psalms with which it is compared, rises out of the fervent glow of a genuine tradition of an event. It does not, like those others, conduce to revive an existing festival rite with a changing word; but it forms itself on the developing festival. And the 'throne festival rejoicing'[88] of the refrain, the great shout 'JHWH remains King for ever and ever!' is neither extra-historical nor characteristically eschatological like the Psalm verses of kindred sound: in occurrence after occurrence of an historical action, between which the doxologies throb with historical reality, it follows at the conclusion as the simple expression of a certainty which seeks to prevail and triumph neither for a now, nor for a then, but for all of history, at the same time, however, over every conceivable temporal limit. In the narrative context of our Book of Exodus the shout runs ahead of the covenant-establishing like a herald.

Through the kingly covenant the staying of JHWH in the camp, His 'indwelling', is granted theopolitical character. His presence is now that of the *melekh*: as *melekh* He dispenses instruction and command; as *melekh* He walks on ahead. In this sense undoubtedly the redactor understood the fact that Moses (Exodus 33:7) pitches 'the tent'— by which he can have meant, if one leaves the section (verses 7–11) in its place,[89] only the 'tent of the leader'[90] ('his own tent' according to the Septuagent and the Peshitta, cf. 18; 7)—outside of the camp at a distance from it, and calls that which henceforth is the place of the kingly audiences 'tent of encounter' or 'tent of the presence' (that is, of the temporary becoming present of JHWH). The high consciousness of having its divine Leader with it will remain with Israel. The trumpet-like blaring jubilation with which Israel at Samuel's time, at David's time, welcomes the arrival of the ark (I Samuel 4:5ff,; II Samuel 6:15)[91] is the very same which the second speech of Balaam evidences (Numbers 23:21): 'Evil is not to be seen in Israel, / JHWH his God is with him / a shout of jubilation for the king within him'.[92] Certainly this verse implies 'that the kingly jubilation is something continuous; that, however, can only mean here: something continually repeating itself in the life of Israel[93]— nevertheless not just every year at a festival of the accession to the throne, but rather as often as an event, perhaps only the re-pitching of the tent of the leader, makes the people overpoweringly sensible that JHWH, its God, with Whom it has established the covenant, is 'with it', present to it, that He is JHWH to it.[94] Gunkel rightly adduces[95] Job 33:26 as evidence for the fact that Israel, that the devout person in Israel, shouts with joy to his God-King wherever He shows His countenance, a passage in which primeval folk experience attains personal expression: 'He beseeches God / and He is gracious to him, / he beholds His countenance / in the shout of jubilation'. The *th*e*rua* in the Balaam speech is undoubtedly understood by the narrator as the jubilation of the multitude around the tent of the leader; by the narrator who has the astrologers and soothsayers peering from the heights into the camp of Israel. Precisely because this people has a God 'with it' Who permits what He is doing to be ascribed to Him,[96] there doesn't need to be any astrology and soothsaying (v. 23). But the speech itself appears to me to have in view the same situation. I cannot concede[97] that this speech, and the one which precedes it, originated with more recent narrative history.[98] One can scarcely understand the Balaam songs according to their nature and their content if one does not presume them inserted into a primitive saga, which, in contrast to them, did not have a fixed wording, but whose form 'each time lay in the hand of the one who, just then, was narrating'.[99] Oldenberg has referred to the fact[100] that such a mixture of fluctuating prose, attaining a lasting form late or never, and verses of fixed form, 'emerged, as it appears, already in the very ancient era of human joy in telling tales as the natural form of artistic narrative'. I see in the Balaam songs remains of a Hebrew formation of this type around which, in the place of and out of the original plasmatic saga, a late, and in all its parts artful, narrative was fashioned. One cannot, naturally, reconstruct the former out of the latter; we are able to know only that about it which we discover from the verses—and, to be sure, from the first two songs; for only from them is a concrete situation to be inferred.[101] That, however, is enough to permit us to perceive the situation in which and with reference to which, in the original context of the saga, the nameless soothsayer narrates in the first two songs, and from which the meaning of that *th*e*rua* is unambiguously disclosed to us. If one does not wish to regard the Balaam passages as post-exilic, that is, as an archaicizing literary production,[102] it seems unavoidable to me to understand them from the point of view of a still unbroken religious and political confidence of the people of a kind that did not return after the division of the kingdom and certainly did not exist under the Omri's (of whose period Mowinckel is thinking). Within the epoch, however, in which there was still an entire Israel—that this epoch does not begin with the monarchy I believe I help to show in this book—it is easy to assign the second passage (as well as the first) with its theocratic bias to the period of the Samuelic crisis, with whose pecularity we frankly have to occupy ourselves in spite of the great literary-critical difficulties, and from which, in spite of every objection, the related passages, I Samuel 15:23a and 29 (self-evidently only they and not the context in which they stand), appear to me also to originate. 'A kingly jubilation', says Gunkel,[103] 'is a jubilation of the kind that the peoples are accustomed to give voice to in the presence of their kings; and Israel breaks forth into such a shouting—thus the passage wishes to say—in the presence of Jahwe, at a time when they were still without secular rulers; and Israel has every reason for so doing: it also has a "king" in its midst'. But is it probable that such an utterance issues retrospectively, out of the midst of habituation to the secular rulership, in a looking-backward that should be called downright romantic, and at the same time in a doubtful ambiguity—for in the meantime *th⁵ruath melekh* had become a profane custom as with the other peoples? To assume that would mean to misunderstand the naive pathos of the songs scarcely less than those do who regard them as post-exilic. It is the pathos of passionate relationship to a reality, to one still present but already seriously threatened, to a religio-political, institutional reality.

Undoubtedly we may perceive in the Balaam passage the conclusion of the productive historical tradition of an early Israelitish divine kingdom, the expression of which has appeared to us as the frame-song of the Blessing of Moses and the main section of the Hymn of the Sea with the brief original closing stanza.

In the Tannaitic tradition, however,[104] knowledge extends to the interrelation of these three passages as the three to be drawn from the Pentateuch for the *malkhiyoth*, the kingly passages which are to be read before God on the day of the new year: 'in order that you make Me king over you'.[105]

CHAPTER EIGHT

CONCERNING THE THEOCRACY

A. THE REDUCTION

THE covenant at Sinai signifies, according to its positive content, that the wandering tribes accept JHWH 'for ever and ever' as their King. According to its negative content it signifies that no man is to be called king of the sons of Israel. 'You shall be for Me a kingly domain', 'there was then in Jᵉshurun a King'; this is exclusive proclamation also with respect to a secular lordship: JHWH does not want, like the other kingly gods, to be sovereign and guarantor of a human monarch. He wants Himself to be the Leader and the Prince. The man to whom He addresses His will in order that he carry it out is not only to have his power in this connection alone; he can also exert no power beyond his limited task. Above all, since he rules not as a person acting in his own right, but as 'emissary', he cannot transmit power. The real counterpart of direct theocracy is the *hereditary* kingship. Hence no leader-like character can belong also to the priestly dynasty: the cultic office is inheritable, the political office plainly charismatic. This was so inviolably established for the tradition, with regard to the pre-Samuelic period, that obviously the attempt was never made to re-colour the reports about it in hierocratic fashion.[1] Thus the Gideon-Abimelech crisis is necessarily a dynastic one, and the Samuelic crisis begins with Samuel's bare intention to bequeath his authority to his sons.[2] There is in pre-kingly Israel no externality of ruler-ship; *for there is no political sphere except the theo-political*, and all sons of Israel are directly related (*kohanim* in the original sense) to JHWH, Who chooses and rejects, gives an order and withdraws it.

The negative, libertarian content of the Sinai covenant appears to correspond to an inclination, operating long afterward, of the wandering tribes of Israel.[3] Although, as far as our knowledge reaches, they never were like the rapacious Bedouin—who still today[4] as formerly

(Judges 6:3) are called 'the people of the East'—genuine nomads, camel-nomads (the camel appears only as transport-animal), but belong to the type of half-settled breeders of small cattle, engaging in elementary agriculture according to opportunity,[5] they also obviously possess that characteristic of resistance against all statics of human power which is certainly universally Arabic and is just mostly highly developed with the pure Bedouin, the 'nobility of the desert'. For these the saying of a popular tribal poet,[6] 'whoever says "I am better than others" is destined for the torment of hell', may be counted as representative. Concerning the pre-Islamic Bedouin we know[7] that no chieftain would have dared to call himself *malik*, that even when his authority (like that of the Israelitish 'judges') went beyond the narrow limits of his own clan in order to embrace several other tribes, his ambition contented itself with the title of a *Sayyid-al-Arab*, of a spokesman of the Arabs; that in general he 'had had no rights in preference to the rest, but only duties', was only 'the first among equals, possessed great authority, but no highest power'; that his power was not hereditary, that rather the members of the tribe after his death could elect one of his descendants as chief, that this, however, did not often happen. Office and clan did not, for them, belong to one another. It remained thus after they had adopted Islam. As the tribe of Azd heard of the death of Muhammad and his replacement by his father-in-law, they raised their arms to heaven and cried[8]: 'What? All Quraish must fancy themselves prophets! That is an unbearable tyranny!' And the poets sang, with a mocking word-play on Abu Bekr, the 'father of the camel-calf': / 'The prophet in death wants to bequeath to us a camel-calf! / By God, that would be the height of infamy!'[9] It is the dynastic principle against which they rebel.

But here, in the early period of Islam, we have not simply a parallel to that negative attitude of the wandering tribes of Israel, but also to the positive one joined to it which is expressed in the Sinai covenant. 'The rulership over men', thus Wellhausen[10] has characterized the fundamental attitude of early Islam, 'befits only God; a human claim of possession thereto, a *mulk* (kingship), is against God; no man has rights in preference to another in this relation which attach to his person and are perhaps capable of being bequeathed.' Still in the period of the Abbasids[11] 'the caliphs with their jurists and theologians had to take their refuge in evasions and legal fictions in order to reconcile the fact of the hereditary princedom with feelings deeply rooted in the folk-consciousness'. We accordingly find in early-Islamic the same popular inclination against hereditary human power as in pre-Islamic times, but a belief has come upon a frame of mind which lent to the original passion that which it needed in order to become historically effective: direction. When the Bedouin says he recognizes no other master than the Lord of the world there is expressed therein still today the old desire for freedom even while it confesses its subjection; a subjection which to understand in purely religious fashion and to understand it merely metaphorically would mean to misunderstand it in equal measure. It is a rudimentary remnant of genuine theocratic enthusiasm which certainly in its deepest roots has sprung from a deeper stratum than that of Islam: 'Nothing remains but the countenance of our King', proclaims an early poetess already before her conversion.[12]

The question why the confederation of half-nomadic tribes wandering out of Egypt did not elevate its human leader as *melekh* can be answered from the point of view of its 'Bedouin-ness'; namely that it was confronted by an *'anawa*, a 'being-bowed-down', subjection to the leader—*'anawa* is not an ethical, but a religious concept—conveyed by an embassy of the one to whom it had submitted, and that it erected the theocracy upon this anarchic psychic basis. In the kingly covenant the 'stiff-necked' people bows beneath the ruler-ship of the divine Liberator who broke the bands of its yoke and caused them to walk erect (Leviticus 26:13). The Tannaites will one day call the personal, daily repetition of this act in the life of every Jew 'the acceptance of the yoke of the kingship of heaven'.[13]

The paradox of every original and direct theocracy, that it involves the intractableness of the human person, the drive of man to be independent of man, but for the sake of a highest commitment, already appears in the Sinai covenant. The existential depth of this paradox shows itself in this, that the highest commitment according to its nature knows no compulsion, that its fulfilment is accordingly surrendered in every moment to the faith-domain of the one who is bound, who, bidden by the commitment, can either strive toward a complete community out of free will, a divine kingdom, or, letting himself be covered by the vocation thereto, can degenerate to an indolent or brutalized subordination. Seen with regard to the political result: the same principle which, where the rightful possessor of the commission, the 'charismatic' man, is there, gives earthly confirmation to his authority, is, where he is lacking, misused to sanction either his foolishness or else empty anarchy. The result of this is that the truth of the principle must be fought for, fought for religio-politically. The venture of a radical theocracy must therefore lead to the bursting-forth of the opposition latent in every people. Those, however, who in this fight represent the case for divine rulership against that of 'history', experience therein the first shudder of eschatology. The full, paradoxical character of the human attitude of faith is only begun in the situation of the 'individual' with all its depths; it is developed only in the real relationship of this individual to a world which does not want to be God's, and to a God who does not want to compel the world to become His. The Sinai covenant is the first step visible to us on the path through the dark ravine between actualization and contradiction. In Israel it led from the divinely proud confidence of the early king-passages first of all to that first form of resignation with which our Book of Judges ends.

Theological vision permits us here to attain to the border of the immanent historical attitude as the only one scientifically possible. A sociological grasp of the problem can help us to find the strictly inner-historical formulation which we need. Nevertheless the sociological 'utopia' of a voluntary community is nothing else but the immanent side of the direct theocracy.

Max Weber has characterized[14] in broad outlines the image of 'purely charismatic' rulership as one by persons who, by virtue of a peculiar 'gift' 'and—if the idea of God is already clearly conceived—by virtue of the divine mission therein contained' function as leaders. Within this 'markedly social structural form' the historical form of the direct theocracy—which to confuse with hierocracy[15] in this context would be especially misleading—is to be understood as that very charismatic which, with its experience of the *charis*, deals seriously with the social and political reality dependent upon it.

This includes first of all—but this many phenomena of the indirect have in common with the direct theocracy—the living acknowledgement of the charismatic man as dispenser of the charisma without whose spirit-blowing he detects in himself no spirit, without whose enabling he, of himself, brings forth no power. In this process, too, so far as we are able to see, the disenchantment of faith was accomplished for the first time in Israel: in place of the magical relationship of the bearer of the spirit and power to the god in Egypt, and of the semi-magical relationship in Babylon which—the first publicly, the second secretly—are inclined to make out of a person a useful bundle of energy,[16] there appears the being-subdued, the 'hearing' and the *'anawa*. The charisma depends here on the *charis* and on nothing else; there is here no charisma at rest, only a hovering one, no possession of spirit, only a 'spiriting', a coming and going of the *ruach*; no assurance of power, only the streams of an authority which presents itself and moves away. The charisma depends here on the *charis* of a God who thus supplies the *ehye asher ehye* of this name-disclosure, in which His unfathomableness for all magic was expressed, to Moses pleading for the granting of a view of His glory (Exodus 33:19): 'I will proclaim / the name JHWH / before thy countenance: / that I am gracious to whom I am gracious, / that I show mercy to whom I show mercy'; a word in which is uttered as the meaning of the name JHWH not 'unvarying faithfulness',[17] nor yet 'grace and mercy',[18] but the completely independent majesty of the divine becoming-present: that the *charis* accordingly stands superior to every enchantment as well as every law.

'The duration of charismatic authority', says Weber,[19] 'is in accordance with its nature specifically labile; the bearer can forfeit the charisma . . . appear to his adherents as "robbed of his power": then his mission is extinguished'. Authority is bound to the temporary proof of the charisma. The direct theocracy of Israel and the indirect which it replaces bear witness to this lability as grounded in the nature of the *charis* itself: the 'prophetic' author of the story of Saul's rejection (I Samuel 15) will give to it, according to the tradition of its content, a presumably quite early expression, but also that which early-deuteronomic (Deuteronomy 3:23ff.) and later passages (32:50ff.; Numbers 27:12ff.) have to report about a rejection of Moses, are attempts to make visible again the obscured essence of a religious tradition.

The paradoxical peculiarity of the direct theocracy in its historical form attains unto utterance, however, only then when the office matures to the point of transforming the charisma 'from a non-recurring, outwardly transitory, free gift of grace of extraordinary times and persons into a permanent, every-day possession'. The charismatic which deals seriously with its experience is now obliged to base its institutional structure upon manifestations of *charis*; to incorporate these, accordingly, as the most real of all, into stable political reality, into permanent presuppositions of political life and action, accordingly to base theopolitics no longer merely on covenant and statute, also no longer simply to verify it in the carrying-out of covenant and statute, but also to exercise theopolitics even when it is a matter of letting the *charis* hold sway beyond the actual charisma.

Weber has recognized [20] the question of the successor as 'the fundamental, first problem in which the charismatic rulership stands when it wants to have itself transformed into a perennial institution'. What herewith results is that 'since it is a matter of charisma there can be no talk about a free "choice" of the successor, but only about a "recognizing" that the charisma is already *at hand* with the pretender to the succession. Thus either it is a matter of waiting for the epiphany of a successor who demonstrates his qualification personally', which, however, endangers the cohesion of the charismatic community, or one seeks to secure continuity, whether the bearer of the charisma itself, as acting in its power, designates his successor, whether the followers after his death identify and acknowledge as such the one presently most qualified, or whether finally belief in a transferability of the charisma through the bond of blood comes into play, in which case, as in the previous one, the charismatic nature of the rulership can still be maintained by means of special consecration, annointing and coronation, a sacrament whose administration by a priestly caste supports its supremacy, a secret or official hierocracy.

Of these possibilities the pre-state Israel knows only the first two, and of these the second, the designation of the successor by the bearer of the charisma, only in one single manifestation. For the Biblical narrative[21] the transfer of the leadership to Joshua is joined to the rejection of Moses: the mission was originally attributed in its entirety to the latter; now another must complete his work. For sociological reflection it is the nearest possibility of a preservation of the charismatic, the 'most adequate form of preservation of continuity of rulership for all originally charismatic organizations'.[22] But the occurrence is in the Biblical narrative absolutely once-for-all: it has Joshua die without having designated a successor, also without even having determined a principle of succession, a fundamentally permanent leadership. To be sure, the Book of Joshua (23:1), in a much discussed opposition to the introduction to the Book of Judges, proceeds from the assumption that Joshua completed the occupation of the land and therewith fulfilled the great mission. Historical investigation must assume a slower tempo for the subsequent settlement only in part by conquest, in part also by means of 'infiltration'[23]; it can ascribe to Joshua no more than the foundation of the work. What might be the reason that he while dying entrusts no one with its continuation, leaves behind no leader for the tribes united under him?[24] That after him no leader of the confederation is there, is a fact that, with all critical caution, cannot well be called into question; traditions of succession usually have an especially intensive and tenacious life. The report of the assembly at Shechem, which in its essential features may be regarded as historical, suggests the thought of a concern reaching beyond Joshua's life. Why do we hear nothing about it? (Muhammad may not be thought of as a parallel, since 'the theocracy was tailored entirely for his person', and with it apparently was joined the belief 'that with his death the hour of the Last Judgment will come to pass'.[25]

The answer to this question must range widely, but it will not thereby deviate far from our object.

As difficult as it also is to sift out of the Book of Joshua the historical kernel of the campaigns of conquest undertaken immediately after the death of Moses, one thing appears to me as certain: that these are the actions of a 'holy' war, and, indeed, of a war which was experienced, not first by its chroniclers, but already by its fighters, as one commanded by and under the command of JHWH. Sagas of a vehemence like those concerning the collapse of the walls of Jericho, like those concerning the standing-still of the sun over the battle of Ajalon, do not grow out of a 'free' people's or poet's fantasy. It is declared in them that something has been done which people will not be able to comprehend hereafter. This deed, this overrunning of the obstacles fancied to be unconquerable to the retrospective consciousness happened because one was subject to a power which willed this, which effected this. But we must comprehend the Biblical concept of the 'war of JHWH' still more exactly.

JHWH is not, as is frequently understood, a war-god; nor a covenant-god developed into a war-god.[26] War-gods help their fighting peoples. They do not, with human and super-human armies, wage their own wars. The mighty-weaponed Ashur helps Sennacherib against Phoenicians, Philistines and Hezekiah of Judah,[27] but he does not command a war with Judah as JHWH with Amalek 'from generation to generation' (Exodus 17: 16). The 'baal of heaven' grants to King Zakir of Hamath power to stand firm against the league of the seven kings under Ben-Hadad of Aram known from the Elisha legend,[28] but certainly Zakir did not feel as one who wages the wars of baal (cf. I Samuel 17:47; 18:17; 25:28; 30:26), and the songs which celebrated his victories are certainly not gathered together in a book of the wars of *baal* (cf. Numbers 21:14).[29] The protector-god wages the war of his protégés; the *melekh* JHWH wages His own war. When Deborah says to Barak (Judges 4:14): 'Does not JHWH go before you?' she speaks not to the devotee of a cult-numen, but to a follower of a divine duke.

In the wars of Israel for Canaan it is naive-theocratic enthusiasm which fights. 'The wild charismatic war heroes of the Israelitish tribes'[30] know themselves not only to be gripped by the power of the *ruach*; they know themselves also to be ordered and incorporated into the conscript army of their King. Even where the saga comes closest to myth it has an odd berserker like Samson (15:18) designated in relation to JHWH as His *'ebed*, as His servant—which is certainly an allusion to 'Nazaritism', but precisely to the primitive Nazaritism of a theocratic consecration of war [31] as it also existed in temporary form when people consecrated themselves to JHWH for defence against His and Israel's enemy and allowed the locks of their heads to remain untouched until the enemy was annihilated (5:2).[32] They even 'come to the help of JHWH among the heroes' (v. 23)—and it is to be expected that He appear with His flashing sword in the midst of the charging host. 'Then the remnant came down, with the nobles the people: / JHWH, come down to me here among the heroes!'[33] cries Deborah at the beginning of her actual song (v. 13).[34] This naive-theocratic enthusiasm extends beyond the epoch of the direct theocracy until the days when David (II Samuel 5:24), setting out against the Philistines, hears JHWH striding along in the storm rushing through the tops of the balsam trees—as He once (Judges 5:4) strode in the crashing of clouds 'from Edom's fields'—striding on before His annointed one, in order to strike the enemy camp. And when David, victoriously returned, immediately brings home out of exile for the Leader-God, Who had to march into battle without His throne, 'the ark of God over which is called out the name of JHWH of hosts Who is enthroned upon the cherubim', as it is called expressing the occupancy with special solemnity[35] (II Samuel 6:2), the Palladium of Israel, with a great dance of triumph of which an old, probably contemporary, song tells.[36] With this dance, in which David, clothed in a garment of the consecrated temple servants,[37] wishes to function only as a follower of his Lord, naive-theocratic enthusiasm comes to an end. According to its nature it reaches no farther than the point at which the dynastic principle attains unto a validity limited only by rebellions.[38] Consequently there could prevail even in its portrayal no back-projecting, but in essence only the genuine tradition of the religio-political, contemporary-historical attitude.

But the point in time, beyond which, while there are war-oracles and, of course, ritual remains, there is nevertheless no JHWH-war to be found any more in the texts, still has a special significance. It is the moment before those campaigns of David which, by means of the final conflicts of liberation and the subjugation of the last Canaanite enclaves, complete the work of the occupation (II Samuel 5), and to which in characteristic fashion the beserker-exploits of chapters 21 and 23 also, for the most part, belong, campaigns which are distinguished by expansive undertakings which are narrated by the historiographer either quite cursorily (chapter 8) or in such a way that one perceives clearly the altered character of the leadership (10:12). This moment is characterized in the 'Deuteronomistic', but for the direct apprehension of the historical perspective which the one responsible for the narrative context intends, indispensable (anticipating, after all, only verse 11) parenthesis 7:1b as the one in which JHWH 'had afforded' to David 'rest from all his enemies round about'. That is set forth in the following speech of God—which is mostly understood as referring to the future and thereby in its fundamental meaning misunderstood: 'I have appointed a place for My people, Israel, / I have planted it, / that it may dwell in its own place'. One cannot say more clearly that here an era comes to an end, the era of that historical action which we call the wandering and settlement of Israel—and therewith also the era of the JHWH-war. The JHWH-war is neither, as one usually conceives of it, the Israelitish war as such, viewed according to its sacral aspect, nor also as has been otherwise asserted,[39] the defensive war alone. With respect to its unity and non-recurring character our differentiation of offensive and defensive war, as great as is its ethical importance, is invalid. It is the one action, taking place on many fronts and covering many generations, which begins with the downfall of the Egyptian pursuing army and ends with the entrance of the ark into the recently conquered Jerusalem. The chroniclers who report this action see its Originator just as little as 'war-god' as the participants themselves saw Him thus; the latter as well as the former see Him as the 'Present One' Who has 'founded' for Himself a people (v. 24). He assists Samson, Samuel, Saul, David against the Philistines, the mighty rivals of Israel for the possession of Canaan.[40] But even before Amos there were those in Israel who knew that just as He had led Israel out of Egypt so had He also led even these Philistines out of Kaphthor, and also that He does not forget this. He *is* not a 'man of war' (Exodus 15:3); He *becomes* one when it is necessary. 'JHWH'—the Present One—'is His name'.

The JHWH-war is the war of the *melekh* Who fulfills His promise. Up until that time, comprising the transitional period of Saul and still including the conflicts of liberation of David, the epoch of the direct theocracy actually extends, which epoch first in Jerusalem is superseded by one of a kingship bearing the divine annointing, but at the same time dynastically warranted. When at that time, as has been assumed,[41] the songs of the wars of JHWH were collected and published as a book, 'under royal incitement or support' perhaps, as a fostering 'of the Israelitish self-consciousness required for the continuation and maintenance of the national affairs of state' and 'as safeguard against the particularism threatening at all times', there speaks in this datum the melancholy humour of human history.

Certainly, however, the JHWH-war, the theocratic-war, is, according to its nature, the common war and the war of the community. The raids and campaigns of expansion of individual clans do not belong to this. But where either, as under Joshua, the great impetus of the tribes breaking forth out of the wilderness, or, as at the time of the judges and beyond, the danger of neighbourly invasions prevails, both are there, the active covenant and the leading, divine, covenant-Lord. To be sure, in the Book of Judges it is only undertakings of ephemeral or permanent confederations of single tribes which are thus reported,[42] but for the narrator—not first for the redactor—Israel is for the time being in the camp of the fighters, and JHWH is 'with him'; and thus it must have been for the core of the participants. The individual tribe is precisely nothing but itself, but where active unification occurs, and it may be only two or three tribes, there is 'Israel'.[43]

The situation will be similar for the actions reported in the Book of Joshua, in so far as an historical basis may be attributed to the narrative—and this appears to me, in spite of the contradictions originated thereby and of the chronological confusion, to prove true for the most important, above all also for the battles against the two leagues of kings so strongly called into question.[44] Only here, if one wishes to understand as historical event the pressing-forward of the Israelitish tribes, hardly sufficiently equipped, against city states well-fortified, well-armed, furnished with a fleet of iron chariots, also—as undoubtedly emerges sufficiently from the Song of Deborah—abundantly protected by alliances, in contrast to the time of the judges, the confederation, acting for the time being militarily is not an event of spontaneous helpfulness or free agreements, but the instrument ready for use in a strongly centralized strategy. One may object that Israel could not have settled first of all in the plain, or else only on its edges. But how—even if the mountain-states were also more weakly organized and more thinly populated[45]—were the mountain fortresses captured, concerning whose impregnable structure we are informed?[46] Also half-nomads are certainly not as mobile as robber-hordes mounted on camels. How were isolated troops without support to venture forth in such a manner as the Israelitish military band must have done in order to contend for the occupied position in which we have to imagine them after Joshua's death? The tribes celebrated in the Song of Deborah are already settled or at least partly-settled small farmers. In order that they could become such, their defensive alliance must have been preceded for a good while by a great offensive one in which people helped one another to win secure positions which could be consolidated, and guaranteed to one another the communications which were indispensable in order to hold them. If we take our cue from the single instance, difficult to date, but to be placed just after the decisive advance of Joshua,[47] of the spontaneous early special venture of a single group, reported in Judges 1:3ff., we must think at the onset of a great, orderly, strategic action engaging separate forces according to plan, an action which is conducted from a fortified base—Gilgal, stone-circle, the Book of Joshua calls it.

I think, however, that not only the reworking of tradition which we know from the Book of Joshua, but even the leader of the action itself, overestimated its consequences, that he imagined the conquered positions to be far more secured, the tempo of their future development faster, the resistances that remained less, than they were. Joshua apportioning the lots to the tribes—this is a thoroughly credible proceeding:[48] he supposes that the JHWH-war, the common action is at an end, the essential is attained, what is yet to be carried out can be entrusted to the individual tribes and clans, a central leadership is no longer required. The casting of the lots is the symbolic act for this. Joshua, the historical Joshua whom we glimpse in shadowy fashion, but like the real shadow of a real person, behind the doubtful book, is from youth up a military man. He trusts in the God Whom Moses has proclaimed and Who has granted to him, Joshua, the charisma. Whether he actually says it or not he puts his trust in the divine Zealot (24:19); certainly he and his house will serve JHWH (v. 15). He is a military man, and he is pious. A theopolitical founder has trained him and has committed to him his work, a theopolitical work, to be continued. He has continued it; he has never felt the theopolitical ardour of his master. The political expression of the theocracy, its only political expression, has been for him the JHWH-war, and this is now at an end. The community led by the charismatic person was necessary for the sake of victory; now it is no longer necessary. He needs to name no successor; the office is disposed of. Joshua at the assembly at Shechem—that, too, is an historical situation; but no longer a religio-political one, only now one in its first part religious, in its second political, including, to be sure, the politics of religion. First he pledges the people anew, but no longer to the *melekh*, now only to God. Then he renews the covenant, no longer, however, between the Lord of the kingly domain and His subjects, but he sets the covenant over the people; he gives, thus we may assume, to the confederation of tribes another, new constitution, that of the sacral organization, another new centralization, the cultic-territorial. He replaces the confederation gathered about the eternal Leader with the amphictyony united for the service of its sanctuary.[49] Outside of the JHWH-war he understands the theocracy in a purely religious fashion, and he gives it a purely religious description. I prefer not to think of this as a real innovation, as an order-altering act. In the covenant of the twelve, whose like we know from Greek and Italian, above all from Etruscan, examples, Joshua has only imported into the primitive system— which like its parallels from Ismael and Edom had an exact genealogical sanction—a form corresponding to the living conditions of the settlement of Canaan. I assume that this older system has its organizational origin in the travel-regulations of the exodus period, and that the first Mosaic 'He established for it statute and law' (Exodus 15:25) which strangely appears fragmentarily immediately after the Hymn of the Sea, represents its establishment just as the same formula—occurring only in two places—with Joshua represents its new formation. This new formation I would rather understand as a reduction, perhaps with technical development, of that which is retained. Political centralization, the invisible one in the *melekh* Himself, a visible one in the bearer of His commission, is not taken over. There remains only the abstract cultic centralization: with a central sanctuary which, according to our texts, sheltered the ark in the tattered, holy tent of the wilderness wandering, with yearly covenant-feasts probably in which the perpetual renewal of the covenant—of the Sinaitic, as whose mere confirmation the Shechemite covenant was intended— was observed, and along with this, connected covenant-assemblies for which, however, scarcely other than cult-administrative concerns were provided for. Certainly JHWH is venerated, afterward as before, as the Lord of the covenant; certainly also His 'mouth' is consulted before political decisions, but for the genuine prerogative of the King not sacrally but really considered, for permanent political initiative, there is no longer any form of proclamation. The institution of charismatic leadership appears to be abolished without being replaced by another expression of direct theocracy. With respect to all the questions of external and internal politics the tribes are referred only to the representative arrangements of each one, to chieftainships and councils of elders. A co-operation is naturally not closed to them, but how much conflicting interests, how much inertia and party-pride hinder a spontaneous co-operation, how ponderously it functions even in the hour where necessity—but precisely one which concerns the different tribes with varying force of actuality—already presses toward action, how much more feebly sounds the confused muttering from below as the peremptory, barrier-breaking, crust-melting voice of the one who knows himself to be empowered by the voice of the *melekh*!

And yet there begins with the Josuanic reduction a new stage of the direct theocracy.

B. THE SECOND STAGE

I have designated as the paradox of the theocratic order the fact that the more purely it occurs the less it wishes to compel obedience; that accordingly it is a strong bastion for the obedient, but also at the same time can be a shelter to the self-seeking behind which he exalts his lack of commitment as divine freedom; that consequently a conflict between the latter and the former blazes forth in which both sides contend in the same name, and always without a clear issue of the quarrel. The theocratic order which, extra-religiously speaking, envisions community as voluntariness, can again and again degenerate into a moderately sanctioned disorder without the conquering powers being encountered in their own radicality. Then a new pronouncement from above, a new charisma, is awaited. Certainly the faithful wait for the grace as that alone which they want to follow, and the most faithful of all profess to do it in order to have to follow no one. The question about the decision would lead us again to the limit of the immanent view of history.

This paradox of theocracy is veiled as long as the original charismatic authority endures; for in the following of the charismatic person opposition does not break forth, and where people rebel against him his punishment descends as the judgment of God. Only when the charismatic authortiy is at an end can the existential problematics, here intended, open up.

While Joshua neither names a successor nor otherwise arrives at an ordinance in order to transform the charismatic authority into a 'perennial institution', he strips theocratic reality of its severe garments of power: now it is surrendered unarmed to the freedom of man. Now where the tribes politically, that is outside of pilgrimage and consulting of oracles, in the broad paths of life have nothing left beyond their separateness but the hiddenness of their God and King, each 'Bedouindom' polarizes itself, so to speak, in them. On the one side appears crass licentiousness and enmity not merely to order but to organization. On the festivals people go to Shiloh, but at home they feed the more convenient *baal's* of which each one is concerned only about his place, but about that completely. People profess to recognize no power but that of JHWH, and know it not. On the other side, however, there now develops the kind of man for whom really 'nothing remains but the countenance of his King'; the King which stands on the alert for a kingly covenant which now dispenses with an earthly executive. We would have little information about it if there were not transmitted to us, perhaps, next to fragments of the single pattern-like remainder of the Book of the Wars of JHWH, 'the oldest coherent historical source of Israel, absolutely contemporary'.[50] In the Song of Deborah there speaks the kind of man who, after the end of the first period, in fact a period of charismatic leadership characterized as succession through surrender, remains faithful to the direct theocracy as the fundamental reality of public life.

If, as we must do in order to grasp the typical, we detach from all that is contemporary the attitude of the song, the attitude of the men who spoke thus, if we disregard, however much it belongs to the sub-

stance of the poem, all its scolding and cursing, boasting and exulting
—the like of which we still find in our time in the political folk-songs
of the Afghans 'from which one can reconstruct the entire history of
modern Afghanistan'[51]—then we see that it has two focal points
which stand in most vital correlation, JHWH and Israel. The importance of both names also emerges in the rhythmic structure of the song:
with evident refrain-intent the first and six other verse lines end with
'Israel', the second and six others,[52] among them the first of the closing
stanza, with 'JHWH', the two first strophes with 'the God of Israel',
and with evident intent there twice follows immediately upon the
praise which the people willingly render the cry: 'Bless JHWH!' The
correlation, however, in which the two stand is of such a kind that just
as one cannot conceive of Israel as mere community of faith, so one
cannot conceive of JHWH as mere Protector God of Israel. This Israel
for whose conception it is not essential how many of the tribes actually
belong to it, but that it is without question a unity qualitatively other
than an aggregate of tribes, is 'JHWH's people' (v. 11) for which He
in order 'to prove His worth to His peasants'[53] not only causes the
stellar army to fight (v. 20), but Himself steps into the battle ranks
(v. 13), and quite like a human commander whose strategic action the
separate troops must 'march to support' (v. 23). Indeed this is 'not a
baal of the land'[54] who clings to spring and soil; He is the accompanying God, the leader of His followers, the *melekh*.

But it is just *this melekh*, Israel's. One must remind one's self what
it means, that the poet in the address to JHWH sees Him coming in
the storm[55] not from the place of the sanctuary, from Shechem or
Shiloh, but from the wilderness, from Sinai,[56] although the army presumably took the ark along with it from the sanctuary[57]: the ark is
precisely the great Sinai-sign, 'the ark of the covenant',[58] and those
who return home behind it look upon it and 'remember' how it once
went on before the people to Canaan as the throne of the Leader, in the
beginning of the many-fronted action stretching over generations, the
'war of JHWH', which is *not at an end* because JHWH's enemies (v.
31) do not wish to permit it to be at an end. For the speaker of the
Song JHWH is not the cultic ('cultic' always to be understood in the
sense of the apolitical sacral order) but the theocratic Lord. To Him,
the Lord of the starry vault (v. 20) *and* of Israel, the speaker points the
'kings', the 'exalted ones' whom he calls upon to listen to his song (v.
3) and to hear how 'the kings of Canaan' were conquered by the

heavenly and earthly hosts of the true King. In all the primitiveness of his word he speaks concerning the holy-political correlation of JHWH and those who love Him: those who love Him, says he, are strengthened on the earth just as in the sky there is the sun which rises in its heroic might (v. 31).[59]

What kind of a man is it who speaks here—who represents the kingly covenant in such enthusiastic rapture, who proclaims anew the JHWH-war, by this time purely defensive, as a breaking of distress (v. 6ff.), who celebrates an acting Israel roused from amphictyonic aloofness and blames or curses the parties which deny Israel and its God? I know no other way to designate this kind of man than the primitive-prophetic.

From the designation of Deborah as 'prophetess' (4:4) it naturally cannot be deduced, if one has to understand as relevant the 'archeological' remark I Samuel 9:9 concerning the term *nabi* which is customarily translated as prophet,[60] that it is late. I relate the term rather to a change in meaning, more precisely: to a meaning-extension of the word—certainly one of a kind essentially other than has been assumed,[61] namely that originally *nabi* is 'the aroused ecstatic who, where he appears as mediator of supernatural revelations, gives these directly by himself', but that the concept was also extended to cover non-ecstatic receivers of such revelations. The author of this gloss to the story about the she-asses of the secret claimant to the throne speaks rather out of the consciousness of a period in which one thought in connection with the word *nabi* primarily of the soothsayers appointed or at least accredited at court, to whom the kings and lords resorted when they wanted information concerning something hidden, whether present or future—and out of whose midst at times the rebellions broke forth (I Kings 22) which gave to the concept of prophet its meaning in intellectual history. Such a soothsayer, thinks the glossator interested in earlier stages of language, was at that time called a 'seer', probably not as a visionary, but as one who merely 'sees' the hidden, as, for example still today with the Rwala Bedouin, the 'knower-of-secrets' knows it.[62] *Nabi* designates, however, both originally and still persisting into recent times, a 'pronouncer',[63] who announces that which is communictaed to him from above in intelligible manner to those below—and that which is addressed to him from below in acceptable manner to that which is above,[64] the bearer of the word in the vertical, the mediating mouth (Exodus 7:1; cf. 4:16) between *elohim* and men. Only in such a definite context are men also like Abraham (Genesis 20:7) or Samuel (I Samuel 3:20) so named. In such a context also the narrator may be calling Deborah an interpreter because she is accepted by him as the speaker of the song entrusted to him which she wishes 'to sing unto JHWH'; Miriam also is indebted for her title (Exodus 15:20) to her song: 'Sing unto JHWH!' When a recent passage, I Chronicles 25:1ff., employs the verb even for the recitation of the temple singers it also means the saying of the word in the correct rhythmically inspired manner to which here as so often the playing of the harp belongs. Certainly the ecstasy (which is reported only in the plural with the communities of interpreters) belongs to this as the change of the soul from which alone from time to time the legitimate 'pronouncing' in every intonation and in every gesture issues forth; it does not, however, determine the *nabi* concept, but the evolution of the word. This needs to be regarded as a Canaanite borrowing just as little as, for example, that Muhammad derived his undoubtedly genuine word-ecstasies from Judaism. Even today travellers encounter a 'man madly rushing along, proclaiming along' (Jeremiah 29:26), one of those simple persons whom the Bedouin call *menahil*, 'dwelling places', of the good spirits namely, and who, when 'the prayer' seizes them, run through the streets prophesying.[65] What distinguishes the prophets of Israel from them generically is certainly the decisive thing which really stands in opposition to everything Canaanite: the genuine gift of the *Word*. But even so this gift must be understood from the point of view of its beginnings. An elementary vocation such as this does not spring up in prepared historical mechanism, but in dark hours of origin, and there it already bears the features in its face which, even in its most sublime moments, can only express themselves, not alter themselves. It is not the case with Israelitish prophetism that it began with wordless-ecstatic transport and that then suddenly its tongue was loosed: just as it is there, it is there as a speaking with heaven and earth, and what gradually comes to pass is only what both of these have to say.

The Song of Deborah is a primitive-prophetic source: with the vision of the beginning which recurs in the proto-prophetic frame-song of the blessing of Moses and the sixty-eighth Psalm which is in nucleus early-prophetic, but also with a late prophet like Habakuk (3:3); with the double promise of the conclusion for the enemies and for the friends of JHWH; above all, however, with its proclamation of the historically real, communally real correlation between God and a unitary Israel. Without applying the word *melekh* to JHWH, without mentioning the *b*ᵉ*rith*, it celebrates and champions the kingly covenant.

Mowinckel[66] has rightly called the Israel of the period of the judges and of the oldest period of the kings 'an exemplar of a unified and splendid primitive culture'. For some important cultures of this type it is characteristic[67] that the most vital material of tradition does not originate wantonly and incidentally, but in strong and ever firmer growing ordered structures which can be made visible in three ways.

First: The primary utterance of that which is to be transmitted has rhythmic (however, not necessarily metrical throughout) definite form, for a song or recitative—which especially with the orientals is enhanced and supplemented by bodily movements.[68] Tradition occurs, even where a developed art of writing already exists, orally and is transmitted by a powerful, rhythmic memory. A writing-down usually does not follow until later; then, probably, rather with the goal of establishing a wording which threatens to become unsure than with the goal of —really senseless—publication, unless political purposes from the outside intervene. On the other hand, often the material of the rhythmic tradition is re-worked by historiographers and other authors, in a literarily valid, multifariously rhythmoid prose, into secondary utterances.

Second: The 'poetizing', that is, the first singing and dancing of the primary utterances, does not proceed from any individuals, but from representatives of exclusive societies in which the poem is kept alive with its melody and its orchestral rendering. The rhythmic memory, which is the element of this preservation, is consequently, according to its nature, not merely a phonetic-musical one, but one involving the entire body. The proclamation of this memory, reproducing the original utterance in its entire three-dimensional form, is, however, not regarded as the mere preservation and reproduction of a received subject-matter, but as the spontaneous production of an enthusiasm which in its corporeality grants to that which is received an immediate life, so that the poem appears as the enduring substratum of an inspiration beginning again and again. That which accordingly is institutionally cared for and protected in the society is the word in its somatic spoken-ness which the danger of scholastic encystation does not threaten so long as again and again something new, stimulating new poetry, new tidings, new ways, presses into existence. Beside this, however, not to be confined by the institutional, the inspiration of the multitude prevails pneumatically, swelling often to raging thiasos-like ecstatics, nevertheless never to be detached from the word, toward which even the wildest rapture strives, even though sometimes confined to impetuous cries which fall short of articulation.

Finally the third: All this is grounded in a naive religious knowledge, a simple consciousness and attitude which seeks, out of the experience of connectedness with the inspiring One, to grasp and to interpret the secret of the relation of above and below.

Into this scheme an early Israelitish *nabi*-dom can be inscribed without difficulty. I see its historical origin in the post-Mosaic and post-Joshuanic convulsions. Problematics of charismatic succession, problematics of the condition of the people, problematics of the theocratic conception, all three basically one, and in addition after Joshua's false termination of the JHWH-war the hardships of the invasion in which the unconquered (and by the unpolitical amphictyony not to be conquered) lability of the external situation manifests itself in a horrible manner. With respect to all this there arises in the passion of the spirit an association of 'speakers' which as association attempted to fulfil that which Moses intended for the people. I dare to assume that in its circle the tradition circulated which is preserved for us in an 'Elohistic' narrative, that is, one developed from *nabi*-ic traditional material, to the effect that Moses, when Joshua asks him to restrain the unorganized interpreters, replies (Numbers 11:29): 'Do you want to be zealous for me? would that all the people of JHWH were interpreters, that JHWH would send the roar of His spirit upon them!' Also they do not plan to keep themselves in closed association; they are concerned with the people of JHWH (Judges 5:11). We may imagine that with respect to Joshua's statutes, on which they place the blame for the troubles of the period, they refer back to the legacy of Moses: for a new, defensive JHWH-war there is needed the reactivating of the confederation of the sanctuary into a politically functioning Israel which places itself under the leadership of its *melekh*. This leadership, the direct divine rulership, must have been for the religious knowledge of the first *nebiim* the secret which they sought to apprehend and to interpret: 'Hear, Kings, / listen, exalted ones, / I will there, unto JHWH / there will I sing, / play the harp unto JHWH / Israel's God.' We are thrown back upon the necessity of concluding from this one salvaged, limited source whatever it itself binds us to conclude with its so common, but if one hears it aright, so thoroughly strange voice. But one cannot, I think, say any more strongly what was to be said than with this dedicative, emphatic 'I', contrasting with the petty kings and the 'empirical' Israel, with respect to whose existence one must abstain from naming a king, this doubled *anokhi*, which cannot be rendered in English in its entire intensity—in the Hebrew verb-form the I is already included, and this *anokhi* amounts to this: I here, however!

Thus we understand that Amos, who indeed wanted to have nothing to do with the guild of prophets of his time (7:14), regarded the original society of the *nᵉbiim*, however, as one of the highest gifts of God to Israel (2:11), imagined it to have its origin in the post-Mosaic epoch and to be closely connected with the JHWH-war against the Amorites.[69] He places it together with the military Nazarites[70] whom we know precisely from the period of the judges—as a troop in the Song of Deborah, in personal enhancement in the Samson saga: 'I Myself have brought you out of the land of Egypt / and have led you forty years through the wilderness, / in order to inherit the land of the Amorites, / and caused some of your sons to arise as interpreters, / some of your youths consecrated for battle, / was it not thus, sons of Yissrael?' The historical action which He began with Moses JHWH continues here with the *nᵉbiim* and military Nazirites. According to the men of the Exodus Amos' message knows them only as the servants of the old divine rulership from which now, in his time, the authority of the divine court grew.

The impression that Amos means with the *nᵉbiim* and *nᵉfirim* the true charismatic leaders of the people of the pre-kingly period, becomes stronger if we remind ourselves that a 'Deuteronomistic' passage of the introduction of the Book of Judges (2:16, 18) knows how to say for the same epoch that JHWH at that time 'caused to arise' for Israel judges who liberated it. Are judges and interpreters connected here only as heroes and singers of heroes? If we recognize in the Nazarites of Amos men dedicated to battle (a merely cultic conception would have no place in this context) we must also concede to the presumed 'prophets' a more active participation in the happening than that through song passages and adjurations with which they accompany the army on its campaigns.[71] They appear to me as the divine-militant society[72] distributed over the land which gives birth to and supports the 'judges'.

The narrator calls Deborah an interpreter first of all because she is acknowledged by him (5:1) as the speaker of the song in which she (v. 12), with a paronomastic *dabri* which perhaps is meant at the same time to derive the duty of the speech from her name, is summoned for the singing of the paean. Then, however, he expands the concept of prophet to her by causing her (4:6) to speak to Barak the divine message which determines the course of things. It is this her direct connection with the 'God of Israel' which the chosen commander wishes to preserve for the army when he poses the condition (v. 8) that she go along. Nevertheless her active participation in the event does not begin for the narrator with the command to fight; he opens the story of Deborah with the report (v. 4) that she 'judged Israel at that time'. Since there is no cause to disallow the author the following sentence which gives information concerning the manner of this judging,[73] we have to understand here, within the double meaning which the verb *shaphat* has in the Book of Judges, not 'vindicating for the oppressed, deprived people its right, to liberate it', but administering justice. The author who doubtless creates from old traditions accordingly knows that the *n^ebia* functioned also outside of the war as leader and arbitrator.[74] I assume nevertheless that perhaps with the redactional connection of chapters four and five—the report got into a false position: it belonged at the conclusion of the narrative, since it is related to the period after the victory at Taanach and relates to the authority which Deborah won by it. At the beginning probably, as in other stories of the judges, there was reported the being-seized by the *ruach* —a report which then, for an unknown reason, became lost.

The motif of the *ruach* leads us into a deeper level of the question about a connection of the judge-like and the primitive-prophetic nature. We know from the narrative of Saul's annointing, which is, to be sure, a hybrid of tale and saga, but of indisputable cultural-historical dependability, that the person whom the Spirit leaps upon for the first time[75] for a while attains the status of the *nabi* and assumes his manner of movement and utterance.[76] The tradition of the pre-Davidic period accordingly knows no other reception of the charisma than the prophetic; even the judge, such as Gideon and Jephtha, also the great berserker, such as Samson, must first of all become a *nabi*. We may here, as scanty as the testimony is, see an indication that the primary historical consideration—the tradition-forming consideration as a history'—of charismatic vocations between Joshua and David was founded in the prophetic experience. 'Then rushed, splitting the air, the roar of the Spirit upon him', 'then the Spirit clothed itself with him'—those are words which, before they could be applied to a third person, must have been spoken in the first, and only a prophetic genius is able to proclaim this sort of thing as something still unsaid. But the primary historical consideration proceeds precisely from people who are themselves bearers of the event. They do not ascribe their own experiences to another human type, the 'judges'; they are not yet especially concerned with interpreter-ship as such and leave behind nothing definite about it. But the judges came forth precisely from their midst, from the community of those susceptible to the Spirit, uninhibitedly surrendered to the Spirit, those men receiving the working of the Spirit as the kingly rule for the life of Israel, from the community by which they are supported thereafter. And they came forth by means of precisely such experiences—in such a way that these experiences brought them forth, snatched them forth. The first authors of tradition who are responsible for the 'anti-monarchical' Book of Judges establish for the reports of vocation the testimony of the summoning *charis* because they know it. But because they knew it they supported the bearers of the charisma.

The *shoptim* concerning whom the book narrates did not judge an Israel of the 'twelve tribes', but at that time the two tribes which were gathered around them. But when the book narrates that they judged Israel—and indeed it is not the later chronicler who first speaks thus: the Song of Deborah already knows of a 'mother in Israel'—this is not vainglory: it has grown from a tradition at whose beginning there was the certainty that wherever the charismatic in the name of the Summoning One was leading and however far this following extended, there was and so far there did extend at the time, the living reality 'of Israel'; for there was and so far there did extend at the time, 'the people of JHWH'—thus actually Israel was in the camp the 'willingly devoted' fighter. This naive attitude, not to be exhibited but to be inferred, will one day, after all manner of subterranean paths and transformations, find its eschatological completion in the doctrine of the holy remnant whose name is Israel and whose king is JHWH.

I have pointed out that early *nabi*-hood has its historical origin in the post-Mosaic and post-Joshuanic convulsions, and I have designated as primary the problematics of charismatic succession. The Biblical report has Moses—for the completion of the limited mission—transfer the leadership to Joshua and has Joshua die without having designated a successor, also without having determined, even rudimentarily, a form of succession, a fundamentally enduring leadership. The cultic centralization, which he leaves behind instead of this, gives way with respect to new situations and tasks. Here begins now, in a community whose nature is only to be surmised by us, the attitude which does not perhaps, as one would expect in terms of theory of history, establish as a guaranteeing principle of charismatic succession, but now deals seriously precisely with the *charis* as a fundamental political reality, that is, with the claim to unconditionness of the divine kingship in a politically active will toward constitution. Without having formulated a new statute, as far as we are able to know, only in this will toward a theocratic real-constitution does the problem of charismatic succession in pre-state Israel enter into its second stage, into that of the fundamental, specific waiting 'for the epiphany of a successor who personally demonstrates his qualification', and to be sure, with changing territorial compass of his sphere of validity, but with the core, remaining essentially the same, of a human type which supports him, and with periods of leadership between the terminating effect of a claim and a new claim of the *charis*—historically expressed: between the death of the subduer of the invasion and the beginning of the liberation from the next one.

Max Weber[77] adduces the Mahdi's as historical example (in addition to the reincarnations of Buddha) of the 'awaiting'. But here, already in the beginnings, the charismatic principle is so mixed up with the dynastic, the awaited bearer of grace with the 'hidden' Aliite,[78] that a comparison would be misleading. Essentially more fruitful, in its similarity as well as in its difference, is an example which Weber does not adduce, that of the genuine, radical adherent of theocracy of early Islam, the 'oldest sectarian division within Islam',[79] the Kharijites (that is, emigrants).[80] Their fundamental attitude corresponds to the attitude whose expression, whose expression in spite of all the literary reworking and theological redaction, is recognizable in the anti-monarchical Book of Judges, whose direct expression was preserved in its oldest part, the Song of Deborah. Also for the Kharijites is 'the unity of the community of the faithful represented by its camp'.[81] They too want to follow as leader who stands at the pinnacle of the theocracy only one whom the Spirit has publicly chosen and who verifies the vocation by the deed. They too 'wait' until he appears. But they assume an attitude of opposition, determined by religious commandment and urging on to the most grusome massacres, to the *ijma*, the 'organized community of all Muslims', an attitude which is strange to the Book of Judges which, to be sure, later on, at the time of the Samuelic crisis, in the religio-political group for which the 'Elohistic' narrative knows only the person-like designation 'Samuel', finds its Israelitish parallel, limited of course to the conflict of the spirit. In any case, here as well as there, 'religion' is 'political; it has the divinely willed community as its goal', as the attitude of the Kharijites has been characterized.[82]

Wellhausen has occasionally[83] opined that the notion of the monarchic prophets in early Islam stems 'from the late Jews', for 'it finds itself typically expressed in the opposition of Samuel and Saul'. These are to be sure, even if one regards the ones in this opposition as products of the theological phantasy of a contemporary of Hosea, not later, but again and again early Jews, and especially if one recognizes the 'Elohistic' narrative as the literary form of an early-*nabi*-ically determined tradition, and recognizes behind the opposition with which it deals an historical one. But the Mohammedan notion of a prophetic ruler may after all be Biblically influenced. The fundamental impetus of the Kharijites against it—out of which their 'waiting' originates,— their resistance to all authorization of rule as hereditary 'private possession for the usufruct of the incumbent', a resistance which Ali is supposed to have comprehended in the formula 'only no rulership', and with which he is supposed to have objected to the necessity of a rulership, just or unjust,[84] is in no case deducible: it probably stems from the primitive Bedouindom of the Mesopotamian steppe.[85] It cannot be explained on the basis of the related tendency which we deduce for the early period of Israel; but probably it can be compared with it for the deeper understanding of both.

Here as well as there is an elementary longing for a freedom which also the pre-Islamic Arabs, in spite of their belief in destiny, at times, quite un-religion-like, may have felt as a divine freedom, perhaps when they, as they appear to have done,[86] called men generally 'the servants of Allah'. In Israel this primitive-Bedouin desire for freedom experienced a heightening whose pure expression according to its negative growth is the Jotham fable, according to its positive growth the Gideon passage. But this positive growth extends nevertheless far beyond all comparability. For the Kharijites want to prevent any one from ruling upon whom the Spirit does not rest; by Gideon's mouth, however, the person on whom the Spirit rests says that he does not want to rule. It is, if one disregards the dynastic concern, a thin, occasionally almost dissolved boundary, this difference between the 'judge' and the 'king', when the king in early Israel derives from the divine annointing alone his right to power. The boundary becomes very definite if we recognize that the judge as such has no right to power. JHWH enables him to do what he has to do in this hour; He does not enable him to be powerful. Certainly he remains until his end the man of his deed, and since he has decided so great a matter the people come to him with their disputes for decision. But the fact of the continuity of the ruling, this marvellous fact that one wakes up in the morning and, without any call from above, hears a question from below, recognizes himself again as the possessor of the grace of ruler-ship, this is strange to him—he wants it to be strange to him. The Kharijites demand that the one who has become unworthy forfeit the rulership. In the narrative concerning the rejection of the first king of Israel we are confronted by something fundamentally related and yet again quite different. The period of the judges, however, lacks the basis for such a demand because it knows no rulership at all outside of the direct operation of the Spirit.

Hugo Winckler characterizes[87] the difference between judge and king as that 'of chosen officials in contrast to a ruler installed by God'. The right of the king is divine, that of the judge stands 'under the divine whose interpreter is the priest'. That may prove true for Carthage; it cannot be reconciled with the Biblical texts. Never is a judge chosen in Israel. Probably, however, the early history of the kings, as it lies before us, knows an action with which the people in-stalls the king previously annointed in the name of God (I Samuel 11:15), or annoints him a second time (II Samuel 2:4; 5:3). Concern-ing an interpretation of the divine law to the judges by the priests our texts know nothing. They have none of the judges consult the oracle, as at that time do the people (Judges 20:18, 28), as later do the Kings (from I Samuel 23:2 on). The anti-monarchical Book of Judges knows no priestly mediation: the *ruach* has seized upon and endowed a man, and that is enough of that. The Spirit seizes upon and endows him not for power and dignity, but only for a limited mission, and also that is enough of that. The king has continuity, his fulfilment is the dynasty; the judge has only his mission. Possessed by the *ruach* he contends against the enemies of JHWH and Israel. Just as it propels a *nabi* about

(I Kings 18:12) it propels him into battle. And in the infusion of the *ruach* he governs judicially the liberated community. He does not judge like the officials appointed by Moses (Exodus 18:22, 26), but like Moses, the '*nabi*', himself: because the giver of the *ruach* is the giver of the law. The *shophet* who at first, Spirit-possessed, became a *nabi*, remains similar to a *nabi*; he remains close to the Spirit. And this only does he want to be; not a confirmed bearer, only the public receiver of the Spirit; not a regent, only a 'servant'.

At one time on the wandering, the '*anawa* of the leader was joined to the 'Bedouin' desire for freedom of the wandering tribes and erected the theocracy upon an anarchic psychic foundation. Underneath the new forms of living of the people-become-settled, which plants fig trees, lays out vineyards, builds towns, and learns to treasure the value of guaranteed security, there persists the old, nomadicizing resistance against the dependency of an autocratic man and his clan. But again there are men there, a kind of man is there, which brings to this intractability a tendency revaluing and sanctifying it as the exclusive commitment to the divine King, and, indeed, in the form of their own person-like '*anawa*, their devotion, their *nabi*-ic, Naziraic enthusiasm, their judicial service and renunciation of ruler-ship. Although there were only a few in whom the tendency attained a pure form their memory remained in the prophetic consciousness. The Amos passage about the 'causing to arise' testifies to this in the choice of words in a promise of Isaiah (1:26): 'I will cause your judges to return as before,/ your counsellors as at the beginning'.

But that paradox of inner antagonism, that an anarchic psychic foundation came to support the structure of the direct theocracy, obscured the crisis of the period of the judges. The self-same institutional interregna which for the one were, for a time, first the standing under the direct rule of the Lord and then the waiting for a new gracious operation of His *ruach*, meant to the other a recovery of judicial discipline and an unleashing of orgiastic local cults. In the abandoned intervals the former believed that they had to approach a highest order not necessitating a human executive; the latter perceived therein the occasion for an aggressive disorder offering advangage and indulgence. And this disorder, completely unconquered by the prophetic community, is almost the only universal constant. Only trouble and tribulation again and again pull together a few tribes for a while and up from flightiness to theocratic obedience. Only seldom, when chaos explodes in an especially visible deed of violence between tribe and tribe, does a punitive action embrace the disunited people.

The outbreak of the crisis did not come from a development of inner antagonism. The strong rivals of Israel from the Aegean, the Philistines, with the superior strictness of their political and military organization,[88] seized the hegemony in Canaan. Now it is no longer single tribes but the people which is threatened in its claim to this land, and that manifestly in its existence. The guerrilla war of sworn military Nazirites brings on mighty berserker-deeds, but no liberation. Great undertakings, if they really were attempted (I Samuel 7), did not extend beyond tactical results (the situation is portrayed clearly enough in 13:19ff.). Then for the first time does the people rebel against the situation which the primitive-prophetic leaders tried, ever anew and ever alike in vain, to inflame with the theocratic will toward constitution. The idea of monarchic unification is born and rises against the representatives of the divine kingship. And the crisis between the two grows to one of the theocratic impulse itself, to the crisis out of which there emerges the human king of Israel, the follower of JHWH (12:14),[89] as His 'anointed', $m^e shiach$ JHWH, χριστὸς κυρίου.

NOTES

===========

INDEX OF ABBREVIATIONS

AJSL: The American Journal of Semitic Languages.
AO: Der Alte Orient.
AOT²: Gressmann, Altorientalische Texte zum Alten Testament, Second Ed.
AR: Archiv für Religionswissenschaft.
ATAO⁴: Alfred Jeremias, Das Alte Testament im Lichte des Alten Orients, 4th Ed.
BASOR: Bulletin of the American Schools of Oriental Research.
BZ: Biblische Zeitschrift.
DB: Hastings, Dictionary of the Bible.
DLZ: Deutsche Literaturzeitung.
EB: Encyclopaedia Biblica.
EI: Enzyklopädie des Islam.
ERE: Encyclopaedia of Religion and Ethics.
ICC: International Critical Commentary.
JBL: Journal of Biblical Literature.
JPOS: Journal of the Palestine Oriental Society.
JQR: The Jewish Quarterly Review.
JThS: Journal of Theological Studies.
KAT³: Die Keilinschriften und das Alte Testament, 3rd Ed.
KB: Keilinschriftliche Bibliothek.
MGWJ: Monatsschrift für Geschichte und Wissenschaft des Judentums.
MVAG: Mitteilungen der Vorderasiatischen Gesellschaft.
NKZ: Neue kirchliche Zeitschrift.
OLZ: Orientalistische Literaturzeitung.
RB: Revue biblique.
RE³: Realenzyklopädie für protestantische Theologie und Kirche, 3rd Ed.
REJ: Revue des études Juives.
RGG²: Die Religion in Geschichte und Gegenwart, 2nd Ed.
RHPhR: Revue d'histoire et de philosophie relgieuses.
RHR: Revue d'histoire des religions.
RLV: Reallexion der Vorgeschichte.
RS: Revue Sémitique.
ThB: Theologische Blätter.
ThR: Theologische Rundschau.

ThW: Gerhard Kittel, Theologisches Wörterbuch zum Neuen Testament.
ThSK: Theologische Studien und Kritiken.
ZA: Zeitschrift für Assyriologie.
ZAW: Zeitschrift für die alttestamentliche Wissenschaft.
ZDMG: Zeitschrift der deutschen morgenländischen Gesellschaft.
ZDPV: Zeitschrift des deutschen Palästinavereins.
ZS: Zeitschrift für Semitistik.
ZThK: Zeitschrift für Theologie und Kirche.
ZWTh: Zeitschrift für wissenschaftliche Theologie.

Chantepie⁴: Lehrbuch der Religionsgeschichte, 4th Ed., edited by Bertholet and
    Edv. Lehmann, 1925.
Fried. Delitzsch, Prolegomena: Prolegomena eines neuen hebräisch-aramäischen
    Wörterbuches, 1886.
Ehrlich, Randglossen: Randglossen zur hebräischen Bibel, 1908–14.
Kautzsch-Bertholet: Die Heilige Schrift des Alten Testaments, 1922–3.
König, Lehrgebäude, Historisch-kritisches Lehrgebäude des Hebräischen, 1881–
    97.
Pauly-Wissowa: Realenzyklopädie der klassischen Altertumswissenschaft.
Roscher: Ausführliches Lexikon der griechischen und römischen Mythologie.
Rob. Smith, Lectures³: Lectures on the Religion of the Semites, 3rd Ed., 1927
    (cited, because of the valuable notes by S. A. Cook, according to this edition
    of the original and not according to the German edition).

CHAPTER ONE

¹ Cf. Granet, *Danses et légendes de la Chine ancienne* (1926), 87ff., 293, 312₁,
426ff., 614; also Granet, *La civilisation chinoise* (1929), 268ff. For the subject itself
cf. Wensinck, 'The Refused Dignity', in *A Volume of Oriental Studies Presented
to E. G. Browne* (1922), 491ff.; Van Gennep, *Le rite du refus*, AR XI (1908), 1ff.

² Cf. Ed. Meyer, *Gottesstaat, Militärherrschaft und Ständewesen in Ägypten*
(1928) 9 (concerning the Theban church-state): 'In Wirklichkeit herrschte
natürlich die Priesterschaft.'

³ Cf. Jakob Burckhardt, *Weltgeschichtliche Betrachtungen* (1905), 106ff.

⁴ Cf. Max Weber, *Wirtschaft und Gesellschaft* (1922), 783.

⁵ Cf. Weber, *op. cit.*, 773.

⁶ Merx, *Die Ideen von Staat und Staatsmann* (1892), 9.

⁷ Reuss and Nowack.

⁸ Lagrange, *Le livre des Juges* (1903), 149₂₃.

⁹ Nor can such a postulative thesis be understood as mere expression of hesitation. The passages adduced by Alfons Schulz, *Das Buch der Richter* (1926), 52,
have no similarity to ours, which do not contain a personal refusal alone.

¹⁰ Budde, *Die Bücher Richter und Samuel* (1890), 117.

¹¹ *Ibid.* Cf. Budde, *Das Buch der Richter* (in Marti's *Handkommentar*), 66;
see also R. Kittel, *Geschichte des Volkes Israel*, 11⁶ (1925), 312, and in Kautzsch-
Bertholet, I, 385.

¹² See especially Wellhausen, *Die Composition des Hexateuchs³* (1899), 222.

[13] Cf. Rob. Smith, *Kinship and Marriage in Early Arabia²* (1903), 198ff., 206ff.; Morgenstern, *Beena Marriage in Ancient Israel*, ZAW NF VI (1929), 91ff. (concerning Gideon's marriage 93); Morgenstern, 'Additional Notes', ZAW NF VIII (1931) 46ff. (concerning Gideon's marriage 49); concerning matrilocal marriage as such, see Briffault, *The Mothers* (1927), I, 268ff., 364ff., 372ff. (Semites), 381ff., 406ff., 416ff.

[14] Gressmann, *Der Messias* (1929), 353.

[15] Galling, *Die israelitische Staatsverfassung* (1929), 16.

[16] *Ibid.*, p. 14.

[17] For a general discussion see Wundt, *Völkerpsychologie* X (1920), 357ff.; for Semites see concerning the South Arabian constitution, M. Hartmann, *Der islamische Orient*, II (1909), p. 349.

[18] The apposition 'sprung from his loins', 8:30, is hence explained; cf. the septuagint 'sprung from the loins of Jacob', Exodus 1:5 (thus also Genesis 46:26); these are the only places where this expression occurs. A legal formula for legitimate descent (Burney, *The Book of Judges²*, 1920, 264ff.; Eissfeldt, *Die Quellen des Richterbuches*, 1925, 56ff.) is therefore not to be thought of; Robertson Smith's reference (*op. cit.*, p. 38) to 'loins' as designation of the paternal clan cannot be adduced for this purpose.

[19] Cf. above, p. 36ff.

[20] Baudissin, *Kyrios als Gottesname im Judentum* (1929), III, 648, asserts that *mashal* appeared to the Hebrews 'as the way of manifesting his function differentiating the king from the tribal prince'; this is said to be clear from Judges 8:23; but the proof for it, *ibid.*, p. 617ff., is not adduced.

[21] This is also contrary to Sellin, *Wie wurde Sichem eine israelitische Stadt?* (1922), 22ff. [Jecheskel Kaufmann, *Kirjath Sepher* X (1933), 65, objects that the contradiction between 8:23, if one sees in it, as I do, an unconditioned refusal, and 9:2 is not thereby removed. But it seems to me indisputable that even with an unreserved renunciation of the office of ruler on the part of Gideon his factual authority can have procured for his clan a power in the land in relation to which Abimelech was well able to present the monarchic sway of the Schechemites as the lesser evil.]

[22] Cf. Buber and Rosenzweig, *Die Schrift und ihre Verdeutschung* (1936), passim, especially the essays 'Die Sprache der Botschaft', 'Leitwortstil in der Erzählung des Pentateuchs,' 'Das Leitwort und der Formtypus der Rede' by Buber and 'Das Formgeheimnis der biblischen Erzählungen' by Rosenzweig.

[23] Wellhausen, *Prolegomena zur Geschichte Israels⁶* (1905), 241.

[24] *Ibid.*

[25] Thus, for example, G. F. Moore, *Commentary on Judges* (1895), p. 230 ('from the last period of the Kingdom of Israel, those terrible years of depotism, revolution and anarchy which lie between the death of Jeroboam II and the fall of Samaria'); Budde, *Handkommentar*, p. 66; cf. the pointing out of the linguistic concurrences in Budde, *Die Bücher Richter und Samuel*, p. 184ff., which, however, seem to me to witness rather for the early development of a specifically prophetic language than for a dependence on Hosea. Cf. also in the next chapter, p. 32ff.

[26] Gressmann, *op. cit.*, p. 212.

[27] *Die biblische Theologie I* (1835), p. 282ff.

[28] Wellhausen, *op. cit.*, p. 245.

[29] Attempts to do this, like that of Wellhausen, *op. cit.*, p. 245ff., seem to me not to have been successful.

[30] 'Legends were narrated from the moment of the experience on.' Herzfeld, 'Mythos und Geschichte' (*Archäologische Mitteilungen aus Iran* VI, 1933), p. 109. Cf. Buber, *Moses*[2], p. 15ff., as well as 89ff.

[31] *Kleine Schriften* IV, p. 74.

[32] *Op. cit.*, p. 417.

CHAPTER TWO

[1] Wellhausen, *op. cit.*, p. 232.

[2] For the meaning of the word cf., for example, Pedersen, *Israel* I–II, English edition (1926), p. 349; S. A. Cook in Rob. Smith, *Lectures*,[3] p. 661; L. Köhler, 'Die hebräische Rechtsgemeinde' (Züricher Universitätsbericht 1930/31), p. 9 [now: *Der hebräische Mensch.*, 1953, 151ff.].

[3] Langdon, *Die neubabylonischen Königsinschriften* (1912), p. 270ff.

[4] L. W. King, *Chronicles concerning Early Babylonian Kings* (1907), II, p. 8.

[5] p. 418.

[6] Along with this basic conclusion it should in no way be said that the Book of Judges reflects the actual course of history in detail, as Baumgartner (DLZ III/4, 1933, p. 1354) erroneously understands me to say; only that it contains and schematically presents in its guiding framework an outline of the actual happening.

[7] Wellhausen, *op. cit.*, p. 232.

[8] Cf. more recently Th. H. Robinson in Oesterley and Robinson, *A History of Israel* (1932), I, p. 138₂, for whom, in spite of the critical consideration, the viewpoint of the redactor presents, 'a wholesome philosophy of history' because the religion of the Israelitish tribes was 'the only unifying force which they possessed'. The *b'alim* are 'disintegrating forces' (*ibid.*, p. 167). It does not follow that in my conception the hiatus between framework and single narratives falls down (Baumgartner, *op. cit.*); it is only reduced to the degree that out of such a 'philosophico-historical' reflection a close, but in its dimensions not dependably recognizable, historical actuality results.

[9] I cannot understand by this an idol in spite of all that has been adduced (cf., however, against the exegetical arguments, especially Caspari, *Die Samuelbücher*, 1926, p. 45ff.); there is obviously something meant, concerning which the reader was sensible, which could be brought against the intention of the author to be faithful to JHWH (cf. further below, note 31). That instead of *ephod*, *elohim* is to be read (cf. Moore EB I, p. 1308ff; Elhorst, *Das Ephod*, ZAW, XXX, 1910, 273ff.; Budde, *Ephod und Lade*, ZAW, XXXIX, 1921, 32ff., 40ff.; Sellin, *Geschichte des israelitisch-jüdischen Volkes*, I, 1924, 134ff.), does not appear to me to be demonstrated. In no place does *elohim* appear as term for an idol; the passages adduced for this, Exodus 20:23 and 32:1 use the word in a special way. The first says, 'Do not make for Me and do not make for yourselves so-called gods which are of silver and gold'; and the second, 'Make us a deity'. Thus both are concerned really with the making of *gods*, not of images. Arnold, *Ephod and Ark* (1917), p.

127ff., can only read *aron* for *ephod* because he makes Judges 8:27b into a deuter-onomic addition: Gideon erected an ark, as JHWH-oracle, as a substitute for the rulership offered to him (*ibid.*, p. 128), but since it was naturally not identifiable with the Mosaic ark the author of the addition is alleged to have rejected it in this way. This ingenious interpretation shatters on the fact that the metaphorical 'whoring' is always related only to a turning away from JHWH to gods, demons or spirits (along with which also the Molochization and Baalization of JHWH is counted); never, however, to the mere opposition of a local JHWH-cult to the official one. That Gideon founds an independent oracle-place is true enough, but it does not become illegitimate until later (cf. note 32). With regard to the *ephod* cf. especially Sellin, *Israelitisch-jüdische Religionsgeschichte* (1933), p. 48ff.

¹⁰ My departed friend Franz Rosenzweig used humorously to construe the initial R as '*rabbenu*' rather than 'redactor' (cf. Buber and Rosenzweig, *Die Schrift und ihre Verdeutschung*, p. 47).

¹¹ Concerning this cf. Pedersen, *op. cit.*, p. 27: 'it is unjustifiable to divide the old narratives of the Book of Judges', an utterance worthy of note despite its all too general formulation with a scholar of such critical brilliance.

¹² Also cf. Burney, *op. cit.*, CXXIff.

¹³ It therefore will not do to concede with Baumgartner, *op. cit.*, p. 1353, the ironic character of the first story, but to ask whether 'along with it the theocratic attitude is given'. Only the whole, seen together, furnishes the proof. From single tales of mockery obviously no theocratic tendency results; but rather from an un-interrupted series which culminates programmatically in the Gideon-passage expanded by the Jotham fable. I do not, however, approve at all of maintaining an 'antimonarchical bias of the single narratives', as Caspari, NKZ, XLVI, 200, represents me to say: the bias was brought to expression in the editorial revision as I have clearly explained on p. 81. That I allegedly prove this bias with the fact 'that the judges fight against *foreign* kings' (*ibid.*) is a scarcely conceivable mis-understanding. Only the manner in which these kings of the narrative are treated in the redaction which lies before us serves me as one of the proofs.

¹⁴ Without his having to be, on that account, identical with the one named in Joshua 10:1.

¹⁵ For this compare Hertzberg, *Adonibezeq*, JPOS VI (1926), p. 213ff. (who, however, also regards Beseq as a divine name and therefore not amended); in opposition cf. Baudissin, *Kyrios*, III, 409ff.

¹⁶ Thus not merely Syriac or Aramaic (Burney, *op. cit.*, p. 5), but also neo-Hebraic. Hence the name Beseq in I Samuel 11:8 could be explained thus by Raschi and other Jewish exegetes (cf. b. Joma 22b). Concerning biased garbling of proper names. Cf. Böhl, 'Wortspiele im Alten Testament' (JPOS, VI, 1926), 202ff.

¹⁷ Cf. Ball, 'Cushan-rishataim', *Expository Times*, XXI (1909/10), 192; otherwise Böhl, *op. cit.*, 203.

¹⁸ Cf. Nöldeke, *Untersuchungen zur Kritik des Alten Testaments* (1868), 180.

¹⁹ Wellhausen, *Composition*, 216.

²⁰ Attempts at explanation like that of Eissfeldt, *op. cit.*, 28ff., 32, do not seem convincing to me.

²¹ Also in I Samuel 12:9 he appears originally to have been characterized (if

his title here is not to be understood wholly as a gloss) as commander-in-chief of the coalition (Chazor is doubtless secondary; perhaps it stood there as a name of the league, a name which was later no longer understood).

[22] Concerning the primacy of the Joshua report cf. Burney, *op. cit.*, 81; Burney, *Israel's Settlement in Canaan*³ (1921), 54.

[23] The first is well presented in Burney, *Judges*, 201ff.; cf. Baudissen, *op. cit.*, III, 91ff. With regard to attempts at solving the second problem by assuming a coalescing of two persons (possibly brothers; see Sellin, *Geschichte*, 35ff.) several objections can be made from the point of view of history of legends (it seems to me, to correspond neither to Rosières' 'law of transposition', cf. van Gennep, *La formation des légendes*, 1912, 284ff., nor to any other known form of coalescing of heroes); cf. also Kittel, *Geschichte*, II⁶, 28.

[24] In reference to Israel see Nöldeke, *Neue Beiträge zur semitischen Sprachwissenschaft* (1910), 75. I consider it to be probable, however, that this is only a question of folk-etymology and that the name originates from a *ssara*, 'ruling' (but in the noun derived from it, *missra*, contained in Isaiah 9:5ff.). Cf. Noth, *Die israelitischen Personennamen*, 1929, 208, and Volz, *Mose*², 1932, 88ff.

[25] For the applicability to Israel König, *Die Genesis*² (1925), 631, has declared himself; for the applicability to Jerubbaal Lagrange, *op. cit.*, 127. [Like Volz, *op. cit.*, 88₁, I consider the interpretation to be 'grammatically difficult to carry through', but it is nevertheless the one popularly given.]

[26] Thus, among others, Gunkel, *Genesis*³, 362.

[27] See Bᵉreschith R. XXXIX 14, Tanchuma on Genesis 12:2.

[28] The controversy (see Burney, *op. cit.*, 210ff. and supplementarily XIVff.) loses sight of the fact that this is a question of water flowing down from above. Whoever wants to get away from 'lapping like a dog' supplies 'with the hand to the mouth'. A contradiction between the two expressions, as several of the old versions assumed it, thus does not obtain. This became clear to me as I visualized the occurrence for myself in 1927 in Eyn Charod.

[29] Nevertheless Lagrange, *op. cit.*, 136, may be compared in opposition to Budde's objections to this probability. (Cf. also Tolkowsky, 'Gideon's 300', JPOS V [1925], 69ff.)

[30] Cf. Caspari, 'Die Personalfrage als Kern der ältesten israelitischen Staatsgründungspläne' (OLZ, XXIII, 1920), 52, whose emendation of the *thoar*, called into question without difficulty, I nevertheless cannot endorse.

[31] Cf. above note 7. If v. 27b is not regarded as secondary (for which no sufficient reason appears to me to have been adduced), then it may be understood from the point of view of v. 33.

[32] Thus we may understand the context of meaning—only very incompletely represented, to be sure—of the redactor who with the report concerning the 'whoring' in v. 27 wants to anticipate the context of v. 33 (see above, note 7): the established Ephod is dedicated by the people after the death of the founder to the 'Baal of the Covenant', apparently a syncretistic divinity (cf. note 21, Chapter IV).

[33] *Prolegomena*, 246.

[34] See Noth, *Personennamen*, 142.

[35] Gressmann, *op. cit.*, 229.

[36] Cf. Ehrlich, *Randglossen* III, 105ff., whose conclusions are nevertheless quite beside the point.

[37] Cf. In my selection of the 'Reden und Gleichnisse des Tschuang-Tse' the extracts 'der Untätige' and 'Der Wolkengeist und der Urwirbel'.

[38] Title of an address of Wellhausen of 1900; cf. below note 7 in Chapter VIII.

[39] *Op. cit.*, 28.

[40] Whether or not, as I assumed in the first edition, it is an expansion of the original state of affairs in a second redaction is irrelevant for my line of argument (against Baumgartner, *op. cit.*, 1352ff.).

[41] See Eissfeldt, *op. cit.*, 12ff.

[42] Cf. Noth, *op. cit.*, 169ff. and recently Eissfeldt, 'Der geschichtliche Hintergrund der Erzählung von Gibeas Schandtat', *Festschrift Beer* (1935), 19ff.

[43] Cf. concerning this Noth, *op. cit.*, 1021.

[44] Something of this opposition, not yet recognized in its significance, may be detected under the covering of the Davidic tendency to moderate history (a little more about this follows in 'Der Gesalbte').

[45] Nevertheless it may be true, as Noth proposes in his *Das System der zwölf Stämme Israels* (1930), p. 102, that we have to deal here with an old motif resting on magical notions.

[46] Cf. Güdemann, 'Tendenz und Abfassungszeit der letzten Kapitel des Buches der Richter', MGWJ, XVIII (1869), 357ff.; Burney, *op. cit.*, 447, 490.

[47] Cf. Noth, *op. cit.*, 121.

[48] The second *dabar* signifies agreement.

[49] The work by Nyberg, *Studien zum Hoseabuche* (1935)—in general quite noteworthy—has unfortunately not differentiated between the passages which refer to the earthly king and those which refer to the *molekh*, but has assigned them all to the second category, having created, in the process, however, a new point of departure for the treatment of the problem.

[50] See Buber, *Das Volksbegehren.* (Cf. also *Der Glaube der Propheten*, 90ff.)

[51] I speak of a 'first' redaction and publication because the later additions speak only against an early dating of the final form of the text.

[52] Wellhausen, *Composition*, 229.

[53] Robert Arnold Fritzsche in a letter to Franz Rosenzweig.

CHAPTER THREE

[1] Why we would have to limit ourselves, as von Gall urges in 'Über die Herkunft der Bezeichnung Jahwes als König' (Wellhausen-*Festschrift*, 1914), p. 154, to Canaanite soil I'm not able to see. Also the allegation that Israel became acquainted with the concept of king 'first on Canaanite soil' (von Gall, βασιλεία τοῦ θεοῦ, 1926, p. 41) is historically unproved and unprovable. [Concerning the question of the 'usual ancient-oriental divine kingship' cf. above the Preface to the Third Edition.]

[2] Eissfeldt, 'Jahwe als Konig', ZAW NF, V (1928), 84.

[3] Cf. also the concept of a *mlk* as cosmic divine kingship in Ras Shamra. [See above, Preface to the Third Edition, 55.]

[4] Cf. Nestle, *Die israelitischen Eigennamen* (1876), 181; Baudissin, *op. cit.*, III, 49ff.; Baudissin, article, 'Moloch', RE³ XIII, 300; Eissfeldt, *op. cit.*; Eichrodt, *Theologie des Alten Testaments*, I (1933), 95ff. Concerning 'counsellor' as the orginal meaning of *melekh* cf. Haupt, 'The Hebrew Noun Melkh, Counsel', JBL, XXXIV (1915), 54ff.; Baudissin, *op. cit.*, III, 613. Already in Gesenius' *Thesaurus, melekh* was equated with consul.

[5] Ed. Meyer, *Gottesstaat*, p. 4.

[6] Cf., among others, Moret, *Du caractère religieux de la royauté pharaonique* (1902), 302ff.

[7] Meyer, *op. cit.*, p. 11, translates 'King who makes kings', which according to a communication from K. Sethe is indeed possible according to the spelling of the text, but in expression thoroughly un-Egyptian. On this point cf. also Sethe, *Amun und die acht Urgötter in Hermopolis* (1929), 12ff.

[8] Sethe, *Urgeschichte und älteste Religion der Ägypter* (1930), 95ff.

[9] Breasted, *Development of Religion and Thought in Ancient Egypt* (1912), 12, 16ff., 313ff. (That this was preceded, as Moret alleges, *Royauté* 71, according to a tradition, by a leaderless primeval period, rests, as K. Sethe has shown me, upon an erroneous interpretation of the text.)

[10] Roeder, *Urkunden zur Religion des alten Ägypten* (1915), 142; literally the 'kingship of men and of the gods' appear as 'one thing'. (Sethe.)

[11] Cf. Breasted, *Ancient Records of Egypt*, II (1906), 76; Moret, *op. cit.*, 9ff.; Engnell, *Studies in Divine Kingship* (1943), 4ff.; Frankfort, *Kingship and the Gods* (1948), 159ff.

[12] Breasted, *Development*, 13.

[13] Erman, *Die Literatur der Ägypter* (1923), 145; cf. Breasted, *op. cit.*, 250.

[14] Erman, *op. cit.*, 373ff.; Roeder, *op. cit.*, 46ff.

[15] Breasted, *op. cit.*, 353ff.

[16] Roeder, *op. cit.*, 6.

[17] Sethe, *op. cit.*, 184.

[18] *Op. cit.*, 64, 69, 81, 101.

[19] Among general presentations of the history of Babylonian religion that of Dhorme, *La Religion assyro-babylonienne* (1910), gives on pp. 121–179 a comprehensive treatment of the subject.

[20] Kugler, *Sternkunde und Sterndienst in Babel*, II, 1 (1909), 138; L. W. King, *A History of Sumer and Akkad*³ (1923), 101; concerning the priestly character of the office see Kugler, *op. cit.*, 140ff.

[21] Thureau-Dangin, *Die sumerischen und akkadischen Königsinschriften* (1907), 36ff.; cf. King, *op. cit.*, 101ff.

[22] Thureau-Dangin, *op. cit.*, 152ff.

[23] Winckler, *Die Keilschrifttexte Sargons I.* (1889), XXVI₆ and *passim*.

[24] KB, I, 16ff.

[25] KB, I, 190ff.

[26] Ebeling, Meissner and Weidner, *Die Inschriften der altassyrischen Könige* (1926), 120ff.

[27] For general presentations of the magic meaning of names, which is entered into in Chapter V, cf. among others Andrian-Werburg, 'Über Wortaberglauben', *Korrespondenzblatt der Dt. anthropol. Ges.*, XXVII (1896), 109ff., reprinted:

Prähistorisches und Ethnologisches (1915), 268ff.; Giesebrecht, *Die alttestament-liche Schätzung des Gottesnamens* (1901), 68ff.; Heitmüller, '*Im Namen Jesu*' (1903), 159ff.; Hopfner, *Griechisch-ägyptischer Offenbarungszauber*, I (1922), 173ff.; Frazer, *The Golden Bough*[3], II (1911), 318ff.; Canney, 'The Significance of Names', *Journal of the Manchester Egyptian and Oriental Society*, No. IX (1921), 21ff.; Canney, *Givers of Life* (1923), 74ff.; Larock, *Essai sur la valeur sacrée et la valeur sociale des noms* (1932). Concerning the meaning of names among the Babylonians cf. Contenau, 'De la valeur du nom chez les Babylon-iens', RHR, LXXXI (1920), 316ff.

[28] KB, I, 16ff.; cf. also the passage adduced under 25.

[29] The difference is clearly recognized in Baudissin, *Kyrios*, III, 638.

[30] Hempel, *Altes Testament und Geschichte* (1930), p. 45, distinguishes the Israelitish king from the Babylonian and the Egyptian on the basis 'that his rela-tion to God is one of calling and adoption, not one of generation'. But this is also true, so far as I can see, for the Babylonian ruler (who never designates himself as begotten by a god and 'born' by a goddess in the sanctuary—see Thureau-Dangin, *op. cit.*, 92ff.—but is said to be adopted by her), but not for the Egyptian. Also it does not seem to me to be true that in the Babylonian as in the Egyptian the two notions run along side by side (Hempel, *Gott und Mensch im AT*, 1926, p. 1341); I find cross-breedings of this kind in Egyptian, but not in Babylonian texts. [In the second edition of the work just adduced, 1936, Hempel remarks on this point: 'Certainly the adoption idea preponderates in the Babylonian by far; but whether in addition "nativism" has disappeared completely in utterances concerning the divine "mother", in petitions to her, and in characterizations of a king as "brother" of a god . . ., seems to me . . . not completely certain.' But the very fact that all sensuous expressions refer to the goddess, not to the god, is a proof for my interpretation. The fact of birth out of the human mother can cer-tainly not be placed into question; nativism is limited to the myth of *begetting*. When Gudea says to the goddess that he has neither mother nor father, that she is mother and father to him, for she has born him 'on a lofty place', he can only mean according to the nature of the case the *'ἄνωθεν γεννηθῆναι*.]

[31] Cf. Kugler, *op. cit.*, 144ff.; Dhorme, *op. cit.*, 169ff.; Christliebe Jeremias, *Die Vergöttlichung der babylonisch-assyrischen Könige* (1919); A. Jeremias, *Hand-buch der altorientalischen Geisteskultur*[2] (1929), 102ff.; Engnell, *op. cit.*, 16ff.; Frankfort, *op. cit.*, 299ff.; Labat, *Le caractère religieux de la soyante assyro-babylonienne* (1939), *passim*.

[32] Cf. Kugler, *op. cit.*, 149.

[33] KB III, 2, 12ff., 64ff.; Langdon, *Die neubabylonischen Königsinschriften*, 98ff., 102ff.; see also Zimmern, 'König Lipit-Ištars Vergöttlichung', *Berichte über die Verhandlungen der Sächs. Ges. d. Wiss., phil.-hist. Kl.*, LXVIII (1916), 16ff.

[34] Winckler, *Die Gesetze Hammurabis* (1904), 2ff.; AOT[2], 381.

[35] Cf. Dürr, *Ursprung und Ausbau der israelitisch-jüdischen Heilandserwartung* (1925), 109ff.

[36] Of the primeval king Yima it says in Yäst 19:34 (Lommel, *Die Yäst's des Awesta*, 1927, p. 179), that as he composed his lying speech in his mind the glory (Lommel: 'the radiance of felicity'; Rudolf Otto rightly prefers to say 'radiance of power') in the form of a bird left him.

[37] Meissner, *Babylonien und Assyrien*, I (1920), 65ff.

[38] Cf. Baudissin, *op. cit.*, III, 252. Several references to connections between Israelitish and South Arabian culture (without consideration of the problem of theocracy) have been made by Montgomery in *Arabia and the Bible* (1934).

[39] Rhodokanakis, 'Altsabäische Texte' (*Sitzungsberichte der Wiener Akademie, phil.-hist.*, CCVI/II (1930), 19ff.

[40] Cf. F. Hommel in Nielsens *Handbuch der altarabischen Altertumskunde*, I (1927), 862.

[41] Rhodokanakis, *op. cit.*, 37.

[42] Cf. Rhodokanakis in Nielsens *Handbich*, I, 120.

[43] Cf. Nielsen, article, 'Sabäer', RGG², V, 3.

[44] Rhodokanakis, 'Die Bodenwirtschaft im alten Südarabien' (*Anzeiger der Wiener Akademie*, LIII, 1916), 174.

[45] Cf. Nielsen, *Der dreieinige Gott*, I (1922), 91.

[46] Rhodokanakis, *op. cit.*, 191.

[47] Rhodokanakis 'Altsabäische Texte' 96.

[48] *Ibid.*, 58.

[49] Rhodokanakis, 'Bodenwirtschaft', 196; *Handbuch*, I, 118.

[50] Rhodokanakis, *Handbuch*, I, 118.

[51] Cf. p. 128ff.

[52] Yet this is already established in the ancient Oriental idea of a king; cf. Mowinckel, *Psalmenstudien*, II (1922), 151. The closest analogy in Israel is II Kings 11:17 (cf. Caspari, 'Das priesterliche Königreich' Th.B., VIII, 1929, 107), except that here kingship and priesthood are allotted to two persons and the office of mediator devolves upon the priest.

[53] For Israel cf. Mowinckel, *op. cit.*, 19, 152ff.; Mowinckel, *Le décalogue* (1927), 123ff.; Noth, *System*, 72ff.; and see further above, pp. 126ff.

[54] Max Weber, *Aufsätze zur Religionssoziologie*, III (1921), 81.

[55] I have followed the assumptions of Rhodokanakis; nevertheless the line of development has not been clearly established.

[56] Baudissin, *op. cit.*, III, 252ff. Cf. also Eissfeldt, 'Götternamen und Gottesvorstellung bei den Semiten', ZDMG, NF, VIII (1929), 21ff.

CHAPTER FOUR

[1] See Eissfeldt, *Jahwe als König*, 84, in which, however, the other possibility is not excluded. Cf. also Eissfeldt in Baudissin, *Kyrios*, IV, 194.

[2] Noth, *Personennamen*, XVIff.

[3] Zimmern, KAT³, 469ff.; Lagrange, *Études sur les religions sémitiques²* (1905), 107; Baudissin, Article 'Moloch', RE, XIII, 274; *Kyrios*, III, 49ff., IV, 24; Jensen, ZA NF, VIII (1934), 236ff. Perhaps this obscure *malik* is a vestige from that primeval period, inaccessible to us, in which the Eastern Semites, too, migrated and settled under the guidance of 'counsellors'—that is, leader-gods. Nevertheless also the national god Ashur carries the title of a *malik ramanishu,* a self-counsellor or self-ruler (Tallqvist, 'Der assyrische Gott', *Studia Orientalia,* IV, 3, 1932, 54). Cf. also above, p. 170, note 4.

[4] Concerning the South Arabian Malik cf. especially O. Weber, *Studien zur südarabishen Altertumskunde*, III, MVAG, 1907, 28 [68]ff.; in condensed form Nielsen, *Handbuch* I, 232ff. Concerning Malik as prince of hell in Islam cf. Montgomery, JBL, XXVII (1908), 41₆₃; Jensen, *op. cit.*, 237.

[5] Cf., among others, Beth, 'El und Neter', (ZAW, XXXVI, 1916), 139ff., 153ff.; and in addition Kleinert, 'El' (*Baudissin-Festschrift*, 1918), 268ff.—My interpretation is not tied to a decision in the etymological controversy (cf. Sellin, *Theologie des AT*, 1933, 4; Eichrodt, *Theologie des AT*, I 86; L. Köhler, *Theologie des AT* [3] (1953), 236; Quell, see entry Θεός in Th W, III, 85). Closest to my interpretation is the explanation of Quell who rightly counts *el* among 'the primeval words of pious speech': 'a potency whose origin man is not able to establish with the means of his knowing', 'the power to which man has not attained'. Only here the *phenomenal* character of this power is not taken into consideration. It belongs to its essence that it appears to man.

[6] I cannot concede that *el* has the meaning of 'lord, owner' of the place to which the *el* attaches (Sellin, *Geschichte*, 47). This meaning comes to the *el* first as *baal*. The *el* himself is indeed always a power manifesting itself at a place, but not yet effective as possessor.

[7] That tribal gods are connected with sagas of wandering is a universal religio-historical fact which one can exemplify equally well in Polynesian or North Indian traditions. Only in wandering does the group become decisively aware of the divinity which belongs to it and which therefore does not stay behind.

[8] The Jeremian 'queen of heaven' does not belong here, since she is no *malk*-consort; that she is 'seated by the side' of JHWH (Nestle, *Die israelitischen Eigennamen*, 177) does not follow from the text. Cf., for example, Tiele, *Geschichte der Religion des Altertums*, I (1896), 357ff.; Baudissin, *Kyrios*, III, 50 (further literature by Moore, article 'Queen of Heaven', EB, IV, 399ff., and Westphal, *Jahwes Wohnstätten*, 1908, 248ff.). Cf. also below, note 18 in Chapter Six.

[9] In Hebrew a person is called *baal* in relation to something with which he is connected in such a way that it belongs to him. The verb lingers intensively in and functionalizes the noun, which I do not regard as denominative, which rather seems to me originally to characterize the act of marriage, of intimate possession. Cf. Buber and Rosenzweig, *Die Schrift und ihre Verdeutschung*, 166.

[10] Concerning water as 'the spermatozoa of the gods' cf. Barton, *Semitic and Hamitic Origins* (1934), 112, 139ff., 160ff., 278ff.

[11] Cf. above the Preface to the Third Edition.

[12] In reference to attitudes toward the ground cf. Robertson Smith, *Lectures* [3], 96ff., 169, 533; Lagrange, *Études*, [2] 97ff.; Wellhausen, *Reste arabischen Heidentums*, [2] 146; Baudissin, *Adonis und Esmun* (1911), 25ff.; Baudissin, *Kyrios*, III, 271ff.; and in addition Alt, Article 'Baal', RLV, I, 305ff.; Noth, *op. cit.*, XVII, 116; Barton, *A Sketch of Semitic Origins* (1902), 104ff., whose problematic assumption of a 'self-watering' female primeval divinity ought to be compared with his *Semitic and Hamitic Origins*, 140ff., 204ff., 210ff.; Sellin, *Geschichte*, I, 124; Oesterley and Th. H. Robinson, *Hebrew Religion* (1930), 122ff.; Cumont, Article 'Baal' in Pauly-Wissowa, I, 2650. Ed. Meyer, *Geschichte des Altertums*, II, 2[2], 140₄, opposes this interpretation on the ground that what is adduced

for it is secondary. But a survey of material known to us (most of it already arranged in outline fashion in Paton, Article 'Baal', ERE, II, 285ff.) indicates that mountain, spring, and tree predominate by far. One can certainly not adopt the all-too-narrow thought construction by Robertson Smith. The fundamental concern here is not water, and certainly not a specific kind of watering, but the mysterious power of natural fertility; the activity of water, especially that of the heavenly outpouring, is only its most mythically clear manifestation (cf. for, example, the ὗε κύε of the Eleusinians and in addition Aeschylus, *Fragments*, 44; for the persistence of the idea in Jewish tradition cf. *Thaanith*, 6b; 'the rain is the husband of the earth' and *Pirqe R. Elieser*, V, where the ground-water fecundation is characterized as illicit wooing of the earth, rain fecundation as her wedded love; here also belongs the Talmudic term 'Baal's field' for a field which needs no artificial watering). If we may well discern in the *baal-marphe* the demon of a healing spring (Paton, *op. cit.*, 289), the *baal-marqod* (cf. among others, Cumont, article 'Balmarcodes' in Pauly-Wissowa, II, 2834ff.), the κοίρανος κώμων, is to be understood most easily as lord of the phallic vegetation dance (cf. K. Th. Preuss, 'Der Unterbau des Dramas', *Vorträge der Bibliothek Warburg* (1927–28, 1930), expecially pp. 58–82; concerning the phallic character of the κῶμος cf., among others, Cornford, *The Origin of Attic Comedy* (1914), 19ff., 48ff.; Gressmann, article 'Religion', RLV, XI, 105, translates inconclusively 'wailing dances', but has in mind 'obscene belly-dances'). His real name, Megrin, signifies perhaps the one who fills the threshing floors (see Clermont-Ganneau, *Recueil d'archéologie orientale*, I, 1888, 94ff., and in addition Lods, *Israël* (1930), 138ff.). And should not the *chamman* stone pillar whose inhabitant is the problematic *baal-chamman* (cf. Meyer, article 'Baal' in Roscher, I, 2870, *Geschichte* II, 2², 152, *Untersuchungen zur phönikischen Religion*, ZAW, NF, VIII, 1931, 8ff.), contrary to Meyer's view, have something to do with 'heat', though not originally with the heat of the sun, and also not with the altar of incense—even if *chammana* signifies such an altar at Palmyra (see Albright, JPOS, IX, 1929, 53; *The Archaeology of Palestine and the Bible*,[3] 1935, 108); nevertheless a divine designation 'lord of the incense altar' is hardly conceivable—but with 'being in heat', in a state of sexual excitement (cf. the Hebrew *yacham*, Genesis 30:38ff., 41, 31:10—from which only a *chamon* or *chaman* could be derived with certainty). The connection of the *baal-chamman* with a divinity *malk-ashtharth* who himself bears the surname *el-chamman* (cf. Meyer, *Geschichte*, 152ff., *Untersuchungen*, 8ff.) is reminiscent of the Deuteronomic *ashthᵉroth ẓon* (7:13; 28:4; 18:51) as well as of the linguistic trace of fertility function of Astarte who is connected in terms of content with the *yacham* of the Genesis passages. Concerning sheep symbols in connection with *baal-chamman* cf., among others, Robertson Smith, *op. cit.*, 477ff.; one might consider the silver band of Batna (Baudissin, *Adonis*, table VI; concerning the Phoenician character, 269ff.) to the right and left of the Baal couple—syncretistically transformed—the two erotics, of which the one rides a ram, the other a sheep.

[13] Cf., among others, Meyer, *Die Israeliten und ihre Nachbarstämme* (1906), 303; Moret and Davy, *Des clans aux empires* (1923), 229ff.

[14] See Nonnos, *Dionysiaca*, XL, 443ff.; cf. the founding of Byblos by the 'malk' (identified variously with Kronos and Heracles) (in Eusebius, *Praep*.

evang. I, 10; see Clermont-Ganneau, *Études d'archéologie orientale*, I, 1880–95, 10). (The assumption by Albright, especially in *Archaeology and the Religion of Israel*,³ 81, 219, repeatedly expressed, that *melqarth* is to be understood as king of the underworld, seems to me to be insufficiently grounded. The fact that his kingship had to be renewed each year by a ritual of re-birth out of fire does not speak for it.

¹⁵ Von Gall, *Wellhausen-Festschrift*, 154.

¹⁶ Baudissin, *op. cit.*, III, 1912.

¹⁷ Mackay, 'The King of Tyre', *The Church Quarterly Review*, CXVII (1934), 239ff., sees (241), and probably rightly, in the *melekh* of Ezekiel 28:12 Melqarth as 'king' of Tyre.

¹⁸ Cf. Paton, *op. cit.*, 284; Baudissin, *Adonis*, 33, far more illuminating than the later interpretation in *Kyrios*, III, 479, 507.

¹⁹ Not as a Baal (Baudissin, *Kyrios*, III, 305), but as a 'dieu de groupe' (Dussaud, *Introduction à l'histoire des religions*, 1914, 77).

²⁰ Baudissin, *op. cit.*, III, 246ff. (see also his *Adonis*, 39ff.). The attempt to discover an original tibal god behind the space-bound place-god Baal is the weakest point in his remarkable posthumous work. The attached genitive which makes an individual proper name out of the *baal* concept never had a band of human beings as subject. In order to be able to understand the Baal as tribal god historically, one would have to assume his division into the many local gods of a tribal region into which gods he had so completely been absorbed that not even his name remained to him—a notion without analogy in the history of religion. That, as Meyer maintains in his *Geschichte*, II 2², 139ff., the *el* of a tribe wanders with it, becomes settled with it, and grows together with its places of worship and is named *baal* as their occupier, would not signify a transformation but a dissolution of the original essence, since the god of a tribe is essentially related to its unity. To be sure, the gods of united tribes can coalesce into a nation god who is really only a tribal god with expanded domain and content, but a tribal god can never be dissipated into gods of localities. If he becomes settled he becomes a territorial god, not a local god. If, however, he enters into a krasis with a place god, then only with one of a place which the immigrated band chooses as a headquarters for itself, and only in such a way that the tribal god overwhelmingly determines the character of the mingling.

²¹ That the '*el* of the covenant' (Judges 9:46) is also called '*baal* of the covenant' (8:33; 9:4) does not signify a preponderance of the *baal*-element in the theocracy: if he becomes partner and protector of a 'covenant' (cf. concerning this the seventh chapter) then the essence of the *baal* has fundamentally changed.

²² The personal name *baal-malk* (Baudissin, *op. cit.*, III, 44ff., 191) seems also to me to mean not '*malk* is lord', but also not '*baal* is king', but (the god) *baal* is (the god) *malk*. Cf. Noth, *op. cit.*, 116ff. In relation to the problem of the god *malk-baal* cf. especially Février, *op. cit.*, 65ff.

²³ Noth, *op. cit.*, 116.

²⁴ Garstang, *The Hittite Empire* (1929), table XXXIV and p. 165ff.; Contenau, *La Civilisation des Hittites* (1934), table XVI, and p. 252, as well as *Manuel d'archéologie orientale*, III (1931), p. 1127ff.; Furlani, *La religione degli*

Hittiti (1936), p. 62ff.; cf. Frazer, *The Golden Bough*[3], IV, 1 (1914), 119ff.; Ramsay, *Luke the Physician* (1908), 171ff.; A. S. Cook, *The Religion of Ancient Palestine in the Light of Archaeology* (1930), 136ff.

[25] Concerning his reappearance on coins of the fourth century as Baal of Tarsos cf. Frazer, *op. cit.*, 118ff.; A. B. Cook, *Zeus*, I (1914), 595ff.

[26] Cf. also Baudissin, *Der gerechte Gott*, 16: 'really the idea of the tribe grown into a person' (in the final edition, *Kyrios*, III, 417ff., deleted).

[27] Not, however, of the animal, as Paton, Article 'Ammonities', ERE, I, 391 maintains. (Among the South Arabians, on the other hand, there is the male variant of Ashtharth, Athtar, the god of *all* fertility; the West Semitic demarcation is not applicable here.

[28] Cf. in addition note 41.

[29] To think of a 'cultic surrender' in the sense of sexual rites (Wilke, 'Kinderopfer und Kultische Preisgabe', *Festschrift der 57. Versammlung deutscher Philologen*, 1929, 138ff.) is forbidden by the very form of dedication which is strange to these; above all, however, the difference in kind between *malk-* and *baal-*gods is not taken into consideration: the former know no sacred prostitution.

[30] See also Eisler, Ιησοῦς βασιλεύς (1928), II, 110₅.

[31] Especially *Wald- und Feldkulte*, I (1875), 463ff., 508ff., 520ff.; II, 302ff. (302₂ calls attention to Semitic material); *Mythologische Forschungen* (1884), 137. Already with Mannhardt, however, the lability of the rite between dedication and sacrifice comes to clear expression. Cf. also Frazer, *The Golden Bough*[3], IV/1, 114ff.; VII/2 (1913), 1–44; Andrew Lang, *Modern Mythology* (1897), 148ff.; Andrew Lang, *Magic and Religion* (1901), 270ff.; Hopkins, article 'Fire-walking', ERE, VI, 30ff.; Eitrem, *Opferritus und Voropfer der Griechen und Römer* (1915), 169ff., 173ff.; Eitrem, 'Die vier Elemente in der Mysterienweihe' (*Symbolae Osloenses*, IV, 1926), 55ff.; Saintyves, *Essai de folklore biblique* (1923), 52ff.; B. Heller, 'Notes de folk-lore Juif', REJ, LXXXII (1926), 301ff.

[32] 21b does not say 'the same' as 20 (see Cornill on this passage), but 21a and b assert two different forms of child sacrifice. For the sentence construction, see Ehrlich, *Randglossen*, V, 55.

[33] Deuteronomy, 12:31; Jeremiah 7:31, 19:5; cf. also II Kings 17:31. On the other hand Chronicles 28:3 seems completely secondary to me, and therefore not applicable as an explanation of II Kings 16:3.

[34] *haabir ba-esh* means unequivocally to lead through the fire. Cf. Numbers 31:23 (lustration). In relation to such an indubitable proof for the construction a passage like Job 33:28 (Eerdmans, *Alttestamentliche Studien*, III, 1910, 120) lacks all conclusive force. The term for the *molekh-*dedication is coalesced from two meanings of the Hiphil, the one just adduced and the one in Exodus 13:12 (as in Numbers 27:7): to commit, to assign, to dedicate. Thus it means: to dedicate by leading through or over the fire (cf. Jensen, *op. cit.*, 236). That this is the 'complete expression' and Exodus 13:12 an abbreviated one (Eerdmans, *op. cit.*) cannot be assumed because of the fact that in 13:15 only the slaughtering, not the burning of the animal first-born is mentioned.

[35] Thus, according to the illuminating interpretation of A. Hillebrandt, *Der freiwillige Feuertod in Indien und die Somaweihe* (1917), 13ff., the symoblic self-annihilation of the *diksha* grew from the original consecration to voluntary

fire-death. (This and other examples I have dealt with in my lecture mentioned in note 47 of Chapter six.)

[36] Cf. Plutarch, *De Iside*, 16; otherwise in the related myth of Demophon (*Hymn to Demeter*, II, 233ff.).

[37] For the whole question cf. the older literature adduced in a note by Moore in the article 'Molech', EB, III, 3184ff.

[38] Ezekiel 16:21 appears to mean that the consecration (*b'-haabir*) degenerates into killing.

[39] Cf. for Phoenicia Eusebius, *Praeparatio evangelii*, IV, 16; for Moab, II Kings 3:27.

[40] In the form of the biblical report we find the former process in II Kings 16:3a (cf. 21:6a), and the latter in 3:27—two passages of characteristic difference in expression and tempo.

[41] In his work *Molk als Opferbegriff im Punischen und Hebräischen und das Ende des Gottes Moloch* (1935) Eissfeldt has enunciated the thesis that the Biblical *lam-molekh* has nothing to do with a *malk*-divinity, that it should be understood after the manner of the Phoenician *molk*—which signifies promise, vow, sacrifice —'as a technical term for this kind of sacrifice' namely, for the offering of children. The thesis is so noteworthy and would be, if conclusive, so consequential in terms of the history of religion that I feel myself obligated to attach here a contribution, however sketchy, to the verification of the arguments.

Eissfeldt takes a votive stele of Saturn, found on Algerian soil in 1930, as his point of departure. The stele's Latin inscriptions relate to a lamb sacrifice presented to Saturn—a sacrifice which is designated as *sacrum magnum nocturnum* and is characterized by the words *anima pro anima, sanguine pro sanguine, vita pro vita*, as well as by *agnum pro vikario* [sic] as standing for a child sacrifice (already in Akkadian sacrificial texts the lamb appears with a similar formula as human substitute; cf. note 41 in chapter VI). Regularly a Punic term recurs in four different transcriptions, of which *molchomor* is doubtless the most correct. In this way the inscriptions are brought together with two Punic ones in which the fulfilling of a vow appears connected with the words *mlk 'mr*, while in others, of a related kind, one finds instead *mlk 'dm* or *mlk 'dn*, or even *mlk bssr*. Eissfeldt, following Chabot, interprets the word-root *'mr* as 'lamb, sheep', *mlk* after the manner of the Syrian verb as 'promise', consequently 'fulfilment of a promise', therefore together: sacrifice of a sheep, analogous with *mlk 'dm*: sacrifice of a human being, and *mlk bssr* perhaps: sacrifice of flesh. Accordingly, Eissfeldt asserts, the Biblical *lam-molekh* is to be understood as designation of a kind of sacrifice. One should read *l'-molekh*; *nathon l'-molekh, haabir l'-molekh* means accordingly: to offer as *molk*-sacrifice, to consecrate as *molk*-sacrifice. It would therefore have to be assumed that we have to deal here with a Phoenician loan-word and thus with a kind of sacrifice taken over from the Phoenicians. Yet Eissfeldt himself does not appear to draw this conclusion. Rather there ensues for him from the 'knowledge that *molek* is not the name of a god, but the designation of a kind of sacrifice' the further consequence that 'the *molek* child-sacrifice belonged from the first to the Jahwe-cultus, or in any case was rooted therein in the seventh or eighth century before Christ'. According to Eissfeldt the Biblical texts confirm this throughout: 'the pre-Deuteronomic parts of the

Old Testament—narratives, prophecies and laws—show with full clarity that child-sacrifice is regarded as a work commanded by Jahwe and pleasing to Him'. As grounds he adduces from the first category Judges 11:30ff. and Genesis 22; from the second, Micah, 6:7, and conditionally Isaiah 30:33; from the third, Exodus 13:2, 11ff.; 22:28; 34:19ff. Only in Deuteronomic and post-Deuteronomic texts is there polemicizing against child-sacrifice. The son-sacrifice of Ahaz and that of Manasseh 'are certainly not judged as idolatry and sin' by the source from which the author of the Book of Kings takes them. 'This discrimination stems rather from the Deuteronomic author of the Book of Kings, and its original text, perhaps along with closer description of the situation which called it forth, represented the decision of the two kings with respect to this most difficult of all sacrifices rather as illuminating example of piety and patriotism. In other words: when the pre-Deuteronomic sagas, prophecies and laws presuppose the custom of child-sacrifice and at latest approve of it in so far as they allow the animal subsitute-sacrifices to be valid in their stead, or allow themselves to be satisfied with the attitude coming to expression in readiness for the offering of that which is precious, the historical reports at our disposal from the pre-Deuteronomic period show us that at that time child-sacrifice was a legitimate part of the Jahwe cultus.'

The interpretation of *molchomor* which Eissfeldt follows is not completely cogent (for the following remarks on this matter I am indebted to A. Spanier's valuable allusions, the most important of which I list under his name. First of all the vocalization of the second component: if we are to think in terms of the Aramaic *immar* it is really understandable that *omor* is transcribed, and not *immor* or *emmor*. I leave the doubling out of account, since it often is ignored in transcriptions. On the other hand, the vocalization is peculiar, since we find no precedent for it either in Akkadian, or in Aramaic or in Ras Shamra (there is always the possibility of a muffling under the influence of the m). And for *mlk*, which in different Semitic languages means to advise, to determine, to decide, to rule (of these the first is especially frequent in Aramaic), the meaning 'to promise' is assured only for *one* Aramaic dialect, namely, the Syrian. 'What is probably involved here is the result of a semasiological special development which was limited to this one dialect' (Spanier), and therefore it is quite doubtful whether one may also assume this meaning for the Punic. Moreover, it is even questionable for the Syrian whether the verb can also have the sense of 'to fulfil a promise', since the only passage adduced for this is designated by the lexicographers as of doubtful transmission.

One may in addition touch upon the problem of why the term was transcribed in the Latin inscriptions if it means nothing other than 'sacrifice of a lamb'— especially since in the one the *agnus* is mentioned particularly. Should one not expect in this passage a magic or sacred formula, the citation of a 'sacred ejaculation' (Spanier) perhaps, through which the substitution of the animal for the human being is made valid, is recognized as valid? Since the verb *amar*, 'to speak', also occurs in the Phoenician, though only in isolated fashion ('which with this type of texts is not surprising', writes E. Mittwoch to me) *malk amar* may plainly be understood as such a sacred cry: the *malk* has spoken! That is, he has pronounced and therefore brought it to reality that the offered sheep is functionally identical with the child which is owed to the god—that it 'is' the child; and the introduction of the cry into the sacrificial formula makes it continually effective, performs the substitution ('vicariate') anew. As far as *mlk 'dm* is concerned, one ought probably to consider (with Lidzbarski, *Handbuch der nordsemitischen Epigraphik*, I, 208; *Ephemeris*, I, 42) an equating with *mlk 'dn* which also occurs in the inscriptions dealt with—the transformation of an n into an m need seem no more strange in Phoenician than in Hebrew, since both languages, for example, have the plural ending *im* instead of the original *in*—especially theophoric proper names like Ebedadom and Adomyathan are to be found (Lidzbarski, *Handbuch*); *malk adon* as sacred cry means: the king is lord (and as such determines the validity). A *malk bissar* finally is to be understood as 'the *malk* proclaims that which is good' (the gracious acceptance of the substitute, namely). There remains many a question to ask; nevertheless it is demonstrated that the problem of interpretation can be solved here too by proceeding from the parallel instance.

In the midst of the Biblical passages which come into consideration, Eissfeld himself, according to the nature of the case, concedes to Leviticus 20:5 a special position, since here *achare ham-molekh* occurs; but that, he asserts, 'does not speak against the interpretation of *molek* as a kind of sacrifice. For if there are preponderantly strange gods after which the Old Testament has the Israelites go whoring, it is also occasionally said of prohibited cultic-mantic objects and practices that the Israelites whored after them, e.g., Judges 8:27 concerning the Ephod, and immediately following our passage—Leviticus 20:6—concerning the dead- and fortune-telling spirits. Notwithstanding the presupposition does not hold good: spirits are certainly mentioned, as well as gods and demons, also an idolatrously usable object in one passage, but never a practice. The metaphor simply does not continue. One cannot find 'whoring after a sacrifice'. The *molekh* as person (or object) is therewith assured.

Instead of *lam-molekh* Eissfeldt wants to read *lᵉ-molekh*. He points out that the Septuagint in the four Leviticus passages where it occurs, translates, in differentiation from the passages in II Kings and Jeremiah, ἄρχοντι without the article, which is of consequence because the translators otherwise, with regard to the rendering of *melekh*, systematically proceed with or without the article. The argument deserves attention. One can also well suppose that the translator has also let himself be guided here by a special motive: he wanted perhaps on the one hand (out of a reserve no longer clear to us today) to avoid the name, on the other hand, however, to do what was possible to prevent misrepresentation of 'the ruler'. It is nevertheless improbable that the diction in these passages would have been transmitted differently than in the others. The rest of the Greeks translate here uniformly: τω μόλοχ, just as the Septuagint does in the other passages.

The new interpretation, says Eissfeldt, was especially suggestive, since with the verbs, occurring in the passages concerned, 'to dedicate' (*haabir*) and 'to give' (*nathon*) the *lᵉ* following them '*more frequently* [emphasis mine] introduces the receiver rather than the kind of dedication or gift'. Accordingly there are passages where with the verbs named in the same meaning the *lᵉ* following them does not introduce the receiver, but the kind of dedication or gift. But such passages do *not* occur with both verbs. When a dative follows *haabir* it is always one of person; by way of exception a second one (Ezekiel 23:37) can follow *this one* which is related to the purpose of the offering. Matters are similar with *nathon*; even the passages to which Eissfeldt particularly calls our attention, where *nathon lᵉ* means to 'do something for a purpose', are not to be adduced here, since in none of them does the verb have the sense of giving and in none does the noun following the *lᵉ* have the sense of a kind of gift. Thus they can afford no occasion for a new interpretation. To be sure, there are within the reports of sacrifice and laws of sacrifice several verbs which at times can be construed with a *lᵉ* related to the kind of sacrifice without a preceding *lᵉ* of person, but here verbs are involved which either do not 'call for the dative' at all or which (*haqreb*) in the ritual language are so extensively technicized that with them one must no longer think directly of the receiver. *Haabir* is here indeed twofold as I have indicated in note 34, but the meaning component 'to assign' has remained so strong and lively that, as was said, no passage is to be adduced in which the directly connecting *lᵉ* would not refer to the receiver. Besides, if one places all the passages side by side where the general child-sacrifice is expressed by a verb with the dative, on the one hand the six with *lam-molekh*, on the other hand the seven others (Deuteronomy 12:31; II Kings 17:31; Ezekiel 16:20, 21; 23:37; Psalm 106:37, 38), one will fully discover from the equivalence of the receiver-dative in the second group that the *lam-molekh* passages also cannot be intended otherwise.

The Old Testament *molekh* is therefore not to be regarded as a technical term for a kind of sacrifice. But on that account it does not also need to be the 'name of the god' 'to whom the children are offered'; Eissfeldt's alternatives are not legitimate. As I have shown above (on pages 111–118), the child-sacrificers did not suppose themselves to serve a god with his own nature and name, but the *melekh* JHWH after the manner of the *melekh*-gods of the neighbouring peoples. What is involved here is a popular degeneration of the JHWH cult, the practice of a popular syncretism beside the religious order of the temple whose mid-point was the valley of Hinnom (II Kings 23:10; cf. p. 113ff. and the related note 34).

That child-sacrifice, however, as Eissfeld asserts, 'was a legitimate ingredient of the Jahwe-cultus' in the pre-Deuteronomic period is something for which an exegetical proof simply cannot be given. The major texts of all three categories adduced by Eissfeldt, the narratives in Genesis 22, the prophetic words in Micah 6, 7, the laws in Exodus 13:2, 11–15, and 34:19ff., proclaim the same battle against degeneration—whether as threatening danger, or as already existing—they all say as the will of JHWH: do not sacrifice, but consecrate and redeem! For Genesis 22 I refer to p. 116ff. That which we find with other Semitic peoples as permissible mitigation (cf. p. 115ff. and in addition notes 42 and 47) solidifies and increases here as originally localized introduction of a sacred validation of subsitution: not the child but the functionally identical animal! (Cf., among others, Wodley, *Abraham*, 1936, 158ff.). It is, therefore, although also disputed, yet in high degree probable that v. 14 belongs to the progress of the narrative, but also that it should identify the mountain of sacrifice with the temple-mountain: the sacrifice of children is heterodox; the temple cult is directed, by the revelation to the tribal father, to the sacred institution of an offering of man *in the* animal. The 'attitude' has here the entirely realistic serious-ness of *intention*. The text, of course, presupposes the custom of child-sacrifice, but certainly not in the legitimate Jahwe-cult, and it certainly does not justify it, also not 'in so far as . . .,' but marshalls against it the primeval establishment of its *anticipated abolition* (cf., among others Welch, *Deuteronomy, the Framework to the Code*, 1932, 14ff., and, by the same author, *Prophet and Priest in Old Israel*, 1936, 78ff.). The Micah verse goes beyond the intent of the demand in that it wishes to set a free and universal regligious ethos in place of one bound to sacrifice. It is completely removed from a 'justification', however relative, of child-sacrifice. But it does not follow from this that its author came upon child-sacrifice as a 'legitimate part of the JHWH-cult'. The representative of the people in whose mouth v. 6ff. are put, prevails from 6b to 7a and from 7a to 7b. The latter is no longer possible for him within the religious order of the temple cult; in order to be able to offer the utmost for expiation, he has to go beyond into the heterodox, but popular shpere. The Exodus passages supplement the Genesis section through the legal fixing of the principle of substitution (that its execution brings not an animal sacrifice, but consecration of Levites and surrender of money, does not, in a negative respect, namely, that of the decline of the existing connection with child-sacrifice, detract from the fact). The explanation that every first-born belongs to JHWH in itself expresses the principle of substitution; for sacrifices of first-born as acts of necessity are certainly performed, but in no tribe still so primitive, so far as we know, is the continuous extermination of the major part of its anticipated future manhood decided or decreed. To extend the demand to *all* first-born means therefore to transform it. The new absolute-ness of the divine claim abolishes, in principle, satisfaction by man-killing. Redemption is thus not secondary, but conceivable as contained in one or another form in the original commandment. Every individual sacrificing of the first-born is by this time reversion, violation of the principle of absoluteness through its material exaggeration. The Deuteronomic and post-Deuteronomic texts do not turn against a legitimate determination of the JHWH-cult, but against the massive associating of the principles '*melekh*-god' and 'child-sacrifice' in the early Semitic conception, thus against the ever-recurring demonization of the achieved religious life by that which is generally Semitic.

With all this it should in no way be maintained that Israel took over child-sacrifice in the post-Mosaic period from the Canaanities. On the contrary it follows from my characterization of the West-Semitic tribal god (see p. 94ff.) that also for the tribes out of which Israel grew the connection of Israel's structure with this form of service would have to have been an original one. Only that in the measure in which JHWH 'emerges from the Semitic *melekh*-ship' (p. 110) the connection is loosened; it is thoroughly credible that the nucleus of the prescriptions of compensation stem from the Mosaic period. I conjecture that first in the period of the kings, after completed amalgamation with the Canaanites, under their influence in many districts (later also at court), the once-abandoned usage springs up again, while in relation to it the compensation is reputed as a weakening of the effect upon JHWH, and the restoration is proclaimed of the original, magical, conjuring connection with the usage made powerful by the extreme character of the offering. The courtly 'false' *n^e biim* may also have had to arrange for this.

Only two passages of the three categories still remain to be discussed: the story of Jephtha's daughter and the Isaiah speech 30:33.

As evidence for the fact 'that child-sacrifice counts as a performance commanded by Jahwe and well pleasing to Him' the saga of the sacrifice of Jephtha's daughter is quite unsuited. There is not a word here that it is to be so interpreted. Neither does JHWH command the sacrifice here, nor does He accept it as well-pleasing. But the story, even in terms of its attitude, does not belong at all in this series. Jephtha does not promise a child-sacrifice, but a human sacrifice. With the first one who steps out of the door of the house he is certainly not thinking of an animal, but obviously not either of any of the women commonly, according to custom, dwelling in the inner chambers, or of the marriageable maidens of the clan, and since he has no son and no un-grown daughter, rather of one of the slaves staying near at hand for greeting and performance of service. Thus modified do we have to think of the psychological background of the saga which in its Cretan variant indeed knows a son, not one who steps out of the door of the house, but only *quae ei primum* [on landing] *occurrisset* (Servius with reference to Vergil, *Aeneis* III, 121; cf. also, however, the variants of Asia Minor, standing between the two, which Baumgartner, 'Jephthas Gelübde', AR XVIII, 1915, 240ff., rightly approximates to the Israelitish one), so that the circle of the possible is drawn much more widely. That it is the only child which as the first one steps out of the door is felt by the narrator to be, as such, a proclamation of the will of JHWH, but nevertheless of a JHWH who punishes the dreadful vow (cf. Lagrange, *Le Livre des Juges*, 217); the redactor took up the narrative—which he could use because it expressed the notion that the dynastic question was not put with Jephtha as it was with Gideon—conceivably without treating it as a problem theologically or without working upon it. A legitimatization of sacrifice stands neither in the narrative nor behind it; it is presented as a misfortune (and indeed as one of a quite extraordinary character as the insertion of the festival of lamentation indicates), not as an agreeable outcome.

With reference to Isaiah 30:33, for whose genuineness Eissfeldt rightly intercedes, I agree with him that here 'Assyria's annihilation under the image of its being offered as a *molekh*-sacrifice' is proclaimed, only (1) not, as he asserts on the *thopheth* in the Valley of Hinnom, but on a *thopheth*, namely an enormous one for which this one merely furnishes the image; (2) accordingly *hukhan* is not to be related, with Eissfeldt, to Assyria, but to the *thopheth*; (3) the pointing *lam-molekh* is indeed erroneous, but the original is not *l^e-molekh*, but *l^e-melekh*: 'For prepared long ago has been a burning-field, even for a king made ready' (Buber-Rosenzweig, *Die Schrift*, XIV, 1930, 123). Also the apocalyptic *thopheth*, Isaiah wants to say, is dedicated like the one in the Valley of Hinnom to a king, but to the genuine *ham-melekh* (6:5). Not a 'silent recognition of custom' is to be envisioned here, not a 'witness for the fact that the prophet, perhaps resigned, has become reconciled with it and has given up the struggle against it', but a powerful irony of the man for whom that which he heard in his calling (6:9ff.), has planted such a different 'resignation' in the soul that he can no more be reconciled ever and with anything. The opinion expressed by Eissfeldt (p. 58, note 2) that the *gam hu* refers to the child-sacrifice of Ahaz corresponds, with variations, to my interpretation, by which the translation adduced above was determined. Behind the vision of the judgment upon the one 'with whom once as rod he smote' (30:31), stands the message to the Hezekiah cozying up to Egypt as formerly Ahaz did with Assyria: upon the *thopheth* your father, who drew the Assyrian into the land, has given your brother to the false king, to the caricature of God; be still (v. 15) and you will see how on the *thopheth* of world history, after a victorious battle which is like the brandishing in the wave-offering (v. 32; cf. the symbolic act, Numbers 8:11, 21), amid great music for the sacrifice, a terrible offering is presented to the King JHWH, which burning He Himself kindles with the breath of His mouth (v. 33). (Cf. Montgomery, 'The Holy City and Gehenna', JBL, XXVII, 1908, 43ff.).

At this point it is also to be judged whether one is authorized to assume that the child-sacrifice of Ahaz and Manasses, of the father and of the son of Hezekiah —if there were sacrifices—were presented by the original text of the Book of Kings in opposition to the later text 'rather as an illuminating example of piety and patriotism'. There is no reason to attribute to the author or redactor of the Book of Kings, who permitted a passage of such 'remarkable frankness' (Eissfeldt) as II, 3:27 to remain as it is, such a meaning-inverting revision. And the author of the book's original text was apparently in popular belief embarrassed as to how it would be if 'one find one's self in the sphere of power of the Moabite god' (R. Kittel); that, however, he regarded the child-sacrifices of Judaic kings —if there were sacrifices—as well-pleasing to JHWH, and rewarded by Him and accordingly equated JHWH with Kamosh is not yet to be concluded from this. But even if he did, it would only mean that he had succumbed to the same popular syncretism, the same Molekhization of JHWH as his kings. What is a legitimate cult-element and what not certainly cannot be concluded from the actions of single monarchs and the records of their chroniclers, but only from the utterances of contemporary guardians of the religious tradition.

I have twice interpolated above: 'if there were sacrifices' and refer in addition to p. 98 and to notes 28–40 to our chapter (especially note 31 where I have added several pieces of religio-historical literature concerning going-through-the-fire). One attains, in my opinion, the entrance to the entire exegetical and religio-historical problem if one has recognized the *lability* of the rite which, according to circumstances, is to be understood as consecratory transfer through the fire and as sacrificial burning in the fire and changes suddenly from the one into the other. The language form of the two passages which refer to the kings' sacrifices points to the former variety (cf. above note 40) just as the form of the others points to passages of the Book of Kings which relate to Israelitish matters, Deuteronomy 18:10, Jeremiah 32:35, and passages of the law of holiness. We find indubitable sacrificial killing of children in Israel in II Chronicles 28:3, Isaiah 57:5, Jeremiah 7:31 and 19:5, Ezekiel 16:20 and 23:37, 39, and in Pslam 106:37. A line of development cannot be derived, but this can be established, namely, that prior to Jeremiah (unless perhaps one wished to regard the passage in Chronicles as pre-exilic) we possess no clear-cut mention of killing. The kings' sacrifices, however, remain in question, since one can detect in the

Chronicles passage surely nothing other than a corruption of the tradition attested by means of the text of the Book of Kings (cf. the Septuagint and the Peshito, as well as II Chronicles 33:6), especially since such an extraordinarily suggestive situation as that of II Kings 3:27 is not reported. It must, however, have been such situations of utmost danger which at times caused a reversion of the rite from a mere consecration by leading-through into a total sacrifice. If one, in addition, considers along with this the first half of II Kings 21:6, one will probably not be able to advocate the opinion that a traditional child-sacrifice at such intervals, in the midst of such a string of superstitious actions, was communicated by the complaining author or editor without special emphasis.

As a result of the research work on the Punic sacrificial inscriptions it ought nevertheless to be specified that the Biblical vocalization *molekh* can scarcely any more be understood, according to the presumption of A. Geiger, *Urschrift und Übersetzungen der Bibel* (1857), 299ff., as a mere stigma-vocalization after the manner of *bothesh*. It is rather to be assumed, as seems to be verified by the transcription in the Latin inscriptions, that the Phoenicians pronounced *mlk* as *molk* in an accented syllable, that the Biblical tradition of vocalization was to point primarily to the Phoenician or Canaanite character of the cult and was determined only secondarily by that otherwise notorious tendency to assimilation.

In summary, the following scheme of the outlines of the religio-historical differentiation may perhaps be justified. Within a West-Semitic rite of child-sacrifice in the cult of the tribal gods there develop as forms of substitution: (1) the animal-vicariate known from Phoenician sacrificial texts and Genesis 22 (also, by the way, lying at the base of the Hittite and Israelitish use of the *s^{e}mikha*), having originated with the Phoenicians presumably under Babylonian influence (the Phoenician formula of equation therefore appears to be borrowed); (2) from the molekhicized popular JHWH-cult in Israel the well-known substitute by fire-consecration of the child devolving upon God in its bondage, a substitute, however, which tends to revert to the original form; (3) from the hierology of the legitimate JHWH cult in Israel the collective redemption, appearing beside the surrender of individuals, of the first-born through the consecration of a sacred tribe or tribal rank, thus, as it were, a substitution of the second degree. The first two of these forms are to be classified with those known to the history of religions which one can characterize as material and functional compensation by human sacrifice. The third, so far as I can see without analogy, is to be regarded as a unique mixed conception, but nevertheless as early (concerning its ancient character cf. V. Rad, *Die Priesterschrift im Hexateuch*, 1934, 91).

[More recently especially Dhorme, *L'evolution religieuse d'Israel* I, 1937, 213ff., and Montgomery, *ICC Könige*, 233ff., who refers to mine and to Dhorme's presentations, have taken a similar position.]

CHAPTER FIVE

[1] That here 'only a leading of the nations to the goal is envisioned' in order to illustrate from this a relationship of Jahwe to Israel' (Baudissin, *Studien zur altsemitischen Religionsgeschichte*, 1911, I, 161), does not quite follow: Amos'

view of the history of nations, as it emerges in 1:3 to 2:3, stands behind it. But even if it did follow, nothing of its unconditional character would in the process be taken from the passage. 'In direct contradiction to 3:2' (Ehrlich, *Randglossen*, V, 254) the verse, thus understood, does not stand in any way: JHWH leads all nations, but only with Israel has He concluded a *covenant*, to which the *yadathi* of 3:2 (cf. note 7 to Chapter Six) points. Ehrlich's 'Do not you behave toward me like the Cushites?' is not supported by the passages adduced for it (see Cramer, *Amos*, 1930, 46), where only a reference to an object (which naturally can also be a person), not a connection with a person is meant.

² That the Samaritan Genesis 48:16 reads *ham-melekh* instead of *ham-malakh*, thus probably understands 'kingly leader', is in any case worthy of note: not without good reasons does A. Geiger, for example, *Urschrift und Übersetzungen der Bibel*, 308, give preference to this reading.

³ Cf. Halévy, 'Antinomies d'histoire religieuse', RS, XIII (1905), 215ff.

⁴ If late, this expression is nevertheless completely in the tenor of the prophetic tradition.

⁵ The 'countenance' is here not 'in a certain sense a parallel to the later notion of the name of Jahwe' (Baudissin, '"Gott-schauen" in der alttestament-lichen Religion', AR, XVIII, 1915, 198). That 'the countenance' of God 'goes' (Exodus 33:14ff.) means only that He *goes before*, so that the opposing enemy meets His deadly shining first (v. 20, cf. Baudissin, *op. cit.*, 184ff.); Israel, how-ever, can walk along behind Him unharmed. Gressmann's 'in His own person' (*Mose und seine Zeit*, 1913, 222) misses the pithiness of the expression. Andre, like Gulin, 'Das Antlitz Jahwes im AT' (*Annales academiae scientiarum Fennicae*, Ser. B, Bd. XVII, 1923), 26ff., misunderstands the relationship of the original refusal (v. 3) to move 'into the midst' of the people—that is, to become specifically present to the people (29:43), to the later agreeing to go on *before* them (to the fact that 34:9ff. follows this, cf. Buber and Rosenzweig, *Die Schrift und ihre Verdeutschung*, 273ff.) and thinks therefore that the countenance here 'has to be interpreted as a kind of hypostasized intermediate nature'. The verse in Deuter-onomy 4:37 depending on our passage means: He has led you out of Egypt through His going-on-before, through His great power. When the enemy does not oppose, but follows, the divine manifestation changes its place so that 'the countenance' is turned again toward that enemy. This is the meaning of Exodus 14:19.

⁶ It is completely incorrect when, for example, Morgenstern, 'Biblical Theophanies', (ZA, XXV, 1911), 149, has the *kabod* of JHWH resting (*shakhan*) continuously on the peak of Sinai. Exodus 24:16a is a *process*. Morgenstern errs just as much when he assumes that the *kabod* moved after the completion of the tabernacle from Sinai to the *kapporeth* of the ark and there took up its permanent place which it left by day only during the leading of the march of the people. JHWH's relationship to the tabernacle is simply not to be conceived of as a static one.

⁷ So also is 'He who dwelt in the thornbush' of Deuteronomy 33:16 to be understood (in opposition to Meyer, *Israeliten*, 4, who assumes an old, later forgotten, folk-belief' according to which JHWH 'in such a bush surrounded by a radiating flame has His authentic and continuous dwelling place'; thus also

Morgenstern, *op. cit.*, 167, as well as 'The Elohist Narrative in Exodus 3:1–15', AJSL, XXXVII, 1920–21, 245ff., who has JHWH 'permanently inhabiting' Sinai and the tabernacle, and also the bush). Only thus can the Massoretic text of the much-disputed temple-dedication passage (I Kings 8:12) be rightly understood. JHWH never declared that He wanted to dwell in the dark. In no passage where 'cloud 'and 'dwell' are brought together does JHWH dwell in the cloud, but the cloud is the one that does the 'in-dwelling'; *ba-'araphel* belongs not to *li-sh^ekon*, but to *amar* (the word order is determined by the rhythm). '*araphel* is, as in Exodus 20:21 (Deuteronomy 4:11, 5:19; cf. also Samuel 22:10), the storm-darkness of the Sinai-revelation. At that time JHWH said He wanted to take up habitation, dwell-in (absolutely the same as in Deuteronomy 33:20; Nahum 3:18, Psalm 55:7), in Israel namely. Had in view here is probably the passage Exodus 29:45a, independently of the question of dating its context surely old, whose wording is repeated in God's speech to Solomon in I Kings 6:13. Thus v. 13 attaches itself meaningfully to v. 12 in our passage: God wants to take up dwelling in Israel on and on for ever; therefore Solomon has built for Him on the mountain-high terrace a pavilion (thus the loan-word is to be understood cf. Fried Delitzsch, *Prolegomena*, 62ff.; Isaiah 63:15 applies the rare and at that time perhaps no longer completely understandable word to the heavenly dwelling). That it is not a dwelling house that is meant, but only a place in which to lodge, a pleasure house as it were, but one in which JHWH in later times could take His residence again and again (v. 13b) the great temple speech sets forth later, especially in 8:27ff., commenting on the old words of consecration.

[8] Here only the pattern of meaning of the narrative is presented, not the question of the historical relation of tabernacle and ark discussed. The present state of the scholarly treatment of this question is characterized by two views standing in utmost opposition to one another: that of Erdmans, *De godsdienst van Israel* (1930), I, 56ff., which regards the ark as well as the tabernacle—the latter in the same sense that I intend in Chapter Seven, p. 133ff.—as Sinaitic and assumes that they are not indeed originally connected, but become so soon (a view which is close to my own: I prefer to assign the instituting of a sacred potency of such a kind as that of the ark to no later period of the Israelitish religious history than the Mosaic), and that of von Rad, 'Zeit und Lade', NKZ, XLII (1931), 476ff., who takes the view of a Canaanite origin of the ark and has it brought into historical connection with the tabernacle only by a 'theological act of the priestly codex'. In relation to the foundations of this assertion several details are to be noted here:

1. The term *li-ph^ene* JHWH does not specify (*op. cit.*, 478) that God dwells in the tabernacle, but that the sacrifice presented to Him at His place of manifestation is accepted by Him, just as the prayer which one prays in or at the temple or even toward it (I Kings 8:28ff.) is received and accepted by JHWH '*in heaven*' (v. 30, 32, 34, 36, 39, 43, 45, 49): the *li-ph^ene* occurs also in this passage (v. 28, where *pan^etha* and *l^e-phanekha* correspond to one another not simply paronomastically, but also dynamically, like the answering movement to the speaking movement).

2. The Solomonic dedication passage does not indicate '*quite* clearly' (v.

Rad, *op. cit.*, 481) that JHWH 'dwells in the darkness of the temple'. It is not a matter of a 'real dwelling in the *d^ebir* (*op. cit.*, 491₂); for '*araphel* never signifies the darkness of a closed space, but exclusively the 'dripping' thunder-cloud. Concerning the meaning of the dedication passage cf. above, note 7.

3. That generally a *beth* JHWH is spoken of, but where no reason against it exists, with preference of an *aron ha-elohim*, cannot (*op. cit.*, 489) be utilized against the original connection of the ark with the JHWH religion. *beth* JHWH or *ohel* JHWH is something which fulfils the function of a house or tabernacle *for* JHWH: in which He sojourns. With *aron* JHWH the danger existed that the genitive would be misunderstood (as the Philistines apparently misunderstood it, in the same way as several modern historians of religion have done so) in such a way that the implement is thought to have the function of a receptacle for JHWH (as for the mummy of Joseph, Genesis 50:26) in which He is contained. Therefore, when appropriate, the more general term was preferred which corresponds almost with the concept of a 'numinous object'.

4. It will not do for us to see—something which v. Rad calls 'most essential' —in the old ark stories (*op. cit.*, 491) 'how inseparably Jahwe was thought to be connected with the ark'. JHWH descends upon it continually; then He sits upon the cherubs just as, in the destructive storm, He 'rides upon the cherub' (II Samuel 22:11; Psalm 18:11) and when He descends upon the cherubs the world must tremble because He then enters upon His kingly office or reassumes it (Psalm 99:1). It does not tremble because He sits permanently, but because He has just now sat down. It is no different in the old ark stories. In I Samuel 4 the ark is captured by the Philistines, but is that supposed to mean that the JHWH 'inseparable' from it now dwells in the camp of the Philistines? He causes His ark there—in the power of its manifested connectedness with Him—to prove its power, but He clings to it just as little as afterward during its stay in Kirjath Jearim, when He is speaking with Samuel elsewhere.

That *yosheb* with the Akkadians does not have to designate 'permanent sitting, inhabiting' (Rohlfs, *Ani und anaw in den Psalmen*, 1892, 37) is demonstrated by such passages as Genesis 18:1; 25:27 (they both dwell in tents, but Jacob loves to abide in them); Jeremiah 36:22.

That JHWH in I Samuel 3:10 after the thrice-repeated call comes and steps up to him, does not indicate (*op. cit.*, 483, 492) that He comes down from the ark. The voice indeed appeared to the one awakened in the *hekhal* to penetrate in to him from without, where Eli sleeps (' in his living room', for the linguistic usage cf. 2:20). JHWH, Who has called from the cloud descending to the entrance of the sanctuary, comes now and 'steps up close', no differently than He, in the more precise report in Exodus 34:5, descends and 'steps up close' (contrary to Klamroth, *Lade und Tempel*, 1932, 24).

One ought not to gather from the first of the two signal-words in Numbers 10:35 (*op. cit.*, 483, 492) that JHWH is bidden to lift Himself up from His throne. Much as the same imperative in Judges 5:12 calls upon Barak to arise and to strike the adversary so Moses here implores the Lord of the ark that He arise with it in order that the enemy scatter. If the idea were a different one it would probably not have been possible, in an historical liturgy from the period of the kings (Psalm 132:8), with the very same imperative and also without a second verb, to call upon JHWH to arise together with His ark to His 'rest-place'. Here indeed the *quma* also applies expressly to the ark!

⁹ Caspari, *Die Samuelbücher*, 476.

¹⁰ A related paronomasia, which relates *melekh* and *halakh* to one another, I find (disregarding mere plays on words like Numbers 20:17 and 21:22) with conscious intention in I Samuel 8:5 and especially 12:2. [This paronomastic or folk-etymological treatment of the word has, of course, nothing to do with its origin and is nevertheless of great significance for its history of meaning (contrary to Caspari's rejection of an etymology, NKZ, XLVI, 199, which has never led me into temptation).]

¹¹ The question of distinguishing the sources may herewith be dismissed. Such analysis is not sufficient, in my opinion, to support the assertion that the expression is lacking for the period in which Israel waged 'the wars of JHWH' (L. Köhler, *Theologie des Alten Testaments*,³ 33).

¹² The *Biblical* material does not lead to the hypothesis of a multitude of war-demons, first expressed as a conjecture by Wellhausen (*Die kleinen Propheten*,³ 1898, 77) and developed by Schwally (*Semitische Kriegsaltertümer* I, 1901, 5ff.). Also Gressmann's assumption of a transfer of the epithet from another god to JHWH (*Der Ursprung der israelitisch-jüdischen Eschatologie*, 1905, 76ff.; *Die Lade Jahves*, 1920, 60) does not need to be discussed in our context. The arguments for the primacy of the sky are given best by Westphal, *op. cit.*, 237ff., 262ff. (cf. also Westphal, *Nöldeke-Festschrift*, 1906, II, 717ff.), the opposing ones by Kautzsch, article, 'Zebaoth', RE³ XXI, 620ff., who, however, weighs pro and con carefully. Concerning the difficulty of the problem cf. especially M. Dibelius, *Die Lade Jahves* (1906), 57ff. J. Hehn, *Die biblische und babylonische Gottesidee* (1913), 256ff., assumes—like others before him—rightly that in the use of the name people thought of 'the divine and human hosts as whose Lord Jahwe is characterized', that the nation named its God thus 'as the God who rules over the hosts of earthly and heavenly beings'. On the other hand, I cannot regard this comprehensive concept as *original*. Concerning the original and its development into the comprehensive concept cf. Hänel, *Die Religion der Heiligkeit* (1931), 197ff., 237ff. I agree also with the supposition of J. Rieger, *Die Bedeutung der Geschichte für die Verkündigung des Amos und Hosea* (1929), 33ff., that by means of the same name two conceptions of God are characterized, 'the old popular one of the God of Israel as the Jahwe of the hosts of Israel, the other higher one of Jahwe Sabaoth, the God of history' (but 'God of history' is sufficient only then when one understands thereby in all seriousness the history of the whole creation in which all powers of nature engage together in serving (cf. Hänel, *op. cit.*, 237ff.), but I must dispute the assertion of an essential difference between the two. It is a difference of degree of development in the sense of my presentation on p. 108ff., even if with Rieger (with whom I agree also in this) it is assumed that Amos 3:13, further 5:27, and (especially) 6:14 'with Sabaoth thought simply of the hosts of the nations': JHWH now goes before as leader for the '*goy*' (6:14) against Israel just as He once went before Israel against the *goyim* of Canaan, but at that time, too, His protection of the army commanded by Him was not prescribed and confirmed in writing, but He stood with the army in a *bᵉrith* (cf. chapter seven) which bound His law and the army's destiny to one another.

[13] Against this, among others, Arnold, *Ephod and Ark*, 144ff.; Torczyner, *Die Bundeslade und die Anfänge des Religion Israels* (1922), 9ff., 74. For this, finally L. Köhler, *op. cit.*, I can hardly conceive of the process of such an abbreviation into something indefinite (Köhler understands *ç'baoth* to refer to the stars): *elohe ç'boath* would be natural as an abbreviation, but hardly JHWH *ç'baoth*.

[14] Whether the name JHWH *elohim* originated from JHWH *elohe elohim* and designated JHWH as chief of the gods (Nathaniel Schmidt, 'Yahwe Elohim', JBL, XXXIII, 1914, 44) or whether, as I assume, it originated from an act of identification, in any case '*elohim*' was understood appositionally by the reader of our texts.

[15] So also Torczyner, *op. cit.*, 74, who connects with this his explanation: JHWH = tumult. Arnold, *op. cit.*, 142ff., wishes to understand the genetive adjectivally, 'the militant JHWH', 'JHWH on the warpath', but the proof for such a construction is lacking; for the two proofs adduced by him are none: the ἅπαξ λεγόμενον *sera anashim* in I Samuel 1:11 means generally 'an offspring of the male gender' (she [Hannah] begs not exactly for *a* son, but male descendants as such), and *ssare ç'baoth* does not mean 'military commanders', but the superiors of individual army units. A singular *ssar ç'baoth* does not accordingly occur (since *ssar ç̣aba* designates the commander-in-chief, the concept 'the leader of an army unit' has to be specified exactly or paraphrased).

[16] Franz Rosenzweig, 'Der Ewige' (Buber und Rosenzweig, *Die Schrift und ihre Verdeutschung*), 205.

[17] Fundamentally Robertson Smith, *The Prophets of Israel*[2] (1895), 386ff. (appealing to Jehuda Halevi's *Kusari* IV, 3—he would, however, also have been able, and with still greater justification, to appeal to the Targum *Onqelos* in the reading cited by Nachmanides for the passage and to the Talmud, *b. b'rakhoth*, 96; cf. Rosenzweig, *op. cit.*, 190ff.). Cf., among others, Skipwith, 'The Tetragrammaton', JQR, X (1898), 662ff.; Spoer, 'The Origin and Interpretation of the Tetragrammaton' (AJSL, XVIII, 1901/02), 33ff.; Hehn, *op. cit.*, 214ff.; G. R. Driver, 'The Original Form of the Name Jahweh' (ZAW, NF V, 1928), 246.

[18] *Kabod* is the radiating and thus manifestation-becoming 'force' or power of a being.

[19] Cf. Aistleitner, 'Zu PS-68' (BZ, XIX, 1931), 40; also see below note 57 to chapter eight.

[20] Gunkel's emendation *m'lakhim* is unnecessary.

[21] The closest analogy is offered by Deuteronomy 6:20, where it is not asked: 'which are the laws?' but: what is the meaning of the laws [known to us]?'

[22] Gunkel, article 'Jahwe', RGG[2] II, 10. Concerning primitive beliefs about names cf. the literature mentioned above, p. 170, note 27.

[23] Cf., for example, Lefébure, 'Le vertu et la vie du nom I En Égypte', *Mélusine* VIII (1896/7), 223ff.; Budge, *Egyptian Magic*[2] (1901), 157ff.; Lexa, *La magie dans l'Égypte antique* (1925), I, 113ff.; H. W. Obbink, *De magische beteeknis van den naam inzonderheit in het oude Egypt* (1925), especially 79ff.; Foucart, article, 'Names (Egyptian)', ERE IX, 151ff. Foucart, article 'Body (Egyptian)', ERE II, 764, characterizes the theory of the name as the basis for more than half of the religious ideas of Egypt.

[24] So in Kautzsch-Bertholet.

[25] Even if, according to the prevailing interpretation of 6:3 only the name *shadday* had been transmitted they would have been acquainted with it and would have had no occasion to ask thus. Nevertheless 6:3b does not refer to becoming acquainted with the Tetragrammaton, but intends the disclosure of its meaning which now follows (cf., among others, A. B. Davidson, *The Theology of the Old Testament*, 1904, 68). [That the Tetragrammaton was known in Israel 'according to the Elohist from the calling of Moses onward'—thus recently, in opposition to me, Grether, *Name und Wort Gottes im AT* (1934), 35—conflicts with the wording of the Massoretic text which deliberately has, and wishes to be understood, not the Hiphil, but the rare Niphal: 'But according to My name JHWH have I not given Myself to you to know.']

[26] This problem is not solved by distinguishing the sources (cf. Galling, *Die Erwählungstraditionen Israels*, 1928, 57ff.).

[27] Rosenzweig, *op. cit.*, 201ff., 207; cf. Driver, *op. cit.*, 24. To the two designations of Dionysos adduced for comparison, Iakchos and Euios, Sabos-Sabazios and Eleleus may still be added; cf. Perdrizet, *Cultes et mythes du Pangée* (1910), 59, 77ff., and Theander, *Ὀλολυγή und ἰά'*, *Eranos* XV (1915), 99ff., especially 120ff. For the problem as such the valuable section, 'Urlaute und Urtermini des sensus numinis' in Rudolf Otto's *Das Heilige*, and respectively, *Aufsätze des Numinose betreffend*, *Das Gefühl des Überweltlichen* (1932), 203ff., are to be compared, where on p. 210 Driver's explanation of the Tetragrammaton is also referred to. In opposition to this Mowinckel assumes in a letter to Otto which the latter adduces, *op. cit.*, 326ff., an original word-form *ya-huwa*, thus 'Oh He!' (*huwa* is the Arabic form for the personal pronoun of the third person), so that the Tetragrammaton is to be regarded not as expansion, but as abbreviation of the original, invoked name. Rosenzweig and I, already in 1925, in our rendering of the Tetragrammaton in our translation of Scripture had proceeded from the supposition that a 'He!'-cry was contained therein, from which then a 'He will be here!' 'He is here!' developed (cf. Rosenzweig, *op. cit.*, 194ff). The idea of a divine name *hu* contained in the Tetragrammaton has presumably influenced the Deutero-Isaiah interpreting *ani hu* (cf. Volz, *Jesaia II*, 1932, 16) and appears to have its effects in Talmudic tradition, *s.b. Schabbath* 104a, *Sukka* 45a; cf. also the passages adduced by Marmorstein, *The Old Rabbinic Doctrine of God*, I (1927), 84, as well as G. Klein, *Der älteste christliche Katechismus* (1909), 44ff. Otto, *op. cit.*, 210, has rightly called attention to the Dervish-cry (*dhikr*) *ya-hu* and the 'I know no other than *ya-hu* [Oh He] and *ya-man-hu* [Oh He who is]' of Dschelaleddin Rumi (see Nicholson, *Selected Poems from the Divani Shamsi Tabriz*, 1898, 126ff., 282). (I have since found in the transcript of an apparently early lecture by B. Duhm on Old Testament theology the sentence: 'Perhaps the name is as it were only an expansion of *hu* = He, as God is named also by other Arabian tribes in times of religious agitation, the One, the Unnamable'. I have also recently had my attention called to Friedr. Delitzsch, *Wo lag das Paradies?* 1881, 166.) [Cf. also König, *Ja-u und Jahu*, 1915, 45ff.; Vincent, *La religion des Judeo-Araméens* (1937), 45ff.]

[28] For this very reason it is false to treat the proper name JHWH as such as proof for an original polytheism of Israel ('The naming of a deity by which it is distinguished from other beings has only one meaning if one presupposes poly-

theism, asserts Gressmann, *Mose*, 426.) Proper names certainly do not arise originally in order to distinguish one person from others, but in order to be able to *address* him, and in order to be able to address him in such a way that he feels he alone is being addressed and he alone answers.

[29] Rosenzweig, *op. cit.*, 204. A related opinion was already advocated by Hehn, *op. cit.*, 228ff.—To Max Weber, *Religionssoziologie*, III, 131, note, it does not seem possible 'to regard the name with Hehn as a theologumenon of Moses, since Jahwe was not only worshipped in Israel'. But disregarding all the relevant religio-historical problematics—it is really not just a question of the name as such, but of its transformation into the Tetragrammaton; and at least this much cannot be doubted, that we find it in extra-Israelitish texts simply as the name of the God of Israel (Mesha-inscription). That it is a 'secondary formation', which originated through 'development' of the shorter name has also been proposed by Van Hoonacker, *Une communauté judéo-araméenne* (1915), 69ff. In addition to him Burkitt, 'On the Name Yahweh', JBL, XLIV (1925), 353ff., has called attention to the participation of Moses in this development. But before him Konrad Müller, 'Jah—ein numinoser Urlaut?' *Kartell-Zeitung, Organ des Eisenacher Kartells Akademisch-Theologischer Vereine*, XXXI (1921), 150ff., apparently without being acquainted with Hehn's and Van Hoonacker's works, in addition to R. Otto (cf. above, note 27) supposes 'the religious act of Moses' to consist in this, 'that by a slight continuation of sound he gave to the irrational, substance-less, numinous primitive sound Yah a rational, substantial content'.

[30] Cf., besides the works named above in note 17, B. Jacob, 'Mose am Dornbusch' (MGWJ, LXVI, 1922), 131ff., as well as Buber and Rosenzweig, *Die Schrift und ihre Verdeutschung*, 162ff., 193ff., 334ff. The connection between the *ehye* and the first sentence of the decalogue is referred to by Trumbull, *The Covenant of Salt* (1899), 150ff.

[31] This is recognized by Grether, *op. cit.*, 7, with the words: 'Exodus 3:14 does not reflect about God's being in the sense of an existing removed from the world or an abstract unchangeableness and eternity'. He continues, however, thus: 'but God is characterized as He who is who He is, that is, who shows Himself to be the one He shows Himself to be'. But this 'that is' is not a step, but a jump. The meaning 'show one's self' can be read from *haya* neither directly nor indirectly. L. Köhler, *Theologie des Alten Testaments*,[3] 235, also rejects the interpretation, but then explains, taking up again a thesis already opposed by Hengstenberg: ' "I am Who I am" is an utterance which refuses information. God does not surrender to Moses the secret of His being (= name). Who God is Moses will see in His effects' (cf. also Dornseiff, 'Antikes zum AT', ZAW, NF XII, 1935, 157). But the questioner appears here behind Moses as *the people*, and God tells him directly with the *ehye asher ehye* the answer which he is to give to the people. And this answer is in no way the refusal of information. It reads: *ehye* sends me to you. Here *ehye* can only be understood as a name. But it can be meaningfully understood only if it says essentially what was said in the entire *ehye asher ehye*: I will be here, close by, present—I am here, I am with you. This is the name which God does not refuse 'His' people (v. 10) whose need He has 'recognized' (1:25). And in the next verse there follows, through the emphatically repeated 'Thus you shall speak to the sons of Israel', the declaration that the

name JHWH, as the name of the Father-God, is disclosed in its meaning through this very *ehye*, just as the latter was disclosed by the preceding and following *ehye* '*im* (the "'im', however, was a reminder for every one who was acquainted with the report and with the other divine '*eyeh* '*im*' of the Biblical narrative). Jehuda Halevi (*Kusari*, III, 4) has God begin, quite in Köhler's sense: 'Why do you seek for that which you simply cannot grasp!' (Judges 13:18 is adduced as comparison), but he has Him continue: 'Tell them: "I will be here" . . .: that I will let Myself be found by them at the time when they seek Me. And they may seek for no greater proof than this, that I let Myself be found with them. And thus will they receive Me.'

Grether, *op. cit.*, 9ff., asserts against the Mosaic origin of the disclosure (of the 'Elohistic interpretation of the Tetragrammaton') that nowhere in the Scriptures is direct reference made to it. But is it not religio-historically suggestive that the resultant disclosure of a secret in decisive form is not discussed again?

[32] See especially Exodus 16:23; 33:19; I Samuel 23:13; II Kings 8:1; Ezekiel 12:25. Cf. Arnold, 'The Divine Name in Exodus, III, 14' (JBL, XXIV, 1905), 127ff., who, however, grasps only the meaning of the pronoun, not, however, that of the verb, and therefore explains the whole passage as unintelligible and as a 'Midrashic gloss' on 14b; a more comprehensive understanding is shown by Jacob, *op. cit.*, 129ff.

[33] Concerning the Oriental connection of the 'way' concept with the idea of king and king-ship cf. Trumbull, *Studies in Oriental Social Life* (1907), 228ff.

[34] Concerning the original meaning of this expression see the comparative study by Gulin, 'Die Nachfolge Gottes', *Studia Orientalia I* (1925), 34ff.

[35] For the historical background cf. Kittel, *Geschichte*, II[6], 401₄. There is as little occasion here as in 10:24 to understand by Assyria the Syrian empire of the Seleucids. The 'Jewish Hellenism of the Diaspora' (Guthe in Kautzsch-Bertholet) was no longer acquainted with this straightforward power of language.

[36] On this point see, in Chapter Seven, p. 129ff.; cf. also p. 22ff.

CHAPTER SIX

[1] This does not mean (according to the thesis of Sellin's *Mose*) a literary, but an existential connection, as will have been shown in the course of these investigations. [I intend, however, with the image nothing small, as Baumgartner, *op. cit.*, 1353, misunderstands me ('the relationship *at most* that of a folded-up to an unfolded leaf'), but something very big, real and important: when one unrolls a leaf there is revealed something previously veiled. 'It is a transformation indeed, but by a logical process of growth which was made possible only by the latent character of that with which it began', thus Woolley, *Abraham*, 246, expresses the same thing in his train of thought.]

[2] That the decalogue is indeed genuine, but that instead of beginning with the I-sentence of verse 2 it is said to begin with the I-sentence of verse 5b (H. Schmidt, 'Mose und der Dekalog', *Gunkel-Festschrift*, I, 1923, 78ff., especially 89ff.) is contrary to the situation. For Israel it is decisive that the speaker is precisely the God who has led, and still leads, it on this journey, Whose act is the experienced liberation. 'Deuteronomic' (disregarding the problematics of this designation)

the sentence is not, but it has influenced the Deuteronomic language. Cf. also
Galling, *op. cit.*, 62.

³ On this point see p. 130ff.

⁴ Cf. Staerk, *Das assyrische Weltreich im Urteil der Propheten* (1908), 14, 20,
22; Cramer, *Amos*, 49ff. For a comprehensive discussion cf. Volz, *Mose₂*, 10ff.

⁵ *Mitteilungen*, II (1887), 330; cf. also Rosenzweig, *Jehuda Halevi, Zweiund-
neunzig Hymnen und Gedichte* (1926), 178.

⁶ Cf. Buber, *Ich und Du* (1923); Ebner, *Das Wort und die geistigen Realitäten*
(1921); Heim, *Glaube und Denken* (1931); Steinbüchel, *Der Umbruch des Denkens*
(1936).

⁷ Cf. E. Baumann, '*jada und seine Derivate*', ZAW, XXVIII (1908), 22ff.,
110ff., who, however, construes the concept too broadly, as does Cramer in his
valuable treatise *Amos*, 55ff. One must try to come closer, in terms of comparative
linguistics, to the original meaning of this 'knowing' (see Grimm's *Wörterbuch*,
under this entry [Erkennen]) as the organic discovering, drawing out and appro-
priating of another existing being. [Only in terms of this original meaning of discovering, drawing out, are such passages to be explained as Genesis 18:19 (where
König's 'I have made him to be My friend' lacks every proof for a possible Hiphil
meaning of *qal*), Exodus 33:12; Jeremiah 1:5. L. Köhler, 'Amos-Forschungen',
Th R IV, 1932, 207, explains the last passage: 'I have known your essence'. But
ought one really to assume in terms of Old Testament concepts that God, before
He forms a man 'in his mother's body' knows his essence—his Platonic idea, so
to speak? And does not the paralleling of the 'sanctifying' speak clearly enough
for the fact that with the 'knowing', too, an *action* of God is meant? Just as He, in
the passages referred to, singles out Abraham, Moses, and Jeremiah from the
totality of men, so He singles out, Amos 3:2, Israel from the totality of the nations. Cf. the image in Deuteronomy 32:11b.]

⁸ Jeremiah 2:11 has only the extreme case in mind. Cf. in addition Caspari,
Die Gottesgemeinde vom Sinai (1922), 146.

⁹ Caspari formulates it correctly, *op. cit.*, 143; they did not wish to dissolve
the relation to God so far enjoyed; only to use it arbitrarily.

¹⁰ See above, p. 182ff.

¹¹ Cf. B. Jacob, *Im Namen Gottes* (1903), 20ff., as well as Buber and Rosenzweig, *Die Schrift und ihre Verdeutschung*, 176ff. One can 'raise up' a lament, a
song, etc. ('to speak with raised voice', as Volz, *Mose²*, 43, has recently asserted,
cannot be meant by the bare *nassa*), but not a name. Psalm 16:4 is no counter-
proof. One can certainly take up a name 'on his lips', but it will not do to understand the decalogue passage as an abbreviation for this. On the other hand, we
have an important parallel in Psalm 24:4, *kᵉthib*: 'he who did not lift up his soul
to that which is false (or: to fantasy)' (the *qᵉre* attempts mightily an identification
of content with the decalogue verse, but its usual interpretation does not support
this). Not a prohibition of false-swearing—whose sphere, moreover, would be
identical with that of false-witness (Exodus 20:16)—is joined to the prohibition
of false gods and of idolatry, but that of the contamination of theocracy and of
worship.

¹² The two branches of a tree-fork are meant (literally perhaps: 'the two
forkings'). This also explains the definite article.

[13] The primary thing with him is not 'the lowing and puffing', as the making of thunderstorms is not primary with Baal (Gressmann, *Mose*, 207; cf. Gressmann, 'Hadad und Baal', *Baudissin-Festschrift*, 198ff.), but the power of generation (cf., among others, A. B. Cook, *Zeus*, I, 514ff., 633ff., 716ff.; II, 1925, 3064). *For this reason* he should be classified 'according to the unanimous tradition of all religions in the near East' as a fertility god, who even as such is often also the storm-god.

[14] Even if, as Klamroth, *op. ct.*, 108ff., assumes, a change of meaning has taken place, the word-usage is remarkable.

[15] Cf. Klamroth, *Lade und Tempel*, 106ff.

[16] It is not necessary to go into the relation of the two narratives to one another. An ingenious explanation of the first as an etiological myth of the Bethel cult is in Oesterley-Robinson, *Hebrew Religion*, 143ff. Cf., however, Klamroth, *op. cit.*, 118ff.

[17] Not really 'to provide Israel with a way-God' (Gressmann, *Mose*, 207), but only to bring to Israel personally its *melekh*-God, Who *as such* is a 'way-god'. (The people indeed demands 32:1—cf. above, p. 166, note 9, concerning the passage—of Aaron that he might 'make a god' for them who is to lead them onward, but in verse 4 they proclaim his identity with the one who has brought them out of Egypt.) Yet it should in no way be concluded from this that the ark 'originally' contained 'a golden calf as Jahwe-image' (Gressmann, *Die Lade Jahves*, 25).

[18] But never in the temple cult, for which Mowinckel, for example ('Wann wurde der Jahwäkult in Jerusalem offiziell bildlos?' *Acta Orientalia*, VIII, 1930, 260ff.) from the fact that Manasseh (II Kings 21:7), beside altars for all sorts of star-gods, also brought an Ashera-image into the temple, draws the conclusion that Ashera was regarded 'as the consort of Jahwä', and, what is more, of a 'Jahwä-Baal'.

[19] Cf. Baethgen, *Beiträge zur semitischen Religionsgeschichte* (1888), 144ff.; Nestle, *Die israelitischen Eigennamen*, 120ff.; Baudissin, *Kyrios*, III, 90ff.; Klamroth, *op. cit.*, 88ff.

[20] Cf. Gray, *Studies in Hebrew Proper Names* (1896), 133.

[21] See Baudissin, article, 'Moloch', RE XIII, 271.

[22] Cf. Meyer, *Untersuchungen zur phönikischen Religion*, 7.

[23] Milcom (thus is I Kings 11:7 to be read, just as the prior 11:5) receives under Solomon a *bama*, but becomes thereby no more the *melekh* or *molekh* in Israel than does Chemosh of Moab who receives the same homage as neighbour-god. And the manifoldly obscure passage Amos 5:26 cannot mean, if one holds fast to the Massoretic text, that an Assyrian astral god grew into an Israelitish tribal god; I understand it thus: or have you perhaps carried your beloved Sakkuth or Kewan as your king, that is, have you carried his throne upon the ark, and not mine? (Sellin's counter-arguments, *Zwölfprophetenbuch*², I, 236ff., do not meet this interpretation. Against his conjecture—established especially in *Kittel-Festschrift*, 1913, 175ff.—cf. Cramer, *op. cit.*, 142).

[24] '*oloth lab-baal* 19:5, which is lacking in the Septuagint, I, too, cannot regard as genuine; nowhere else is the God who receives these dedications or sacrifices (here clearly the latter) called *baal*. It is a gloss which—with insufficient

means—attempts to direct the thoughts to Melqarth the Tyrian *baal*, the only one who, as a syncretism of *malk* and *baal*, therefore came into consideration. Also *bamoth hab-baal* (19:5 and 32:35) for *bamoth hat-thopheth* sounds peculiar.

[25] Concerning the struggle against it cf., among others, Weber, *Religionssoziologie*, II, 202ff.

[26] Cf. especially Hosea 2:10; on the other hand (with Sellin, *Geschichte*, 124) Isaiah 28:16–29 may not be adduced for this, since it deals not with the Baalic natural fertility, but with the cultivation instructions of the divine leader of the people, instructions which have nothing to do with Baal. Whether or not 'in by-gone ages Jahwe is the God of the steppe and of the roving nomad' (Budde, 'Das nomadische Ideal im AT', *Preussische Jahrbücher*, LXXXV, 1896, 62)—I believe that He simply cannot be so defined in any stage—Biblically He is throughout the Leader, familiar with the wilderness, who leads through the wilderness and out of it, the Lord of the wandering and of the settlement, who loves to abide in the steppe and yet teaches agriculture to His own.—With respect to Baalization cf. also L. Kohler, *Theologie des AT*[3], 57ff.

[27] Cf. Weber, *op. cit.*, 148.

[28] It is unimportant for our context whether one thinks here of the Phoenician or of the Greek cosmogony or of both.

[29] *tholedoth* does not mean 'origin' in Biblical Hebrew. Some one's *tholedoth* are his lineage of descendants, not his lineage of origin (the referring back to Abraham is only prooemium). *tholedoth* also never means 'history' (so, for example, Eerdmans, *Alttestamentliche Studien*, I, 3): in Genesis 6:9 it does not simply introduce the narrative, but points to the following verse. In 37:2, in any case, it means descendants: history of the sons of Jacob, not history of Jacob, —also here it does not simply introduce; therefore there is also no cause to detach verse 2a from what follows.—That with 2, 4a we have to do with a separation (for *ele* cf., for example, the word-usage in the Esau-genealogy in Genesis 36), is demonstrated by the forced nature of every attempt to connect the cosmic passage with the following narrating account, which no longer deals with the natural universe (in the cosmic sense), but with the historical (thus the 'anthropoligical') universe.

[30] That Ezekiel did not have the Exodus passage in view (so Smend on this passage) is therefore not easily conceivable.

[31] Rothstein in Kautzsch-Bertholet.

[32] The ambiguity consists in this, that in the introductory passage, Exodus 13:2, just as in 22:29, there is no talking about a redemption of the human first-born; that thus, if one wishes, one may interpret its redemption, 13:13, only as allowed, not as commanded.

[33] The objection of Tiele, *Geschichte*, I, 350, that one would expect the altar for child-sacrifice to be in the temple itself rests upon a failure to recognize the fundamental fact that a *heterodox* JHWH-cult is involved. The *lahem* (Ezekiel 16:20) which Tiele, *op. cit.*, 351 (wkth an inexact citation) adduces as argument, for the difference of the addressee of the sacrifice means: those caricatures there, not: those gods. The only Biblical author who knows how to say anything else is a very late Psalmist (106:36ff.) for whose diaspora-theological construction of history there are, as receivers of the sacrifice, demons as well as Canaanite idols.—

The supposed meaning for *gillulim* is only intended folk-etymologically; cf. Baudissin, ZDMG, LVIII (1904), 405ff.

³⁴ Cf. Baudissin, article, 'Moloch', RE XIII, 272ff., and recently Eichrodt, *Theologie des AT*, I, 69.

³⁵ Eerdmans, *op. cit.*, III, 129, indeed maintains that Ezekiel declares 'with clear words' that JHWH has commanded the Israelites 'to throw into the fire everything which parts the mother's womb', but I am not able to find words of this content in the text. (For the meaning of the requirement of first-born cf., among others, Menes, *Die vorexilischen Gesetze Israels*, 1928, 33ff.)

³⁶ It is also understood thus by Baudissin, *Kyrios*, III, 612s.

³⁷ I do not, as does B. J. Herrmann, for example, regard v. 32ff. as having been added by Ezekiel after 586, but only verse 32, which interrupts the continuity, as of later origin.

³⁸ Cf. Smend on the passage.

³⁹ That the chapter 'cannot be Ezekiel-ish' (Hölscher, *Hesekiel*, 1924, 110) this, from a point of view which is not able to regard the employment of a traditional pattern of language, and traditional formulas in a given context requiring them, as a proof of inauthenticity, is as little to be conceded as that the imagination of the author is inadequate or that 'his situation' is the exilic: it is the situation of his prophecy, not his own situation.

⁴⁰ Neither emendation nor deletion is necessary. This is not about Milcom, who as foreign tribal god indeed could receive a *bama* assigned to him, but never, at least under Josiah, could be named beside JHWH, but about 'their king'. Three categories are distinguished: those who worship 'the host of heaven' (and JHWH only as *primus inter pares*); those who worship a mixture of JHWH and *molekh*; an those who turn away from JHWH completely (v. 6). These last are no longer numbered among the 'worshippers'; we would certainly not call them atheists, but perhaps practising agnostics. All together they are characterized as 'the remnant of *baal*: there is the ancient faithlessness, but in this syncretistic or indifferentistic form.—For 'swearing' = confessing cf. Jeremiah 12:16. Here one would translate verbally: 'to swear themselves to JHWH and (at the same time) to swear by their *melekh*'. Naturally that is 'a sharp opposition' (Tiele, *op. cit.*, I, 350); it is indeed intended as the sharpest possible. But the demonism of this opposition consists in the very fact that it does not become conscious of the two elements being united as opposition.

⁴¹ Dussaud, who in his book, *Les origines cananéennes du saerifice israélite*² (1911) manifests understanding for the meaning of the *sᵉmikha* (27, 72ff.; cf. also *Syria* ,XVI, 1935, 272), assumes, p. 158, without proof material, as 'probable' that the rite had also been practiced by the Phoenicians. The North-Semitic texts which we know do not report a *sᵉmikha*. The most important is the much-discussed oath which, around 750, Mati-ilu of Arpad, during the slaughter of a ram, gives to the Assyrian king (and breaks): 'This head is not the head of the ram; it is the head of Mati-ilu . . .' (see Peiser, 'Studien zur altorientalischen Altertumskunde', II, MVAG, 1898, 2[228]ff.), corresponds to the well-known 'exchange' or 'substitute' formula from Babylon for the sacrificial lamb (Zimmern, KAT³, 597; Ebeling, ACT², 330) so closely that one is inclined to regard it as Babylonian also. What we are able to conclude from Punic inscriptions (cf. **note**

41 to Chapter Four) demonstrates as common only the Semitic variety of the substitutionary usage, not a particular ritual form. On the other hand the *Hittite* variety of the *s^emikha* must be considered (Friedrich, 'Aus dem hethitischen Schriftum II', AO, 1925, 11ff.; Gustavs, 'Kultische Symbolik bei den Hethitern', ZAW NF, IV, 1927, 139ff.; cf. also Pettazzoni, *La confessione dei peccati*, II, 1935, 214ff.).

The Biblical variety contrasts decisively with it in this, that with the former the sacrificial animal is supposed only to ransom from a pestilence then raging, while in the Old Testament rite the animal is intended to help change the relationship between God and the man threatened by no immediate danger. Common to neither is, as Gustave, *op. cit.*, 140 asserts, the transferring of evil by the laying on of the hand (cf. concerning this especially Frazer, *op. cit.*, VI, 1ff.). In the Biblical ceremony it is not an evil, but a function, an 'office' that is transferred. Whether the Hittite usage of clothing a sacrificial lamb as a human (Sommer and Ehelolf, 'Das hethitische Ritual des Papanikri von Komana', *Boghazköi-Studien*, X, 1924, 12ff., 79) came close to this intention cannot yet be decided on the basis of the texts at hand. Cf. also note 46.

42 Dussaud's conjecture (*op. cit.*), 72₆ with regard to Numbers 27:18 (with Dussaud Deuteronomy 34:9 is erroneously adduced) by means of which he attains the meaning: 'You shall lay your hand upon him in order that the spirit be in him', is not only linguistically impossible, but also proceeds from a factually incorrect assumption: a transfer of *ruach* of this sort is not known in the Old Testament for which the 'spirit' is no controllable substance or power (both in Volz, 'Die Handauflegung beim Opfer', ZAW, XXI, 1901, 93), but the 'blowing' from above (cf. Buber and Rosenzweig, *Die Schrift und ihre Verdeutschung*, 42ff., 16off.). The action of Moses is neither 'transfer of spirit' (thus recently Pettazzoni, *op. cit.*, 295) nor mere 'consecration to office' ('simply the consecration to office', asserts Holzinger, but what does the action mean in this consecration?) But also Deuteronomy 34:9, where, for example, Médebielle, 'Le symbolisme du sacrifice expiatoire' (*Biblica*, II, 1921), 284, finds the transfer explicitly expressed, wants merely to say that Joshua at this time, after Moses has identified him functionally with himself, he is the one whom the *ruach* 'fills'; it is here also, however, not Moses who puts the *ruach* into him.—The 'fulness' of the *ruach* is probably to be distinguished terminologically from the simple, as it were, dispositional *ruach* (Numbers 27:18). It is connected with the specific task (cf. Exodus 31:3).

43 Cf. Meyer, *Israeliten*, 560₁.

44 Cf. recently Pettazzoni, *op. cit.*, 201ff.

45 So, for example, Galling, *Der Altar in den Kulturen des alten Orients* (1925), 76.—Eichrodt, *Theologie des AT*, I 79, wants rather to assume less than a substitution, and summarizes the counter-arguments as follows: (1) that the sacrificial animal is not regarded as impure, but as most holy; (2) that the slaughter is performed not by a priest, but by the giver of the offering; (3) that substitution through a meal-offering is permissible; (4) that the offences atoned for by sacrifices are not sins unto death. To this one may reply: (1) that the sacrificial animal does not take upon himself (in contradistinction to the *asasel*-goat) the sins, but only the function of atonement; (2) the slaughter is performed by the giver of the offering as the one minded to offer himself, or in a case where the giver is a multi-

tude (Leviticus 4:15) 'one' on its behalf—in no case is 'performance of the death-penalty' involved; (3) substitution through meal-offerings is permissible only in the special cases which are enumerated in Leviticus 5:1ff., and in which (just as in a simple trespass-offering 5:14–26) no *s^emikha* takes place; (4) *every* sin is 'sin unto death', but there are sins in which the sacrifice finds its value-limit; these are the ones upon which the death-penalty stands.—On point (3) it may also be pointed out that in Jewish tradition the meal-offering of the poor counts before God 'as though he had offered himself unto Me' (Yalqut on Leviticus 2:1).

⁴⁶ In the cult of the Syrian mother-goddess this was arranged in such a way that the offerer, kneeling upon the fleece of the slaughtered sheep, drew its head and paws over his head and thus, as sheep, prayed to the gods (Lucian, *De dea Syria*, 55). Cf. in addition Rob. Smith, *Lectures³*, 474ff.; on the subject as such cf., among others, Diels, *Sibyllinische Blätter* (1890), 69ff., 122.—That the *s^emikha* —as presumably the later Jewish tradition partially asserted (cf. Lauterbach, article, 'Semikah', *The Jewish Encyclopedia*, XI, 182ff.), and in more recent time Bähr, *Symbolik des Mosaischen Cultus*, II (1839), 338ff., was first to assume ('the willingness to offer that which is one's own completely to Jehovah') says nothing else 'but that the close relation between offerer and sacrifice is to be brought to expression in the sense of a declaration of will, of the one offering, of the sur-render of his property' (Eichrodt, *op. cit.*; cf. also Matthes, '*Der Sühnegedanke bei den Sündopfern*', ZAW, XXIII, 105ff., 118ff.) is refuted, for example, by the con-secration of Levites in Numbers 8, where first, verse 10, the people identifies itself functionally with the Levites and these in turn, verse 12, identify themselves in the same way with the sacrificial animals (the second part of the action remains unexplained in Bahr's discussion, *op. cit.*, 342).

⁴⁷ I have provided the proof first of all in my Frankfurt lecture, 'Glaube und Brauch' (W.-S. 1930/31).

⁴⁸ Cf. also van Hoonacker, 'Le voeu de Jephté' (*Le Muséon*, XII, 1893), 76ff. and Procksch in *Deutsche Theologie*, II (1929), 131ff. (with reference to *kopher* cf. the rendering in Buber-Rosenzweig and in addition to this Buber and Rosen-zweig, *Die Schrift und ihre Verdeutschung*, 146ff.).

⁴⁹ Cf., however, Alt, 'Zur Talionsformel' (ZAW NF, XI, 1934), 304ff.

⁵⁰ For Babylonian material see the works cited above in note 41, as well as Dhorme, *La religion assyro-babylonienne*, 272ff.; cf. also Dhorme, 'Le sacrifice accadien' (RHR, LIV, 1933) 110ff. For Phoenician material see Eissfeldt, *Molk*. (cf. note 41 in Chapter Four). In later Judaism the custom of '*kappara*-killing' on the eve of the Day of Atonement is to be compared, where the redemptive character of the slaughtered cock is expressed in the recited Scriptural passage, Job 33:24 (whose ending is understood as validation-pronouncement of the re-demption) and 'life-breath for life-breath' (Exodus 21:23), as well as in the saying, 'This is my substitute, this is my exchange, this is my covering (*kapara*)'. It is significant that in the Geonaic period one applied the custom to lambs and per-formed the *s^emikha* along with it, which later passed out of use in order that the rite could not be mistaken for a sacrifice (which was forbidden outside of the temple cult). Cf. Brück, *Rabbinische Ceremonialgebräuche* (1837), 25ff. (whose attempt to explain the origin of the custom is, however, a complete failure);

Scheftelowitz, *Das stellvertretende Huhnopfer* (1917); Lauterbach, 'The Ritual for the Kapparot-Ceremony', in *Jewish Studies in Memory of George R. Kohut* (1935), 413ff.; Lauterbach, 'Tashlik', (*Hebrew Union College Annual*, XI, 1936), 262ff. The Mohammedan formula reads: 'My God, this sacrificial animal represents me, its flesh my flesh, . . . its body my body'; see Garcin de Tassy, *L'Islamisme d'après le Coran*[3] (1874), 228.

51 Concerning Protestantism as a religio-historical category cf. Frick, 'Der katolisch-protestantische Zwiespalt', *Kairos*, 1926, 345ff. and *Vergleichende Religionswissenschaft* (1928), 86ff.

52 On Genesis 22 cf. my essay 'Genesisprobleme' (MG WJ, LXXX, 1936), 85ff.

53 How deeply this matter has affected Jewish tradition can be seen from the material gathered together with exemplary care by M. J. bin Gorion, *Sinai und Garizim* (1926), 129ff. In the prayers, especially in the liturgy of the New Year as of the day of judgment and of renewal, Abraham's performance of the 'binding' is remembered as the carrying-out-by-intention of the divine will with non-resisting heart, and in the prayer before interment one thinks back in the same sense of the carrying-out-by-intention on the part of the son, 'who was bound like a lamb'. Isaac's carrying-out-by-intention is virtually understood as activity. Concerning 'with all thy soul', Deuteronomy 6:5 the Siphre observes (*Siphre zu Deuteronomium*, ed. Horovitz-Finkelstein, 58): 'like Isaac who bound himself upon the altar'.

54 I supplement the Biblical account in terms of the related narrative from Byblos by Diodorus 20:14 (cf. A. B. Cook, *Zeus*, I, 722) whose 'Kronos' (cf., for example, Lagrange, *Études*[2], 104ff.; Baudissin, *Adonis*, 60, *Kyrios*, III, 102) is certainly a *malk*-god. For his identity with the *malk* (andros) of Plutarch, *De Iside* 15, see Clermont-Ganneau, *Études* I, 10.

55 *Thamim* means unitary wholeness (not 'completeness'), so that no appearance of part is different from the rest. The related *shalem*, on the other hand, points to inner non-resistance. *thamim* therefore relates more to life, *shalem* more to soul. The person is *thamim*, his heart is *shalem*.

56 Cf. Volz, *Mose*[2], 35: 'The community of Moses was already "theocracy".' Volz maintains, however (*op. cit.*, 79), and rightly (contrary to the first edition of his book as well as Caspari and Sellin), that the concept of community does not suffice, that rather 'the religion of Moses was fashioned in the framework of a folk mode of existence'.—On the federation of tribes which calls itself Israel cf. also Sachsse, *Die Bedeutung des Namens Israel* (1922) 91: 'As covenant-name Israel from the very beginning possesses a sacral-religious meaning'. Presumably the original meaning of this name, precisely as covenant-name, is: '*el* rules, *el* is Prince' (cf. p. 168, note 25), and it expresses concerning the Godhead as such precisely that which the close of the sea-hymn proclaims concerning JHWH (cf. p.131ff.), as 'the visible programme of the rulership of God'. (Volz, *op. cit.*, 88). But the name need not yet on that account have been coined by Moses; it can be pre-Mosaic and can have received through Moses only a renewing interpretation, just as the Tetragrammaton had been newly interpreted by him (probably in expanding by means of the fourth character; see above, p. 25ff., 104ff., and 190ff.)

CHAPTER SEVEN

¹ The meaning of *ssepher* in this place is to be determined independently of II Kings 23, where the 'book of the covenant' represents a variation for 'book of instruction' (22:8). The latter is a legitimate concept; the *thora* is recorded in a book—to the *b'rith*, on the other hand, there pertains not a book, but a document. The variation in II Kings 23:2 is motivated by the fact that the discovered is immediately (v. 3) used as the documentary foundation of the renewed covenant. Thus the 'document' arises again from the 'book'.

² In no case is it to be assumed (however one answers the especially difficult question of sources here) that the account of this event represents a later *tradition* with respect to the meal-account in verse 11 (cf. recently Mowinckel, *Décalogue*, 119): The common meal belongs to the *b'rith* (thus Pederson, *Der Eid bei den Semiten*, 1914, 48ff. rightly in opposition to Krätzschmar, *Die Bundesvorstellung im Alten Testament*, 1896, 46), but is not to be regarded as a central ceremony for Israel since it precedes the real concluding of the covenant in general (and, to be sure, introduces it, cf. Pedersen, *Israel* I–II, 305), at times even (Genesis 26:30ff.; the decisive moment is naturally that of the oath) by a whole night. It would therefore be too little for the sacramental representation of such an important event. In addition there is the fact that verse 11b by itself cannot be understood as covenant-meal since the participation of the divine partner would be expressed first through the sacrificial action, which is lacking here and for which possible omission there is nothing to be said, since the redactor certainly had no reason to avoid a supplementing of the peoples' sacrifice, which was performed below, by one which those summoned to the summit offered. Mowinckel wrongly construes the event (*op. cit.*, 115) in such a way that it is those summoned upon the mountain who eat with JHWH as one eats with a man. It will not do to speak of a 'sacrificial meal on Sinai' (Gressmann, *Mose*, 183), since, if one treats the version of chapter 24 which lies before us as a unitary context, both events, sacrifice and meal, occur spatially as well as in significance on a different plane; but when verse 5 and verse 11 are separated from one another the meal remains indeed a sacred, but in no way bilateral, event. The conciseness of verse 11b conflicts with the suggestion of a sacrificial banquet; precisely the same ones who behold, and only they, take part in the meal. For the 'very high altar' of verses 3–8 Steuernagel, 'Der jehovistische Bericht über den Bundesschluss' (ThSK, LXXII, 1899), 349ff., has rightly made significant the officiating of the 'young men of the sons of Israel'. [What Quell, under the entry διαθήκη, ThW II, 124₆₈, adduces against my simple statement that the sacrifice takes place at the foot of the mountain, the meal, however, upon the mountain, has not become clear to me. In his thesis that the representatives of the people held a meal upon the mountain near to God 'and then quite self-evidently' with God (cf., for example, Eissfeldt, article 'Mahlzeiten', RGG² III, 1856, 'in the sight of the deity and that means with the deity'), the self-evidence does not seem to me in any way assured: the fire had already consumed God's share of the sacrificial substance below at the foot of the mountain. What is needed is to take seriously the two acts of the event in their separateness.]

[3] Cf. especially Trumbull, *The Blood Covenant*[2] (1893) *passim*; Rob. Smith, *Lectures*[3], 314ff., 479ff., 691ff.; Hartland, *The Legend of Perseus* II (1895) 237ff.; Pedersen, *Der Eid bei den Semiten*, 21ff.; MacCulloch, article, 'Covenant', ERE IV, 206ff. The adducing by Curtiss, *Ursemitische* Religion (1903) 242ff., of the blood-sprinkling of the Ismaïlis in which, according to his opinion, the same 'age-old Semitic custom' has been preserved, does not belong in this context at all.—For the general problem cf. also Marrett, *Sacraments of Simple Folk* (1933) 163ff.

[4] Cf. Max Weber, *Religionssoziologie* III, 83.

[5] Wellhausen, *Reste*[2], 127, where in note 1 there is a passing reference to our passage as to the attestation of an occurring sub-species.

[6] That the sprinkling of the altar at sacrifices is prescribed does not make it here into an 'offering' (Krätzschmar, *op. cit.*, 84). The sacrifice is performed in v. 5. Moreover, in Deuteronomy 12:27, to which passage Krätzschmar appeals, what is discussed is not the sprinkling but the 'pouring on' of the blood, which is quite a different story.

[7] Wellhausen, *op. cit.*, 128; cf. also Goldziher, *Muhammedanische Studien* I (1889), 67.

[8] Pedersen, *op. cit.*, 26. That 'the appeal to the age-old universally Semitic covenant rite' is 'quite weak' (Krätzschmar, *op. cit.*, 85) is an untenable assertion, all the more since the sacrificial element occurs in Arabian usage (cf. Wellhausen, *op. cit.*; Jaussen, *Coutumes des Arabes du pays de Moab*, 1908, 13; Pedersen, *op. cit.*, 27). Rob Smith (*Kinship*[2], 61) characterizes the Exodus 24-rite as 'quite similar', and that is certainly quite apt for the *form* of the rite, if one separates it from the situation (altar and people as partner);—its peculiarity lies precisely in this, that it is performed between heaven and earth.

[9] Caspari, NKZ, XLVI, 202, has me saying that only the covenant of Sinai is an act between God and man. I say something quite different: that *such a ceremony* between God and man occurs only here.

[10] The ethological material for comparison is treated exhaustively by Frazer, *Folk-Lore in the Old Testament* (1919), I, 391ff., the classical and the Nordic material by Eitrem, *Beiträge zur griechischen Religionsgeschichte*, II (1917), 8ff.; but Zachariae, 'Scheingeburt', *Zeitschrift des Vereins für Volkskunde*, 1910, 150ff., reprinted as *Kleine Schriften* (1920), 245ff. (cf. note 16) has compiled the most important material from antiquity.

[11] The Jeremiah account alone is supposed to have refrained from playing off the 'old Hebraic blood rite reported in Genesis 16' (Krätzschmar, *op. cit.*, 84) against the Exodus text allegedly proven thereby as late. It ought not to be concluded from the fact that in Genesis 15, in distinction from Exodus 24, no mediator functions (*op. cit.*) that here we have to deal with a 'much more ancient covenant ceremony' Baentsch, 'Exodus-Leviticus' in *Göttinger Handkommentar*, 216): the mediator does belong to the covenant between God and *people* in Israel as well as in South Arabia; he does not belong to the covenant between God and an individual.

[12] Meyer, *Israeliten*, 560; cf. Frazer, *op. cit.*, I, 399ff. A related interpretation of the rite, the two partners as halves of an organic whole, we find already in Jewish philosophy of religion around 1400; see Albo, *Iqqarim* XLV.—B. Jacob,

Das erste Buch der Tora (1934), 405, has recently attempted a symbolic interpretation which may hold good for the animals (the three cut to pieces as the three generations of servitude, the undismembered birds as the generation of liberation), whereas the explanation of the walking-through of the torches, namely that, besides the concluding of the covenant (which rite Jacob leaves unexplained), they, too, signify 'that the living God walks through the periods of servitude and yet unites those who are divided' seems to me thoroughly speculative.—That the walking-through of JHWH signifies participation in the consumption of a covenant-meal whose remnants Abraham afterwards enjoys (Zolli, *Israele*, 1935, 268ff.), is in terms of the wording of the text completely unfounded. Such an action of the heavenly fire would certainly not be expressed by means of *'abar*.

[13] Therefore this rite also cannot with Meyer (*op. cit.*) be regarded as the Judaic form of the concluding of a contract.

[14] Cf. Pedersen, *op. cit.*, 61. The text does not justify speaking about a covenant of the lords 'with their slaves' (Hempel, article, 'Bund', RGG² I, 1359): the slaves are only the object, not the participants, in the action.

[15] Procksch, *Die Genesis*² (1924), 110.

[16] Cf. Pedersen, *op. cit.*, 50ff. Eitrem, *op. cit.*, 14, objects that it 'would have to be explained', then, 'to whom and how the sacrifice was offered;' but both points emerge sufficiently from the Genesis-account. [Quell, under the entry "διαθήκη" TH W II, 118, objects that the Jeremiah passage refers to 'the legal transaction practiced among men'. But the term *lᵉ-phanai* which occurs as it does here, emphatically uttered in the first person, and may in no way be treated as 'an elegant expression', signifies the sacred character of the event and in any case conveys the thoughts to a sacrificial action.] Certainly the parallels treated by Eitrem, *op. cit.*, 8ff., point mostly to an 'ancient rite of lustration'. That, however, the Biblical ceremony does not have a lustrative, but a sacrificial character, is not to be explained by a 'variation of *interpretation*', and to lump both together, as Frazer, *op. cit.*, 409ff., tries to do, simply will not do. This is rather a matter of a transformation in the *nature* and *structure* of a magical act by its absorption into a religious context. Pilcher, 'Covenant Ceremony among the Hebrews' (*Proceedings of the Society of Biblical Archaeology*, XL, 1918), 13ff., has correctly recognized wherein that consists which the lustrative act and the *bᵉrith*-act, so similar to it, have religio-phenomenologically in common: 'Both include a new situation. In the act of lustration the devotee strides through the animal, and when he steps forth he believes himself to be in a new condition, a condition of purity. In a similar manner he moves in the act of a vow through the animal and steps forth in a new condition, the condition of obligation. . . . The body of the sacrificial animal is consequently a gate through which the devotee moves into a new domain'. On the other hand, Pilcher has not recognized that both acts are to be deduced from a remarkable group, not considered by van Gennep in *Les rites de passage* (1909), of 'rites of passage', which Zachariae, *op. cit.*, has treated in connection with the Old Testament rite of 'walking-through'—an especially characteristic Indian rite of regeneration, 159ff. (*Kleine Schriften*, 266ff.)—and which I characterize as 'renewal from out of the body of an animal'.—It should be mentioned that Th. H. Robinson, 'My Blood of

the Covenant' (*Marti-Festschrift*, 1925), 235ff., characterizes the ultimate meaning of the walking-through as well as of the Sinaitic blood-sprinkling as the restoration of an 'identity' of both partners, but that in the process of achieving his purposes he misunderstands the former and exaggerates the latter.

[17] Concerning the situation, cf., for example, B. Volz, *Der Prophet Jeremia*[2] (1928), 321.

[18] Jaussen, *op. cit.*, 361ff.; Eitrem mentions it, *op. cit.*, 11.

[19] Since the Assyrian *birithu* means fetter and the Talmudic *berith, birith* means thigh-band, I believe that ploughshare-rope (see Levy, *Wörterbuch über die Talmudim und Midraschim*[2] I, 267; cf. also 288) despite the dissent which has been expressed (cf. Pedersen, *op. cit.*, 45) may be derived from it (cf. also Karge, *Geschichte des Bundesgedankens im AT*, 1910, 227ff.). Concerning the difficult word usage in Ezekiel 20:37 see Valeton, 'Das Wort *b'rith* bei den Propheten', ZAW XIII (1893), 256; Krätzschmar, *op. cit.*, 167; and especially F. Perles, JQR, XVIII (1906), 384, and 'Analekten zur Textkritik des AT', N.F. (1922), 103ff. I understand the sentence in which, in my opinion, the image of the flock of sheep from the first half of the verse is adhered to: and bring you into the 'enclosure of confinement', that is, into the confining enclosure (for the Massoretic cf. Luzzatto, *Erläuterungen*, 1876, 162, and Ben Jehuda, *Thesaurus* VI, 31402, both of whom erroneously bring *b'rith* into connection with the following *u-barothi*, which has merely a paronomastic relation to it.

[20] I cannot accede to the diverging explanation of Pedersen (*op. cit.*, 46), since I regard the meaning 'decidere' for *karath* as late and derivative. Cf. also Quell, *op. cit.*, 108.

[21] Cf. Buber and Rosenzweig, *Die Schrift und ihre Verdeutschung*, 68ff.

[22] Cf. S. A. Cook in Rob. Smith, *Lectures*[3], 665. Max Weber, *op. cit.*, III, 141, correctly points out that the confederation of tribes in the pre-state period could decide on new statutes only on the basis of a *b'rith*. Concerning the uniqueness of the Sinai-covenant cf. also Eichrodt, *Theologie des AT*, I, 11. [I do not, by the way, say in the least, as Caspari, NKZ, XLVI, 203, understands me, that the rite was performed only at that time, but that, preceisely because it is the first time, it is only *reported* here.]

[23] Cf. bin Gorion, *op. cit.*, 363ff. That one would have to 'choose either for Shechem or for Sinai' because it would not do 'to regard the events in Shechem as a repetition of those from Sinai' (Menes, *Die vorexilischen Gesetze Israels*, 42) rests just as does B. Luther's consideration (in Meyer, *Israeliten*, 550) to the contrary, that 'the same event is recounted to us twice', on a failure to recognize the principle, attested by Biblical and South Arabian sources, of the *renewal* of a covenant (see above). Nor can one deduce from an analysis of the so-called 'book of the covenant' 'that the Shechem tradition merits preference' (Menes, *op. cit.*), since the identity of this law-book, at least in its present version, with the 'document of the covenant' of 24:7 cannot be proved (cf. my *Moses*[2], 123). Noth, *System*, 68ff., characterizes it rightly as an 'illicit act of violence simply to put aside the Sinai tradition for the sake of Joshua 24'.

[24] Cf. Mowinckel, *Décalogue*, 116.

[25] Cf. Pedersen, *op. cit.*, 61, with whom I am not able to agree that Joshua

allows himself to be acknowledged as chief of the people. The concluding of the
b'rith is here nevertheless the formal confirmation of the preceding sanction of
the people. *karoth b'rith* with *l'*, with exception, to be sure, of a late passage
(II Chronicles 29:10), does not mean as it does with *eth* 'to enter into a covenant
with some one' (Pedersen, *op. cit.*), but to establish a covenant for some one,
to accept some one into a covenant.

[26] Sellin, *Geschichte* 98. The assumption of Sellin (*Gilgal*, 1917, 53) that
the blood-sprinkling is in Joshua 24' only presupposed, not narrated', contradicts
the fundamental uniqueness of the covenant-establishing characterized above.

[27] And indeed not just a part of the people, but the whole: contrary to
Sellin, *Geschichte*, 98; cf. also Sellin, 'Seit welcher Zeit verehrten die nord-
israelitischen Stämme Jahwe?' (*Oriental Studies dedicated to Paul Haupt*, 1926),
126ff.; Noth, *op. cit.*, 69ff., 87ff.

[28] This also counts against the thesis brought forward by Steuernagel,
'Jahwe und die Vätergötter', (*Festschrift Beer*), 63ff. There is no occasion to
explain verse 16 and the verse 20 which refers to the *me-asob* as secondary
('E²'). The inconsistency alleged by Steuernagel between v. 3ff. and other
passages exists only if one understands with him 'all the gods of the fathers of
Israel' as included under the gods to be given up and regards JHWH as the God
only now to be chosen. If one understands, however: 'It will not do to avow
one's loyalty to JHWH and to carry along the *theraphim*; to serve this God *and*
others means to give Him up. Therefore you will have to decide unequivocally',
—then there is no inconsistency at all. As soon as one visualizes such survivals
religio-historically, the Joshua of chapter 24 may be interpreted without difficulty:
'harmless' household gods of this sort are secretly carried along by the women
(Genesis 31:34) and for a long time escape discovery until a thorough purifica-
tion takes place (cf. Genesis 35:2).

[29] If one regards the Genesis text as a parallel narrative projected into
primeval history (cf. Steuernagel, *Die Einwanderung der israelitischen Stämme*,
1901, 87) the argumentation is weakened once more.

[30] Sellin, *Geschichte*, 98. Concerning the historical extent of the Exodus
tribes one assertion seems impossible to me; an 'extra-Egyptian Israel' (Eerdmans, *Alttestamentliche Studien* II, 1908, 59) can, to be sure, be conjectured from
extra-Biblical material, but cannot be proved from the Biblical text. The equation
chabiru = lost-tribes (cf., among others, Barton, 'The Habiru of the El Amarna
Tablets and the Hebrew Conquest of Palestine', JBL, XLVIII, 1929, 144ff.;
Böhl, *Das Zeitalter Abrahams*, 1931, 30ff., 44ff.) appears not to be sufficiently
substantiated. On the problems of the *chabiru* cf. Speiser, 'Ethnic Movements in
the Near East', *Annual of the American Schools of Oriental Research*, XIII (1933)
and the special printing, 13ff.; Noth, 'Erwagung zur Hebräerfrage', *Festschrift
Otto Proksch* (1934), 99ff.; Julius Lewy, 'Les Textes paléo-assyriens et l'Ancien
Testament', RHR CX (1934) 29ff.

[31] As bin Gorion, *op. cit.*, 366, also emphasizes.

[32] Cf. Noth, *op. cit.*, 73ff. and in the next chapter, p. 157ff.

[33] Cf., among others, Trumbull, *op. cit.*, 147ff.; Trumbull, *The Threshold
Covenant* (1896) 193ff.; Marti, *Geschichte der israelitischen Religion*⁵ (1907), 44;
Pedersen, *Israel*, 268; Oesterley-Robinson, *Hebrew Religion*, 139ff.; H. W.

Robinson in Peake, *The People and the Book* (1925), 357ff.; Rüsche, *Blut, Leben und Seele* (1930), 308ff.

[34] For what follows cf. Buber, *Moses²*, 111ff.

[35] Gressmann, *Mose*, 185.

[36] Vischer, *Jahwe der Gott Kains* (1929), 26.

[37] Weber, *op. cit.*, III, 127, cf. 140. Pedersen, *op. cit.*, 32ff. has shown that the *bᵉrith* is not the solemn concluding of the covenant, but the covenant-relation itself.

[38] Concerning the compatibility with Exodus 3:13 and 6:3 see above, p. 28ff. and 104ff. (in opposition to Gressmann, *op. cit.*, 33ff., Galling, *Erwählungstraditionen*, 56ff., Alt. *op. cit.*, 12ff.).

[39] Gressmann, *op. cit.*

[40] Pedersen, *Israel*, 306.

[41] And indeed not the one originating first with the redactor, but already the one—according to the prevailing interpretation—originating with the Elohist to which 3:13 as well as 24:8 are ascribed.

[42] That this primitive scheme of organization has an historical background, Meyer, *Israeliten*, 98, has recognized from a quite different point of view which sees the tradition as rooted 'in the age-old politico-religious organizations of Kadesh corresponding with the simple relationships and viewpoints of a wilderness tribe' (cf. also 501ff.). His assertion that in the division of authority between Moses and the newly-installed functionaries who are only delegates and representatives there is 'established theocracy, *that is, government by priests*' already 'in full rigour as the only authorized organization of the people', is disproved by the very fact that Moses' successor, to whom his prerogatives pass, is an Ephraimite (the limitation pronounced in Numbers 27:21 and its carrying-through in the Book of Joshua is surely secondary—cf. also note 21 to Chapter Eight below—the Book of Judges knows nothing more of it, and, too, Eli has no political authority). Moses is indeed the one who performs the initial consecrations, that of the sanctuary and that of the priesthood, for the narrative of the original priests, but only in these non-recurring cult-establishing functions; his office as leader is by nature un-priestly and does not pass over to the priesthood. The administration of the Urim and Thummim involves the tendering of answers in special moments of crisis, but not initiative leadership. The tabernacle-oracle of the Exodus history is initiative; but it does not bequeath its character to any priestly institutions. What we find in the way of initiative utterance from this time on—also vis-a-vis the kings—has an almost exclusively prophetic character.

[43] It can therefore probably be granted that the people lacks—as does every primitive people—'the clarity and judgment requisite for a compact' (Caspari, *Gottesgemeinde*, 141), but 'compact' is here much too narrow a concept for the *community-establishing* act, to enter into which the people possesses the requisite *objective* qualifications. Certainly none of the narrators and of the prophets who refer to the Sinai-covenant says that Israel at that time 'out of necessity sold itself to God' (*ibid*). They emphasize again and again the reciprocity of the restriction. [According to Steuernagel, *Jahwe und die Vätergötter*, 69, with the establishing of the relationship by means of the blood of the covenant 'strictly

speaking the existence of such a relationship since the time of the fathers, that is, the identity of Jahwe with the gods of the fathers, was ruled out'. The existence of *such a* relationship—namely of the definite one between God *and people*—certainly; but the existence of a relationship as such, and along with it the identity of JHWH with the god of the fathers, certainly not.]

[44] *Der Eid*, 52ff., especially 63. Cf. also Quell, *op. cit.*, 123: 'Occurrence and meaning of this convenant find an analogy in the act of state which hands over the kingly power to a man (cf. especially I, p. 11).' [Caspari, NKZ, XLVI, 203, objects that only through the concluding of the covenant does David become a deliberate partner; but for the narrator he is one, as II Samuel 5:3 once more confirms, even before this by means of the divine election.]

[45] Cf. also above, p. 39.

[46] Sellin, *op. cit.*, 85.

[47] Mowinckel, *Décalogue*, 115ff. Cf. Mowinckel also in *Psalmenstudien* II, *passim*, and article, 'Drama', RGG[2] I, 2000ff. I find the interpretation, according to the generally held suggestion of Luther in Meyer, *Israeliten*, 550, to the effect that the report is constructed 'on the basis of the ritual of Shechem', first detailed in Jevons, *Comparative Religion* (1913), 29, who understands the Sinai-covenant as the 'interpretation' of a yearly covenant-feast.

[48] For the underlying approach cf. Wensinck, 'The Semitic New Year and the Origin of Eschatology', *Acta Orientalia*, I, 1923, 158ff. who limits himself, however, to the derivation of the Biblical cosmogony from the cult-drama. For the concept of 'projecting' cf. H. Schmidt, *Die Geschichtsschreibung im AT* (1911), 8ff.

[49] RGG[2], I, 2003.

[50] Cf. beside the designated works of Mowinckel and Wensinck: Volz, *Das Neujahrsfest Jahwes* (1912), 14ff., 33, 35ff.; von Gall, βασιλεία, 19ff.; H. Schmidt, *Die Thronfahrt Jahwes* (1927); Böhl, *Nieuwjaarsfeest en koningsdagen in Babylon en in Israel* (1927); Kraeling, 'The Real Religion of Ancient Israel', JBL, XLVII (1928), 133ff.; Oesterley in Hooke, *Myth and Ritual* (1933), 122ff.; A. R. Johnson in Hooke, *The Labyrinth* (1935), 85ff.; Pedersen, *Israël*, III–IV (1934), 330ff., concerning material for comparison, 557ff.; Hempel, *Gott und Mensch*[2], 69ff., 180; Krauss, *Die Königsherrschaft Gottes im AT* (1951), *passim*; Engnell, *Sakrales Königtum im AT* (1955), 62ff.; essentially restrictive, Gunkel, *Einleitung in die Psalmen* (1928), 100ff., even more so, von Rad, under the entry 'βασιλεύς' Th W, I, 567ff. Cf. also Hempel, 'Jahwegleichnisse der israelitischen Propheten', (ZAW, NF, I, 1924), 79s, and on the problem of an Israelitish cult-drama see Quell, *Das kultische Problem der Psalmen* (1926), 48ff. In opposition to the interpretation, above all Eissfeldt, *Jahwe als König*, 97ff., Baudissin, *Kyrios* III, 190ff., and after that—especially in opposition to the derivation of eschatology from the cult—Cramer, *Amos*, 144ff. (Pap, *Das israelitische Neujahrsfest*, 1933, does not do justice to the importance of the cultic sphere and therefore not to the problem either). Noth has dealt with 'the historization of myth' in an essay of the same name in *Christentum und Wissenschaft*, V (1929), 265ff., 301ff.; cf. in addition Weiser, *Glaube und Geschichte im AT* (1931), 23ff., and concerning the New Year Feast 40ff.

[51] *Décalogue*, 119.

[52] *Ibid.*, 115.

[53] Cf. Gray, *Sacrifice in the Old Testament* (1925), 200: 'The occasion here described is unique: and so, in some respects, is the ritual.'

[54] Cf. besides the works adduced above in note 3: Rob. Smith, *Kinship*[2], 56ff.; Doughty, *Arabia Deserta*, II, 41.

[55] Now compare Nyberg, *Studien zum Hoseabuche*, 7ff.

[56] Winternitz, *Geschichte der indischen Literatur*, I, 34. Cf. Oldenberg, *Aus Indien und Iran* (1899), 22ff.: 'The memory of spiritual brothers "rich in hearing"—what we today call well-read was at that time called rich in hearing—took the place of monastery libraries'—concerning the tradition of the Avesta text H. Lommel (who completely rejects the hypothesis of a long oral transmission presented by Nau, 'La transmission de l'Avesta', RHR, XCV, 1927, 149ff.) writes to me: 'Perhaps the tradition is so deficient precisely because it was not purely mnemonic as in India where the best text-tradition existed because it was for such a long time only mnemonic.'

[57] Cf., among others, de Slane, *Journal Asiatique*, III Ser. VII Bd. (1839), 371ff.; Nöldeke, *Beiträge zur Kenntnis der Poesie der alten Araber* (1864), Vff.; nevertheless compare also, on the one hand, Ahlwardt, *Bemerkungen über die Echtheit der alten arabischen Gedichte* (1872), 1off., on the other hand, Krenkow, 'The Use of Writing for the Preservation of Ancient Arabic Poetry', in *A Volume of Oriental Studies presented to E. G. Browne*, 261ff.

[58] Cf. Hackmann, *Religionen und heilige Schriften* (1914), 17ff. That which Caesar (*Bell. Gall.* VI, 14) reports concerning the disciples of the Druids in relation to the holy verses transmitted to them: *neque fas esse existimant ea litteris mandare*, receives a significant and confirming amplification in that which the chief treatise of ancient Irish law, the *Senchus Mor*, tells about its preservation; there have worked together for this, it says in the preface, 'the joining together of the memories of two old men, the transfer from ear to ear, the recited presentations of the poets' (*Ancient Laws of Ireland*, I, 1865, 3off.)—Concerning the function of oral tradition in the development of the Talmudic teaching cf., among others, Michael Guttman, 'Zur Entstehung des Talmuds' (in *Entwicklungsstufen der jüdischen Religion*, 1927), 44ff.

[59] Weber, *op. cit.*, III, 141.

[60] 'With the god Nin-gir-su Uru-ka-gi-na has bound the word concerning this', that is, has made this agreement, or has established this arrangement (Thureau-Dangin, *Die sumerischen und akkadischen Königsinschriften*, 52ff.; Deimel, 'Die Reformtexte Urukaginas', *Orientalia*, number 2, 1920, 9; differing, but—as a communication to me from E. Ebeling confirms—doing less justice to the text, Barton, *The Royal Inscriptions of Sumer and Akkad*, 1929, 84ff.). Cf. also Meissner, *Könige Babyloniens und Assyriens* (1926), 21; L. W. King, *A History of Sumer and Akkad*[3], 184.

[61] Meissner, *Babylonien und Assyrien*, I, 148.

[62] Thureau-Dangin, *op. cit.*, 5off.; Deimel, *op. cit.*, 8; Barton, *op. cit.*, 8off.

[63] Numbers 12:3; for the concept cf. Zephaniah 2:3: 'who do His law' (even as that under which they have bowed down: concerning 'those bowed down', on the Day of Judgment 'the fuming' of JHWH will move away without doing them harm). Jesus Sirach (45:4) connects the *'anawa* of Moses with his

emuna. Rahlfs, *'Ani und 'anaw in den Psalmen* (1892), 64ff., has clarified the linguistic foundation. He formulates aptly: "*anaw* has religious significance' and means 'placing one's self before God in the position of a servant' or 'bowing one's self under the will of Jahwe'. [This part of Rahlf's thesis is in my opinion not shaken by the essay of Birkeland of the same name (1933); except that the sphere of validity of the word's religious significance is restricted.]

⁶⁴ For Urukagina cf. Deimel, *op. cit.*, 4; King, *op. cit.*, 177ff.; for Kariba-ilu see p. 96ff.

⁶⁵ I regard the construction *ha-adon* JHWH, which occurs only in these two passages as old (cf. Baudissin, *Kyrios* III, 179) and the *ha-adon* JHWH *ẓᵉbaoth* in Isaiah (cf. concerning this *op. cit.* III, 193ff.) as its development.

⁶⁶ Cf. Eerdmans, *op. cit.*, IV (1912), 121ff., in all that is essential an incontroverted argumentation; Kugler, *Von Moses bis Paulus* (1922), 49ff.; also Weber, *op. cit.* III, 78; further, Ramsay, *Asianic Elements in Greek Civilisation* (1927), 40ff., especially 49ff., and Jirku, 'Das israelitische Jubeljahr', *Reinhold-Seeberg-Festschrift* (1929), 170ff., as well as Buber, *Moses²*, 209ff.

⁶⁷ Weber, *op. cit.* III, 145, speaks rightly of 'the rhythmic ancient speaking of God'. Cf. Volz, *Mose²*, 81, and on the passage as such, Buber, *Moses²*, 120ff.

⁶⁸ As Caspari, 'Das priesterliche Königreich', Th B VIII (1929), 105ff. (cf. also Caspari, *Die Samuelbücher*, 116) asserts, the word means 'reign' as it does nowhere else (Genesis 10:10; royal domain, Jeremiah 27:1, kingly ruling, but not static reign in the sense of an established power of office as Caspari understands it), thus also not in I Samuel 10:18 where it is used tendentiously for the enemy nations in contrast to the hitherto king-less Israel (cf. above, 69ff., 81ff., 83). In the immediately following masculine there comes to expression the fact that the peoples are involved, not the states. The Phoenician linguistic usage from which Caspari starts is different from the Biblical Hebraic. (It does not appear to me to be necessary with Caspari to treat the *cstr. mamlekheth* as an independent noun; on Micah 4:8 cf. König, *Lehrgebäude*, II, 182.)

⁶⁹ That the 'to me' refers to the King of this royal domain should not be called into question; *mamlakhthi* (for example in II Samuel 3:28) means: my royal domain; when something becomes 'to me' a *mamlakha* that can only mean: it becomes my royal domain (contrary to Caspari who unjustifiably, *op. cit.*, 110, construes thus: 'Jahwe says that people and *mamleket* are to belong 'to Him'. This JHWH does not say, but rather: those who are addressed are to become 'to Him' a *mamlakha* and a people—which is something quite different). Just as previously 'you become to me a *sᵉgulla*' means: I become the owner of this property, thus 'you become to me a *mamlakha*': I become the king of this royal domain.—On *sᵉgulla* it may further be noted that I am not able to endorse the interpretation of Caspari, 'Beweggründe der Erwählung nach dem AT' (NKZ XXXII, 1921), 209ff., to the effect that it is related to the Assyrian *sukallu* and that Israel is therefore designated by JHWH as His deputy, as theologically enticing as this is. The Arabic (cf. J. Barth, *Etymologische Studien*, 1893, 64, as well as the lexicons of Ben Jehuda, Brown-Driver-Briggs, and König under this entry) which Caspari does not consider, denotes 'share' unambiguously, that one does not need to adduce as primary the Assyrian *sugulu* rejected by Caspari. [Caspari refers me, NKZ, XLVI, 1951, to the fact

that Arabic political development is more recent than the Sumerian-Babylonian; but stateless nomads also know special interests.]

⁷⁰ Cf. Baudissin, *Studien*, II, 19ff. and in addition Nöldeke's judgment, *Liter. Centralblatt*, 1879, 361; Lagrange, *op. cit.*, 145ff.; Eichrodt, *Theologie* I, 139. Material for comparison is compiled in F. Pfister, article, 'Heilig', RGG² II, 1715ff.

⁷¹ Cf. Dillmann-Ryssel on the passage.

⁷² Cf. Baudissin, *Die Geschichte des alttestamentlichen Priestertums* (1889), 191ff.; Kugler, *op. cit.*, 243ff.; Paton, 'The Use of the Word Kohen in the Old Testament' (JBL XII, 1893), 2ff., who also in Job 12:19 argues for profane *kohanim* (for the interpretation of Exodus 19:6. Paton, *op. cit.*, 11ff., does not draw the correct conclusion); Dhorme, *L'évolution religieuse*, 225.

⁷³ Wendel, *Säkularisierung in Israels Kultur* (1934), 291, objects that a priest can 'nevertheless, "at the same time," indeed as such, be a friend of the king'. But from I Chronicles 27:33 it follows unambiguously that it is not friendship that is meant, but a court-office of the direct service of the king, an adjutancy: *ra'a* means to have directly to do with someone, to stand in direct relation to someone; the two concepts are related.

⁷⁴ Cf. Baudissin, *op. cit.*, 61.

⁷⁵ For a reason unclear to me, Galling, *Die israelitische Staatsverfassung*, 10, identifies this *yᵉshurun* with Jerusalem; there is nothing about 'Jahwe on Zion' in the song. When Deutero-Isaiah and the author of the Song of Moses (Deuteronomy 32) use the word one ought not to infer absolutely the lateness of the blessing-framesong: Isaiah 44:2 employs the sacred old word in order not to weaken, but to strengthen the tone of verse 16 in the repetition; and the irony of Deuteronomy 32:15 looks with obvious intention to texts like Deuteronomy 33:5, 26.

⁷⁶ The correct interpretation of syntax and meaning of the sentence at the same time in Noth, *op. cit.*, 721.

⁷⁷ Sellin, *Geschichte*, 99.

⁷⁸ Thus, for example, Sellin, *op. cit.*

⁷⁹ Only one who fails to recognize such great historical import as this in the frame-song can say with Caspari, NKZ, XLVI, 201, that 'the preservation of these verses' can be understood 'most easily in application to a regular cult-celebration', and that the king is 'the *incumbent* at whose sanctuary the celebration, perhaps at his ascension to the throne, takes place'.

⁸⁰ Sellin, *Zur Einleitung in das AT* (1912), 36ff.; Sellin-Rost, *Einleitung in das AT⁸* (1950), 37ff.; Gressmann, *Messias*, 229ff.; Burney, *Judges²*, 109; Phythian-Adams, 'On the Date of the "Blessing of Moses" ', JPOS, III (1923), 158ff.; Blau, 'Zwei dunkle Stellen im Segen Moses' (in *Jewish Studies in Memory of George A. Kohut*), 93.

⁸¹ One does not need to make the dating of the presumably independent frame-song dependent upon the dating of the blessing (cf. on the latter, however, for example, Kittel, *Geschichte*, II⁶, 16); I can in no case, on the basis of its style, regard it as more recent than the blessing.

⁸² Gressmann, *op. cit.*

⁸³ *Op. cit.*; the formulation of the conclusion has unfortunately remained obscure.

⁸⁴ Sellin, *Der atltestamentliche Prophetismus* (1912), 138, *Einleitung*⁷, 22; Gressman, *op. cit.*; Galling, *Erwählungstraditionen*, 6, also contends for an early dating, although later.

⁸⁵ H. Schmidt, 'Das Meerlied', ZAW, NF, VIII (1931), 59ff.

⁸⁶ *Op. cit.*, 61; cf. also Mowinckel, *Psalmenstudien*, II, 111ff.

⁸⁷ *Gesammelte Abhandlungen* (1866), 37.

⁸⁸ H. Schmidt, *op. cit.*, 65.

⁸⁹ Cf. concerning this Buber and Rosenzweig, *Die Schrift und ihre Verdeutschung*, 266ff.

⁹⁰ Concerning leaders' tents and their significance cf. R. Hartmann, 'Zelt und Lade' (ZAW XXXVII, 1918), 217ff.; Morgenstern has compiled some supplementary material in 'The Book of the Covenant" (*Hebrew Union College Annual*, V, 1928), 94ff.

⁹¹ It will not do, from the viewpoint of the first of the two passages, to understand *thᵉrua* in both of them as a war-cry (von Gall, *Zusammensetzung und Herkunft der Bileam-Perikope*, 1900, 28); both must contribute equally to the ascertainment of the common meaning. Schwally, *op. cit.*, 25, also gives the literal sense as 'war-cry', but defines this more exactly as 'cry of allegiance to Jahwe'. With the very same cry of allegiance, for which the 47th Psalm is the liturgical source, the multitude receives Saul as king (I Samuel 10:24).

⁹² That JHWH here is 'equated with the Canaanite God "Moloch" ' (Galling, *op. cit.*, 8; cf. Gressmann, *Die Anfänge Israels*,² 1922, 125). I believe I have refuted in the previous chapter, p. 111ff; there never was a god with this name. 23:22 does not give evidence for an 'animal form of divinity' (Galling, *op. cit.*; cf. Gressmann, *op. cit.*; Mowinckel, 'Der Ursprung der Bileamsage', ZAW NF VII, 1930, 268); the *el* does not have horns like those of a wild ox, but 'like the ure-ox's horns is He to him', that is, He furnishes to Israel, at whose head He marches, the mighty defence which is furnished to the wild-ox by his horns; the *kᵉ* in *kᵉ-thoaphoth* comes into its own so much more strongly, and the suffixes in *'immo, bo, lo*, which are at the same time voice stops, harmonize neatly.

⁹³ Mowinckel, *Psalmenstudien*, II, 43; cf. Mowinckel, *Bileamsage*, 267.

⁹⁴ See above, p. 103ff.—[That which J. Kaufmann, *Kirjath Sepher*, X, 65, says to me by way of objection, namely that from 24:7, for which he rejects my reading (see below), it follows that it cannot be JHWH who is meant with the *melekh* in 23:21, lacks conclusive-force. Even if the two songs are regarded as contemporaneous, one should start out from 23:21b, which reveals its meaning clearly by means of its parallelism. How the Massoretic text of 24:7 is to be understood remains, then, a problem for itself. Cf. further below, note 99.]

⁹⁵ *Op. cit.*, 108.

⁹⁶ l. poel.

⁹⁷ Cf. Mowinckel, *Bileamsage*, 264.

⁹⁸ The validating reasons for this are:

1. The two songs 'demand to be understood from out of the existing context'. But that in the situation of the speaker which comes to expression in them may be apprehended entirely from the point of view of the basic parts of the original saga we ourselves could deduce from them. And that *it* is to be attributed

to the period of the Omrids, of this the demonstrations of Mowinckel, *op. cit.*, 251ff., have not been able to convince me. The psychological pre-supposition for the regarding of Moab as the destruction-desiring enemy was given by the conflicts with Moab in the period of the judges: first the invasion, which is reported in Judges 3:12–21 (concerning its historicity cf., among others, Lods, *Israël*, 401ff.; Garstang, *The Foundations of Bible History, Joshua Judges*, 1931, 269ff.) and in which according to the text it is not at all 'really a single tribe, Benjamin, which is involved', merely because the liberator belongs to it; after that, whether in Judges II Moab is the original enemy (cf. Burney, *op. cit.*, 298ff.) or only stands behind the action, the campaign of Jephtha (cf. on this Auerbach, *Wüste und Gelobtes Land*, I, 1932, 104ff.). Certainly the Balaam saga reckons with an entire Israel; but this speaks forth, one would think, from the Song of Deborah strongly and unambiguously enough—the Balaam saga also does not presuppose a different Israel than the one which lives therein. The question of an historical nucleus of the saga (cf. Böhl, *Kanaanäer und Hebräer*, 1911, 62), which does not yet seem to me to be disposed of by Mowinckel's arguments, is here disregarded.

2. The two songs are said to be dependent upon the two following. But why 23:9a is supposed to be dependent on 24:17a and not either the other way around or neither of the two (that is, all the songs originating from the same school of poets) is not clear; this is the way it is with 23:24a and 24:9a which appears to me rather as a development of the former, and the juxtaposition of 23:24b and 24:8b is not really conclusive. I regard the third and fourth songs as more recent, since the name *bil‘am* son of *b‘or* seems secondary to me (see further below); 24:15–21 points to a Davidic time of origin ('more recent than David's kingship over all-Israel'—so Mowinckel, *op. cit.*, 250—it need not be, however: such a thing is composed during the lifetime of the celebrated hero).

3. The content of the two songs is said to prove that they are more recent. To begin with, it is said, here the reference to King Agag and the prophecy about David and about the conquest of Moab and Edom has disappeared, apparently because these features no longer mean anything for this time.' But first of all 'agag' does not seem to me to be genuine: what kind of glorification of the King of Israel is this supposed to be, that he is exalted even above the prince of the Bedouins? I read Adad = Hadad (on the style of spelling cf. I Kings 11:17): the prophet, who actually comes from Aram (cf. Kraeling, *Aram and Israel*, 1918, 36ff., as well as Daiches, 'Balaam—A Babylonian bārū', *Hilpert-Festschrift*, 1909, 60ff.) and has only been mixed up with the Edomite king known from Genesis 36:32, says about JHWH the King of Israel that He will be exalted over Hadad, the Aramaic god; 'Agag' was made out of this when *malko* was related to the human king and 'Adad' consequently was no longer understood (Agag was a famous prince of antiquity—that sufficed, since one didn't know what else to do), but the text which was available to the Greeks and to the Samaritan did not know what to do with Agag, understood the verse eschatologically and found in Gog a worthy opponent of the king of the last times. [Nevertheless—this may be noted with regard to objections to my reading by Hylander, *Der literarische Samuel-Saul Komplex* (1932), 191₃, and J. Kaufmann, *Kirjath Sepher*, X, 65—the correctness of my interpretation would remain un-

touched even if the reading were not to prove to be right: also the Massorretic text can better have reference to JHWH than to the earthly ruler. The struggle against Amalek is JHWH's own struggle—cf. p. 142ff. and in addition p. 216, note 28—and that He is exalted above him can have a symbolic and in the context a suitable meaning rather than when the same thing is proclaimed about David, for whose glorification, as was said, it appears less suited.] Secondly, it is quite appropriate to the style of composition of the whole that the prophecy of 24:17ff. occurs only once and that until it begins everything is kept general. And thirdly, the first two songs need only to be from a pre-Davidic period in order to nullify the argument.

Then 'the martially-triumphant mood of a young conquering people', which comes to expression in the third and fourth song, is said to have disappeared in the first two; it echoes only softly in the 'rather stereotyped' image of the lion. But this image is set forth precisely here, and only the terse wording of 24:9 can be called stereotyped; and furthermore the ure-ox horns in 23:22 are no gentler than those in 24:8, except that here the image is detailed and there only indicated, so that thus the two images, that of the lion and that of the wild-ox, on the whole counterbalance one another in the two songs.

Further, the poet is said to wish for himself in the first song the quiet death of such pious and 'righteous' people, a sign of later origin. But *yashar* means, originally and here, not really 'righteous', but upright, in good condition, worthy, able (which even Mowinckel himself, *op. cit.*, 267, points out)—thus no proof for lateness; and nothing is said at all about being 'pious'. It is certainly by no means correct that the honorific name *yᵉshurun* connected with *yᵉsharim* (cf. Bacher, 'Jᵉschurun', ZAW, V, 1885, 161ff.) occurs only in later texts; the frame-song of the Blessing of Moses has been relegated by Mowinckel, *op. cit.*, 268₉, to a late period merely because it presupposes 'the idea of kingly rulership and of the accession to the throne on the part of JHWH'!

Further, it is said that 'the idea of God in the songs according to the Elohist is clearly more recent than in the two other songs', for in these JHWH is said to be 'quite naively conceived in animal form'; at least He has 'horns like those of the wild-ox'. I have rectified the meaning of the image above; but apart from this it is just the same, word for word, in the second of the 'Elohistic' songs, 23:22—and yet from the repetition of the same words in the third song its greater age is supposed to follow!

The last objections go deeper:

The declaration in 23:19 is said to show a more reflective concept of God than that of the older period. But the idea of the succession of Biblical concepts of God upon which this objection rests has originated from the late-dating of just such passages as this, whose late-dating in turn is based upon the former idea—a fateful circle, without the overcoming of which we could not attain unto a genuine historical understanding of Old Testament belief in spite of all our accumulated knowledge of details. This understanding cannot be separated from that of the *struggle* for the concept of God as a struggle already beginning in the earliest times.

Further: the tendency to religious isolation which comes to expression in 23:9b as well as in Deuteronomy 33:28, is said to be Deuteronomic 'as a consciously emphasized idea'; that is, it belongs probably to the period of around 500 (thus according to Hölscher toward whose 'solution of the Deuteronomic question' Mowinckel inclines). But in the Deuteronomic passage *badad* is a synonym of *betach* and can mean nothing else but 'alone' in the sense of 'unmolested, unhindered' (cf. Micah 7:14; Jeremiah 49:31; Psalm 4:9). It is also to be understood this way here if only one grasps the key correctly. That Israel does not need to reckon itself among the *goyim* does not concern its 'religion', but its *b'rakha*, its abundance of blessing (cf. concerning this concept Mowinckel, *Psalmenstudien*, V, 1924, 6ff.; Pedersen, *Israel*, I–II, 182ff; Arabian parallels in Westermarck, *Ritual and Belief in Morocco*, 1926, I, 35ff.): by virtue of it Israel, for the speaker, is exempted from the vicissitudes to which the others are exposed and consequently from their transitoriness (nevertheless they can participate in Israel's *b'rakha*; see Genesis 12:2ff. and cf. with it Numbers 24:9b; cf. also Pedersen, *op. cit.*, 193ff.). Moreover, the possessor of this *b'rakha* is especially exposed to unfavourable external influences (cf. Westermarck, *op. cit.*, 229ff.). 'Religious' isolation in the sense of later times does not need to be thought of here (cf. also above, p. 129: covenant fulfilment = preservation of the *b'rakha* = separateness) as little as with the *qadosh* of Exodus 19:6: Israel is singled out and unshackled; for it is chosen and blessed. This is a quite early idea. (Just as Exodus 19:6 is not Deuteronomistic, but Deuteronomy-determining—cf., for example, Dillmann-Ryssel on the passage—so I Kings 3:8 is not to be regarded as revised, but—cf., for example, Eissfeldt in Kautzsch-Bertholet—to be assigned with its context to the ancient chronicler). The choosing and blessing God is an ancient oriental conception which received its great animation in Israel through the believing experience of a *community*. (The appreciation of the fundamental importance of this element is what I miss, for example, in J. M. P. Smith, 'The Chosen People', AJSL, XLV, 1929, 73ff.)

Further: 'The strong emphasis of the difference between the prophets of Israel and the "sorcery of the heathen" ', the conception 'that prophecy is *the* characteristic feature of Israel' is said to characterize the songs as late. But 23:23, to which this is related, speaks not at all of the prophets, but of the 'leader-oracle' of the wilderness journey toward which the passage, like the saga as such, now points. The *initiative* character of the leader-oracle is accentuated: here the people does not need to come to a soothsayer, since 'for the time', that is, at least in view of the new situation shaping itself, Israel is told from above that which it is necessary for it to know, just now, of the purpose of God (cf. note 42).

Finally: 'the allusion to the feast of accession to the throne' in 23:21b is said to point in the same direction; everything speaks for the fact 'that this feast, or more correctly: the interpretation of the old autumn- and new-year feast as a feast of Jawä's accession to the throne is said first to have been adopted in the Assyrian period under Babylonian influence' (269). Thus Mowinckel finds in the 'cry of allegiance to the king' (267) which can be completely explained from the familiarity of an early period with the moving out of the ark of the covenant into war, an allusion to a feast whose existence in the accepted sense after all was not proved, but was inferred only from liturgically or allusively understood texts; concerning this he now assumes that it first 'gained entry at the end of the pre-

Exilic period, perhaps in the Assyrian epoch' and as a feast of accession to the throne 'under the influence of the Babylonian religion' (v. Gall, βασιλεία τοῦ θεοῦ 21, whom Mowinckel, *op. cit.*, 267₃, follows as he corrects his earlier dating of the feast in the older period of the kings); and now the late-dating of the Balaam passage, among other things, is proved with this!

[99] Oldenberg, *Die Literatur des alten Indien* (1903), 125. The prose narrative, precisely because it is regarded as generally known, is not written down, but 'left to the improvisation of the preacher' (Winternitz, article, 'Jataka', ERE, VII, 491).

[100] *Op. cit.*, 45.

[101] From which (see above) their being more recent is not inferred with Mowinckel, *op. cit.*, 248ff., 264ff.: they originated with the saga; the others perhaps composed independently of the saga were incorporated later in it, or in its already fixed literary elaboration. Nothing results for the dating if one does not, with Mowinckel, *op. cit.*, 251ff., regard the saga itself as later; for which, however, even if one does not confuse it with the narrative, a proof cannot be adduced.

[102] Thus Diehl, *Erklärung von Psalm 47* (1894) 8ff.; v. Gall, *op. cit.*, 16ff.; in opposition especially Gray, *Commentary on Numbers* (1912), 343ff. and on the separate verses, particularly on 23:7 and 19.

[103] *Op. cit.*, 108.

[104] *b. Rosch Haschana*, 32b.

[105] *Op. cit.* 16a.

CHAPTER EIGHT

[1] Cf. J. Kaufmann, 'Probleme der israelitisch-jüdischen Religionsgeschichte' (ZAW, NF VII, 1930), 27.

[2] Certainly I Samuel 8:1 means first of all that he installs them as his assistants (Budde, *Die Bücher Samuel*, 53; R. Kittel in Kautsch-Bertholet, 419, note a); that this, however, is done, and is so understood, with the purpose of making the office hereditary follows from verse 5. The sense of the conversation is: your death is imminent, your sons have no charisma, the land needs a hereditary charismatic, and this is (according to ancient oriental belief) only to be guaranteed through a dynastic kingship.

[3] Cf. on this, among others, Oesterley-Robinson, History I, 105ff.—Titius, *Die Anfänge der Religion bei Ariern und Israeliten* (1934), 54, compares with the Teutonic.

[4] Musil, *Arabia Petraea*, III (1908), 22.

[5] Cf., among others, Meyer, *Israeliten*, 303ff.; Eerdmans, *op. cit.*, III, 38ff.; Max Weber, *Wirtschaft*, 811, *Religionssoziologie*, III, 43ff.; Mauss, 'Critique interne de la "Légende d'Abraham",' REJ, LXXXII, 1926, 35ff.; Albright, *Archaeology and the Religion of Israel*³, 96ff.

[6] Musil, *Rwala*, 477.

[7] Nallino, 'Sulla costituzione delle tribù prima dell' Islamismo' (*Nuova Anto-*

logia, XXVIII, 1893), 615; Wellhausen, *Ein Gemeinwesen ohne Obrigkeit* (1900), p. 7. For the relationships in the present era cf. especially J. L. Burckhardt, *Notes on the Bedouins and Wahabis* (1830), p. 66.

[8] Lammens, *Le berceau de l'Islam*, I (1914), 423ff.

[9] *Op. cit.*; cf. Wellhausen, *Skizzen und Vorarbeiten*, VI (1899), 7ff.

[10] *Die religios-politischen Oppositionsparteien im alten Islam* (1901), 14; cf. also Wellhausen, *Das arabische Reich und sein Sturz* (1902), p. 5.

[11] Nallino, *op. cit.*

[12] See Nöldeke, *Beiträge zur Kenntnis der Poesie der alten Araber*, p. 159ff.; on the supposition expressed by him, p. 1604, of a 'Muslim variation' according to Sura 55:27, cf. Brockelmann, 'Allah und die Götzen', AR, XXI (1922), 1082.

[13] M. Berakhoth, II, 2, cf. also II, 5; not 'of the kingdom of heaven', as, among others, Bacher, *Die Agada der Tannaiten*, II (1890), 312, translates: *shamayim* is a divine designation, and *malkhuth* means kingship, to be king, and then kingly power, kingly rulership, kingly function (cf., among others, E. Landau, *Die dem Raume entnommenen Synonyma für Gott*, 1888, 17ff.; Dalman, *Die Worte Jesu*, I², 1930, 75ff., and recently especially Kuhn, under the entry 'βασιλεύς', ThW, I, 570ff.). Concerning the supposition of the kingship of heaven at Sinai see *Melkhiltha*, ed. Horovitz-Rabin, 219, 222.—Schechter, *Some Aspects of Rabbinic Theology* (1909), 66, thinks improperly with the Mischnic concept of something 'primarily mental'; it is intended, in the performance of daily prayer as well as in the dying words of the martyr, as a theo-political act in the most exact sense.

[14] *Wirtschaft*, 140–8, 753–78.

[15] Cf. concerning this Weber, *op. cit.*, 779–817 (without consideration of our problem).

[16] Cf. Hubert and Mauss, 'Esquisse d'une théorie générale de la magie' (*L'année sociologique*, VII, 1904), 84.

[17] Holzinger in Kautzsch-Bertholet on the passage; so understood, the divine utterance may indeed appear as 'a thought-sequence of an already genuinely advanced theology'.

[18] Baentsch on the passage.

[19] *Op. cit.*, p. 755.

[20] *Op. cit.*, p. 763.

[21] In Numbers 27 the first, second, and fourth part of verse 21 is to be dismissed as hierocraticizing revision. 21 a and b interrupt the continuity; '*al piw* in c can in accordance with v. 17a only refer to Joshua: the Urim do not have in the narrative, as said, this meaning of an initiative-oracle one is in duty bound to consult; the end of v. 21 is clumsy. Presumably also in v. 19 the mention of the priest is secondary. The divine utterance would then read: 'Take unto you Joshua son of Nun, / a man in whom spirit is, / and lay your hand on him: / set him before all the congregation, / present him before their eyes / and give of your glory to him, / in order that they obey (him), / all the congregation of the sons of Israel / at his bidding shall they go forth, / at his bidding shall they return'. Thus JHWH fulfils directly the petition of v. 17. If one restores the text in this manner it no longer contains, at least in terms of the transmission of content, any late elements. Linguistically *hod* remains questionable, but the conception need not be

Iranian; it can be the primitive one (the same seems to me to be true for Exodus 34:29, cf. concerning the primitive origin of the Iranian conception Moulton, *Early Zoroastrianism*, 1913, 277; on the motif of veiling cf., for example, Frazer, *The Golden Bough*[3], II, 120ff.), just as well as the conception which underlies the *elohe ha-ruchoth* here and in Numbers 16:22: in our passage *elohe ha-ruchoth* and the *asher ruach bo* (v. 18) are meaningfully connected; this *ruach* is one of the *ruchoth* which are bestowed upon 'any flesh whatever'. The Hiphil forms in v. 17 are directly reminiscent of those in II Samuel 5:2; the rhyme rather sounds ancient.

[22] Weber, *op. cit.*, p. 764.

[23] Alt, *Die Staatenbildung der Israeliten in Palästina*, p. 6.

[24] If, as is customarily assumed, Joshua had been *only* the leader of the Joseph tribes, it would remain unexplained, how such an extension of his sphere of influence, as it would then lie before us in the book, could be undertaken and be carried through without Judaic objection; when and where are we to imagine a redactor who would permit an Ephraimitic wording of the tradition to flourish thus? One would certainly not have received the document of a Samaritan tradition in Jerusalem if one possessed material contradicting it. However, if one perhaps at the time of the formation of the tradition had reason to be silent about Juda in order, as Kittel, *op. cit.*, I[5·6], 428, asserts, 'to show the placing of Juda also in the ancient period as free from objection' and to cause the ancient, certainly much blamed separation to be forgotten, it ought not to be assumed that one would have allowed Ephraim to be exalted in so unlimited a fashion if one could avoid it—naturally not through a limitation of the military actions to the house of Joseph which would compromise the others, but through interpolation of leader-stories of other tribes into the narrative.

[25] Wellhausen, *Das arabische Reich*, p. 21; cf. also Casanova, *Mohammed et la fin du monde* (1911), *passim*, whose conclusions nevertheless—as Joseph Horovitz has confirmed in conversation with me—are for the most part erroneous.

[26] So Schwally, *Kriegsaltertümer*, p. 2; Weber, *Religionssoziologie*, III, 140; cf., on the other hand, the comprehensive presentation in Hempel, *Gott und Mensch*[2], pp. 33ff.

[27] KB II, 91ff.; AOT[2], 352ff. The Assyrian concept of 'enemies of the god Ashur' (cf. Tallquist, *Der assyrische Gott*, pp. 93ff. (comes closest, after all, to the Israelitisch conception.

[28] See Lidzbarski, *Ephemeris für semitische Epigraphik*, III, 3ff., 6, 10ff.

[29] Concerning the 'book of the wars of JHWH' it may probably be assumed that it was an early collection of 'carmina of the occasion' (Caspari, 'Was stand im Buch der Kriege Gottes', ZWTh, LIV, 1912, 137) concerning 'the ancient struggles for the possession of the land' (Dillmann-Ryssel on the passage) and that the separate parts thus resembled the Song of Deborah (Caspari, *op. cit.*, p. 130); cf. Meinhold, *Einfuhrung in das AT*[2], p. 105.

[30] Weber, *op. cit.*, p. 138.

[31] Samson's 'Nazirite-hood' is originally the obligation of life-long conflict against the Philistines, to endure until their complete subjugation (cf. Lagrange, *Juges*, p. 261); the birth-legend then transformed this into public cult. Concern-

ing the Nazirites cf., among others, Sellin, *Beiträge zur israelitischen und jüdischen Religionsgeschichte*, II/1 (1897), 127ff.; Budde, 'Das alttestamentliche Nasiräat', *Die Christliche Welt*, XLIV (1930), 675ff.; Eichrodt, *Theoligie des AT*, I, 159ff.

³² Cf. Schwally, *op. cit.*, p. 69; Sellin, *Geschichte*, pp. 128ff.; Arabic materials in Wellhausen, *Reste²*, p. 122, Jaussen and Savignac, *Coutumes des Fuqarâ* (1914), p. 73. The 'war-hair of the enemy' in Deuteronomy 32:42 is probably nothing more than a metaphor with the late poet.

³³ The accents, in my opinion, yield a stronger meaning than the usual sentence-divisions. The imperative (cf. Gesenius in the Thesaurus), it seems to me, may be represented as archaic; in the first half *yarad* is to be read.

³⁴ In 2–12a Deborah is sung-to; at the invitation of 12a she begins her song with 12b, first of all, transported back in thought to the moment before the battle, her battle cry.

³⁵ Cf. Giesebrecht, *Die alttestamentliche Schätzung des Gottesnamens*, pp. 21ff.; Dibelius, *Die Lade Jahwes*, p. 25. On the question of authenticity cf. the same, 21ff.; Gressmann, *Die Lade Jahves*, pp. 19ff.; Torczyner, *Die Bundeslade*, pp. 23ff.

³⁶ v. 14ff. with the threefold 'And David' is a verse quotation. The narrative itself cannot be much later; cf. Rost, *Die Überlieferung von der Thronfolge Davids* (1926), 37ff.

³⁷ That the *bad-ephod* (whether *bad* actually means linen—cf. among others Elhorst, *Das Ephod*, 266ff.—is unimportant here), 'as the two examples of Samuel and David teach' belongs 'to the robe of the priest of the covenant' (Gressmann, *op. cit.*, 32) I am not able to comprehend. Besides, there must have been 85 priests of the covenant at the time of the murder of the priests of Nob, (I Samuel 22:18); cf. Elhorst, *op. cit.*, 265 (the Septuagint text, in my opinion gives a less acceptable picture than the Massoretic), whose interpretation 'oracle pouch' (see also Grimm, 'Ephodentscheid und Prophetenrede', *Hommel-Festschrift* II, 1918, 316ff.) does not seem to me to be justified by the texts.

³⁸ Concerning a related development on another basis in Babylon see Caspari, *op. cit.*, 133¹.

³⁹ Caspari, *op. cit.*, especially 143.

⁴⁰ Cf. especially Alt, *Staatenbildung*, 1ff.

⁴¹ Caspari, *op. cit.*, 155.

⁴² The punitive campaign of the 'people of God' against Benjamin (20ff.) is indeed a 'holy war' in the amphictyonic sense (see further below), but in spite of all the theocratic terminology not a war of JHWH, since the account contains nothing about a charismatic leader. These problematics come to an obviously unintentional expression in the strange dissimulation of the oracle in 20:18–25.

⁴³ The chronicler of the Jephtha story certainly does not want to glorify Judah and Benjamin in the process, but from Judges 10:9 in connection with 12:1ff. one can infer the existence of the coalition. On the question of sources cf. Burney on 10:8 (that Judah and Benjamin were exposed only to 'raids' does not follow from the text).

⁴⁴ Concerning the southern league cf. Kittel, *op. cit.*, I⁵˙⁶, 433ff.; Garstang, *op. cit.*, 169ff.; Alt, 'Josua' (in *Werden und Wesen des AT*, 1936) 24ff.; also H. M. Wiener, 'The Conquest Narratives' (JPOS IX, 1929) 13ff., concerning the

northern league cf. Garstang, *op. cit.*, 183ff. Chazor as well as Jabin are to be stricken from the Book of Judges. On the significance of the victory over the Jabin-coalition cf. Alt, *Die Landnahme der Israeliten in Palästina* (1925) 20, 33. On the occupation as such cf. Albright, 'The Israelite Conquest of Canaan in the Light of Archaeology', BASOR, LXXIV (1939), 111ff.

⁴⁵ Cf. Alt, *op. cit.*, 34.

⁴⁶ Cf. the general sketch in Vincent, *Canaan d'après l'exploration récente* (1907), 47ff.

⁴⁷ Kittel asserts: after the conquest of Jericho; Sellin assumes earlier (*Gilgal*, 1917, 69): after the victory of Joshua over the southern league. That the highway leading to the south was blocked by the fortress of Jerusalem, to which Steuernagel, *Einwanderung*, 75, and Auerbach, 'Untersuchungen zum Richterbuch I', (ZAW, NF VII, 1930), 287, and *Wüste und Gelobtes Land* I, 78, call attention, need not be contradicted if the report of a battle at Jerusalem has an historical core (cf., among others, Wiener, *op. cit.*, 15, 21), in such a way that either the city temporarily fell into the hands of the immigrants (cf. Hertzberg, *op. cit.*, 213ff., recently de Groot, 'Zwei Fragen aus der Geschichte des alten Jerusalem', *Werden und Wesen des AT*, 193), or that it was indeed not conquered, but an agreement was arrived at whose consequences are expressed in that '*eth*' in Joshua 15:63 and Judges 1:21 (cf. Dalman, 'Die Stammeszugehörigkeit der Stadt Jerusalem', *Baudissin-Festschrift*, 108) and which also made possible the march through (cf. also Kennett, *Old Testament Essays*, 1928, 26ff.). Beside these possibilities there is to be noted the hypothesis represented by Wiener (most recently in *op. cit.*, 11ff), and supported in terms of textual criticism, of a northern flanking of Jerusalem above Rama (with which he identifies the Bezek of Judges 1:5). Steuernagel's (*op. cit.*), 76 and Auerbach's (*Untersuchungen*, 287ff., cf. *Wüste*, 101) identification of the 'city of palms' in Judges 1:16 with Thamar in the extreme south of the wilderness of Judah (cf. also Olmstead, *History of Palestine and Syria*, 1931, 252) is illuminating, but instead of *eth bʹne* one should read *el bʹne*. The Kenites, of whom we have not heard in the Book of Joshua, push in a concerted manner (cf. also Garstang, *op. cit.*, 205ff.) from the south up to Judah; they 'go in' and 'settle with the people'—idioms which are explained so much more easily than if the Kenites had moved together with Judah. With this the arguments of Meyer (*Israeliten*, 76) correct in themselves, brought forward against Steuernagel's Thamar-hypothesis, are answered.

⁴⁸ Cf. Alt, *op. cit.*, 26ff.

⁴⁹ The concept of the Israelitish confederation has been developed by Max Weber in the third volume of his *Religionssoziologie*, to be sure, in a broader sense embracing statehood within which he recognizes in the pre-state period 'amphictyonic ritual acts' (98) in Shechem and Shiloh. Alt (article 'Israel', RGG² III, 438ff.; cf. also *Staatenbildung*, 11, and *Josua*, 27ff.) has pointed out that the pre-state alliance of tribes may be most easily thought of 'in the form of sacred associations around common sanctuaries (so-called "amphictyonies"), which under certain conditions could attain political influence without, however, taking independence away completely from their members', and that this association had to date from a very early period. In his important work, *Das System der zwölf Stämme Israels* (1930), Noth has established the historicity of an Israelitish sacred

covenant of twelve and has attempted to explain its origin—the latter from premises whose correctness, to be sure, I am able to acknowledge only in part.

[50] Budde, *Die Bücher Richter und Samuel*, 101. For the high altar of the Song of Deborah cf. Albright, 'The Song of Deborah in the light of Archaeology', BASOR, LXXIV (1936), 26ff. For the song as such cf. Buber, *Der Glaube der Propheten*, 20ff.

[51] J. Darmesteter, *Chants populaires des Afghans* (1888/90), CXCIXff.

[52] Instead of *amar malakh* JHWH in v. 23 one should read, with Burney, *aror*.

[53] Cf. Budde on the passage [Sellin's defence of the Septuagint interpretation, 'Das Deboralied' (*Festschrift Otto Procksch*, 1934), 151, has not been able to convince me either linguistically or factually; Budde's plausible interpretation of *pirsono* as an objective genetive he simply disregards]. In this phrase the end of the epoch of nomadic living, the securing of a settled way of life is clearly expressed.

[54] Kittel, *op. cit.*, II[6], 67.

[55] It will not do to understand the direction of origin in mere meteorological fashion; the great storms in Palestine come from the south west (cf. Lagrange on the passage, also in opposition to Westphal, *Wohnstätten*, 54).

[56] Thus, even if the meter-interrupting, but very much dependent on the Song of Deborah, recurring *se sinay* in the sixty-eighth Psalm is left out of account. As a simple gloss on the plural *harim* it can only be understood with difficulty, especially if one regards the core of the Psalm—for which, in my opinion, new verses were composed in the course of the years until it attained its present form—in opposition to the opinion of Gunkel and others, as an 'ancient hymn of victory' at the bringing home of the ark, from the period of the unified Israel, and in adition if one observes that in it 'there is nothing about a human king as such' (Torczyner, *op. cit.*, 62; also König, *Die Psalmen*, 1927, 419ff.). Following a suggestion of Rosenzweig (cf. the translation of the passage in Buber-Rosenzweig), that the words in the Song of Deborah refer to Tabor; it (too) is a Sinai (for from it the divine power has been revealed to us). The Psalm then applied the phrase to Sinai itself, newly interpreted and understood as a parenthesis: this is Sinai!

[57] Cf. Torczyner, *op. cit.*

[58] Concerning the age of the designation cf. Torczyner, *op. cit.*, 31 (in the list Numbers 14:44 is missing). That in doubtlessly old passages, such as I Samuel 4:3ff., one deletes the word *b'rith*, occurs because of an opinion against which the previous chapter is directed.

[59] On the genuineness of the closing verse cf. Moore, Lagrange and Burney on the passage; that it does not submit to the strophic scheme is to be explained from the character of the refrain.

[60] I have dealt with the concept and problem of the prophetic mission in my books *Moses*[2], 75ff., 193ff.; *Der Glaube der Propheten*, *passim*; *Die chassidische Botschaft* (1952), 128ff.; *Sehertum* (1956).

[61] Hölscher, *Die Propheten* (1914), 125ff.

[62] Musil, 'Miszellen zur Bibelforschung' (*Die Kultur* XI/4) 10; Musil, *Rwala*, 400 ff. As in the Biblical narrative the lost she-asses, so here the lost camels are 'seen'.

[63] On the hitherto unclarified etymology cf. successively König, *Der Offen-barungsbegriff des AT* (1882), I, 75ff., *Theologie des AT*[3.4] (1923), 50ff., *Geschichte der alttestamentlichen Religion*[2] (1924), 140, as well as the general sketch in van den Oudenrijn, *De prophetiae charismate* (1926), 26ff. On this point cf. Sellin, *Der alttestamentliche Prophetismus*, 9ff. [Recently noteworthy is Albright, *From the Stone Age to Christianity*[2] (1946), 251ff.: 'The correct etymological meaning of the word is rather "one who is called (by God), one who has a vocation (from God)", as appears from the fact that this is almost always the sense which the verb *nabû*, "to call", has in Accadian, from the middle of the third millennium to the middle of the first.']

[64] The concept 'speaker of the deity' (Kittel, *op. cit.*, II[6], 329) is too narrow, as a comparison of several of the passages adduced by me demonstrates; Kittel must accordingly understand the designation of Deborah imprecisely (*op. cit.*, 23, 67) and regard the term *nabi* 'in the technical sense' as more recent. In actuality the pointing of the word from below upward cannot be separated from the concept of prophet. The people come to Isaiah not simply for prophecy, but also for prayer (II Kings 19:4), and Jeremiah, especially, is not simply an emissary, but also a spokesman. Cf., among others, Hertzberg, *Prophet und Gott* (1923), 146ff.; Cramer, *Amos*, 69ff.; Hempel, 'Die israelitischen Anschauungen von Segen und Fluch' (ZDMG, NF IV, 1925), 80ff., who, however, brings intercession and blessing too close to one another: they are phenomenologically different, since the former is an action directed 'upward', the latter one directed 'downward'. On Abraham cf. Buber and Rosenzweig, *Die Schrift und ihre Verdeutschung*, 236ff.

[65] Cf. Doughty, *op. cit.*, II, 108ff.

[66] *Psalmenstudien* II, 148.

[67] In this context I can summarize several results of comparative research.

[68] Cf. the important book by Jousse, *Études de psychologie linguistique* (1925), 133ff.

[69] The context forbids thinking of 'men like Elijah and Elisha' (Fascher, προφήτης, 1927, 125). The context is: once I destroyed the Amorite for your sake and by means of one called from your midst; now, however, since you 'have prostituted the name of my sanctifying' (v. 7), I Myself will do the same with you (v. 13ff.) and, just as I chose you out of all people, so I will punish you above all (3:1ff.). In relation to the post-Joshuanic warriors v. 11 is no longer 'hard to imagine in the mouth of Amos if one holds against his rejection of the prophets which lies in the word 7:14; then still 'it remains completely obscure wherein one should recognize the "benefit" of the Nazirites' (Weiser, *Die Prophetie des Amos*, 1929, 95). I cannot here enter into the question of genuineness, which I regard as doubtful only in the case of v. 12. Also in Hosea 12:10ff. the awakening of the prophetic mission follows upon the Exodus-deeds of JHWH.

[70] Cf. Sellin, *Beiträge* II/1, 135; Eichrodt, *Theoligie* I, 159.

[71] So Hölscher (concerning Deborah), *op. cit.*, 91ff., 120ff.

[72] Cf. Volz, 'Der eschatologische Glaube im AT' (*Beer-Festschrift*), 78.

[73] Cf. Kittel, Lagrange, Burney, in opposition to Moore.

[74] A characteristic example for the connection of a community of prophetic spokesmen with judicial functions is afforded by the Irish 'seers', the Filid. Cf. d'Arbois de Jubainville, *Introduction a l'étude de la littérature celtique* (1883), 296ff.

[75] Actually: draws near cleaving the air (cf. also Volz, *Der Geist Gottes*, 1910, 221). The hypothesis of Canney, *Journal of the Manchester Egyptian and Oriental Society*, 1917–18, 65ff., that the *ruach* cleaves, penetrates the *man* is already untenable because of the '*al*. On the other hand the attempt of Joüon, 'Notes de lexicographie hébraïque', *Melanges de l'université Saint-Joseph* X (1925), 39ff., to separate the Hebrew verb from the Syrian, which clearly means to cleave, and to ascribe to it the meaning 'aller droit vers', is unnecessary and founders on II Samuel 19:18, where only the meaning 'wade through' does justice to the situation (cf. Buber-Rosenzweig). Yet I also cannot, with Hempel, OLZ XXIX (1926), 266, regard 'the *quick* hurrying' as the decisive meaning; the *ish maẓliach* (Genesis 39:2) is not one who reaches the goal quickly, but one who advances to it *through all obstacles*. Cf. also Hylander, *Der literarische Samuel-Saul-Komplex*, 158₁.

[76] That we have to do here with a 'mimic' (rather orchestric: it is not a matter here as with a mime of imitating, but of directly expressing, gestures) chanting Caspari, *Samuelbucher*, 102₁, following the Targum, has rightly recognized (see above, p. 153ff.); only it must be maintained that it is not a general-cultic, but a specifically *nabi*-ic performance to which there is attached an ecstatic psychic change. [I do not in any way think of a 'blurring of the line of demarcation between judge and prophet' (Baumgartner, DLZ III/4, 1352). For the leader-charismatic, just in terms of the Old Testament, the *nabi*-ically characterized reception of the Spirit is the necessary *transition*, as I Samuel 10:6, 9ff. attests most plainly.]

[77] *Wirtschaft*, 763.

[78] Cf. Goldziher, *Vorlesungen über den Islam*² (1925), 215ff., and the literature adduced there on p. 363.

[79] Goldziher, *op. cit.*, 195ff.

[80] Cf. Goldziher, *op. cit.*, 191ff.; Wellhausen, *Oppositionsparteien*, 3ff., *Arab. Reich*, 38ff.; van Vloten, *Recherches sur la domination arabe* (1894), 34ff.; Muir-Weir, *The Caliphate* (1915), 266ff., 272ff.; Margoliouth, article 'Khawarij', ERE VII, 692ff.; Levi della Vida, article 'Kharidjiten', EI II, 970ff.

[81] Wellhausen, *Oppositionsparteien*, 15.

[82] *Ibid.*, 16.

[83] *Das arabische Reich*, 5.

[84] asch-Schahrastani, *Religionsparteien und Philosophenschulen*, üb. Haarbrücker I (1850), 132; cf., however, another tradition in Caetani, *Annali dell' Islam* X (1926), 102.

[85] Even if Wellhausen's (*Oppositionsparteien*, 8ff.) historical arguments against Brünnow (*Die Charidschiten unter den ersten Omayyaden*, 1884, 8ff.) prove to be right, Brünnow's insight that in the position of the Kharijites something primitively Bedouin is expressed, remains intact: their postulates are determined by the accepted religion, but in the manner of this being-determined there are age-old instincts at work. Concerning that which is Bedouin in the Kharijite position cf. also Muir-Weir, *op. cit.*, 266ff. The peculiarity of the Kharijites is not shown in the fact that they 'condemned both opponents as transgressors on the basis of religious considerations and wanted to keep the cause of Islam pure' (Ed. Meyer, *Ursprung und Anfänge des Christentums* II, 1921, 284, where the Pharisees

are compared with them), but in the character of those considerations: that they wanted to recognize no power which does not establish their origin by grace.

[86] Wellhausen, *Reste²*, 224₅; Brockelmann, *Allah und die Götzen*, 115.

[87] KAT³, 214; cf. on the other hand, for example, Margoliouth, *The Relations between Arabs and Israelites* (1924), 25, which refers to South Arabian linguistic usgae.

[88] Cf. especially Alt, *Staatenbildung*, 4ff.

[89] I, with Klostermann against the erroneous deliberation of Wellhausen, *wich'yithem*: 'then shall you live, / so you, / so the king, who after JHWH your God, entered upon the kingship over you'.

SUBJECT INDEX

milk, see malk
moab: Phedu-sacrifice of Arabs in, 122
molekh, see melekh
Moses, 26, 51, 57, 72, 115, 133, 147, 154, 155, 161; Blessing of Moses, 37, 130-132, 135, 152; death of, 142; rejection of, 141; religious heritage of, 27-36; Sinai covenant, 92, 100-106, 121-135
Moses (Buber), 47, 49
"Mountain of God" concept, 31-36
Mowinckel, S., 134, 153; dating of Balaam passages, 17; on Sinai covenant, 126, 127, 128
Muhammad, 137, 142, 152
Mysteries, Greek, 115
Myth: as language of faith, 14

Nabataea, 96
nabi, 151-152, 154, 156, 157, 160, 161
Name, "to appoint a name," 74
Nativism, 89
Nature: Semitic experience of, 95-97
Naville, 18
nebiim, 155
nebliim, 30
Nielsen: on JHWH as king, 49
Ningirsu, 129

obed, 32
Odin, 103
Oldenberg, 134
Omri, 134
Orient: divine kingship in, 52-54, 84-93
Osiris, 88

Palmyra, 96
Patriarchs: covenant with, 124; patriarchal narrative, 118
Pedersen, Johannes, 126
Pentateuch: divine kingship, 37
Pharaoh: divine rulership of, 87-88
Phoenicia, 96
Politics: religion and, 119
Priesthood: separate from political office, 136
Prolegomena (Wellhausen), 67
Prophetic texts: divine kingship, 37, 38
"Prophetocracy," 30
Prophets: protestantism of, 116
Proton, 58
gadosh, 130

Ras Šamra Mythologie und biblische Theologie (Nielsen), 49
Ras Shamra, 46, 51; on Baal, 55
Re, 85
Re-Arum, 87
Redactor concept, 18
Religion: history of, 48; politics and, 119

Rigveda, 39; see also Vedas
Rosenzweig, Franz: 13, 32
ruach, 160, 161; being-seized by, 156-157
"Ruler" concept: in biblical history, 61-62
Rulership, divine, see Divine kingship

Saba, 129; kingship-of-God tradition in, 90-92
Sacrifice: child sacrifice, 98; Genesis narrative, 122-123; to melekh, 98; Phedu-sacrifice (Arabian), 122; ritual of, 30; at Sinai, 121
Samson story, 68, 77, 78, 83, 143, 144, 156
Samuel, Books of, 15, 83
Samuelic crisis, 76, 82, 103, 133; dynastic character of, 136
Samuel-Saul story, 83
Sargon of Assyria, 88
Saul, 42, 63, 73, 79, 131, 144, 145; rejection of, 140
Sellin: on Jotham fable, 75
semikha, 115
Sennacherib, 103, 142
Servant figure, 92, 108
Sexuality: Near Eastern pathos of, 112-113
Shechem, 73, 74
shophet, 161
shophtim, 76
Sidon, 80
Sinai experience, 33, 100-106; sacrifice at, 121; significance of, 35-36; see also Covenant
Sisera, 70
Soil, divine ownership of, 92, 129
Solomon, 79, 125
Song of Deborah, 26, 53, 70, 146, 158; direct theocracy, 149; significance of, 149-153; see also Deborah
Song of the Sea, 37
South Arabia: theocracy in, 86-87, 90-92
Staerk, 18, 43
Syria, 96

Tannaitic tradition, 135, 138
Theil, Carl, 14
Theocracy, 136-162; in Babylonia, 86-87, 88-90; Caspari on, 22-25; charismatic rulership, 139-142; definition of, 23-24; direct theocracy, 56-58, 136, 139-162; in Egypt, 86-88; and historical scholarship, 59-60; in Israel, 22, 93; paradox of, 138-139, 148-149; pre-exilic, 30; pre-state, 22, 23-25; primitive theocracy, 83-85; rule-of-priests equation, 30; in South Arabia, 86-87, 90-92; Theban theocracy, 87;

SCRIPTURE INDEX

73 74 75   12 11 10 9 8 7 6 5 4 3 2 1